LOCAL
AREA NETWORK
DESIGN

INTERNATIONAL COMPUTER SCIENCE SERIES

Consulting editors   **A D McGettrick**   University of Strathclyde
J van Leeuwen   University of Utrecht

OTHER TITLES IN THE SERIES:

Programming in Ada (2nd Edn.)   *J G P Barnes*

Computer Science Applied to Business Systems   *M J R Shave and K N Bhaskar*

Software Engineering (2nd Edn.)   *I Sommerville*

A Structured Approach to FORTRAN 77 Programming   *T M R Ellis*

The Cambridge Distributed Computing System   *R M Needham and A J Herbert*

An Introduction to Numérical Methods with Pascal   *L V Atkinson and P J Harley*

The UNIX System   *S R Bourne*

Handbook of Algorithms and Data Structures   *G H Gonnet*

Office Automation: Concepts, Technologies and Issues   *R A Hirschheim*

Microcomputers in Engineering and Science   *J F Craine and G R Martin*

UNIX for Super-Users   *E Foxley*

Software Specification Techniques   *N Gehani and A D McGettrick* (eds.)

The UNIX System V Environment   *S R Bourne*

Data Communications for Programmers   *M Purser*

Prolog Programming for Artificial Intelligence   *I Bratko*

Modula-2: Discipline & Design   *A H J Sale*

Introduction to Expert Systems   *P Jackson*

UNIX™ is a trademark of AT & T Bell Laboratories.

LOCAL AREA NETWORK DESIGN

Andrew Hopper
Steven Temple
Robin Williamson*

University of Cambridge, England
* now at IBM Zurich Research Laboratory

ADDISON-WESLEY
PUBLISHING
COMPANY

Wokingham, England · Reading, Massachusetts · Menlo Park, California
Don Mills, Ontario · Amsterdam · Sydney · Singapore · Tokyo
Madrid · Bogota · Santiago ·San Juan

Cover shows patterns of iterated non-linear mappings using computer graphics by Barry Martin.
Typeset by Columns, Reading.
Printed in Finland by Werner Söderström Osakeyhtiö, member of Finnprint.

British Library Cataloguing in Publication Data

Hopper, A.
  Local area network design.—(International
  computer science series)
  1. Local area networks (Computer networks)
  I. Title   II. Temple, S.   III. Williamson, R.C.
  IV. Series
  651.7 TK5105.7

  ISBN 0–201–13797–6

Library of Congress Cataloging in Publication Data

Hopper, A. (Andrew)
  Local area network design.

  Includes bibliographical references and index.
  1. Local area networks (Computer networks)—Design
and construction.   I. Temple, S. (Steven)
II. Williamson, R. C. (Robin C.)   III. Title.
TK5105.7.H67 1986   621.398'1   85–26782
ISBN 0–201–13797–6

ABCDE 89876

Contents

Foreword

The coming into use of wide-band local area networks in the late 1970s was a signal event in the development of the computer field. These networks were developed by computer engineers who perceived that the use of computer techniques, rather than telecommunication techniques, would permit the attainment of high bandwidth, low error rate, and low cost. As the authors of this book point out, the new wide-band local area networks came just when they were needed to enable the low cost computers then being installed in large numbers to share peripherals; at the same time they made possible a new approach to the design of shared computer systems.

The Ethernet represented original thinking. Rings had been discussed in the literature for some time, but fears about reliability held back practical developments. The construction of the Cambridge Ring was an act of faith in the reliability of TTL MSI packages – an act of faith which was wholly justified by results.

Local area networks are introduced in this book as fast communication systems; they can equally be regarded as slow computer buses. A typical local area network is roughly three orders of magnitude faster than an ordinary telephone line and one order of magnitude slower than the Synchronous Backplane Interconnection in a VAX-11/780. For comparison, a jet aircraft is about two and a half orders of magnitude faster than a bicycle.

It is clear that the development of local area networks still has a long way to go. This is especially true of rings, a subject about which the present authors are uniquely qualified to write. I welcome this book as a timely contribution to the literature.

Maurice V. Wilkes
Maynard, MA

Preface

Over the last decade there has been a revolution in the application of semiconductor devices such as microprocessors and memories. The cost of these devices has fallen at a rapid rate, typically by a factor of two every two to three years, while their power and complexity has risen at a similar pace. As a result, systems built from these devices have found their way into all walks of life and continue to do so. In particular, one system, the computer, is now an essential tool in many industries, businesses, universities and other places of work. With the ever increasing number of computers has come the need for communication between them, for the exchange of data, programs, messages and other forms of information. Computer networks came about to fill that need, providing communication paths between computers connected to them.

One form of network, the local area network or LAN, evolved to satisfy a particular requirement. As the cost of semiconductors fell, it became cheaper and cheaper to make computers of ever increasing power. Indeed, it became possible for each user to have his or her own 'personal computer' where, in the past, he or she would have had a share in a mainframe computer. Unfortunately, while the cost of the semiconductor parts of the personal computer was small, the cost of peripherals such as printers and disk drives remained relatively high. In order to reduce the effective cost of these peripherals a means of sharing them between many users, each with their own personal computer, was devised. This involved connecting their computers together with a fast communication network and having sufficient peripherals attached to various of these computers to serve the needs of the computing community. In this way the peripherals were shared between the users and an additional advantage was the ease with which users could communicate with each other and access data in common storage. The network which was used to connect the computers was normally fast, carrying more than 1 million bits per second (1 Mbps), and relatively small, covering the building or site in which the users worked. Such networks first appeared in the late 1970s and were named local area networks (LANs). Their first use was in peripheral sharing, as described above, and today this is still their major use. Many other applications have since been found and include process control, data gathering and digital telephone systems.

Who will read this book?

This book will provide primary reading material for undergraduate courses in local networks and background reading material for courses in data communication in both computer science and engineering. It will also be of interest to computer scientists and engineers in general, who wish to become acquainted with LANs. The professional engineer who is involved in the design of a LAN may also find it useful.

About this book

In this book we concentrate on the hardware side of LAN design. For a computer to be able to make use of a LAN it must have both the hardware which performs the LAN functions and software to control that hardware. We have concentrated our effort in describing the hardware because that is our particular interest. However, experience has shown that when developing a LAN system it is normally the software which is the more expensive, the more troublesome and the more time consuming part of the development.

This book is not a comparative survey of commercial LANs, rather, we have chosen to write about a variety of LANs, pointing out their interesting features. We do describe some commercial networks including the most popular, the Ethernet. The focus of the latter half of the book is a LAN known as the Cambridge Ring. Because we have had first-hand experience with this network, we have used it to illustrate many aspects of LAN design. We describe the Cambridge Ring hardware, the protocols it uses, the methods by which it is interfaced to a variety of computers, its performance and a large-scale application. Although some of the things we have to say are specific to the Cambridge Ring, most of the points apply to any LAN. We hope that the reader will be able to appreciate that, for many applications, the type of LAN used is of little consequence, despite what manufacturers claim in their advertising material.

Outline of the book

In Chapter 1 we describe the various types of computer networks which exist and then concentrate on LANs and describe their particular characteristics. A brief survey of LAN protocols is then followed by a discussion of LAN applications. Chapter 2 describes the various components which make up a LAN. We discuss the types of transmission systems and the means by which computers transmit data. Chapter 3 begins by classifying LANs according to their topology and then describes four LANs including Ethernet. In Chapter 4, ring LANs are discussed, including the IBM token ring. Chapter 5 begins the description of the Cambridge Ring with a discussion of the hardware, the protocols used and implementation in VLSI. Chapter 6 discusses interfacing computers to local networks and gives some examples of interfacing a variety of machines to the Cambridge Ring. In Chapter 7, a large-scale application of the

Cambridge Ring is described and some performance measurements made on this system are reported. Chapter 8 describes a new local network that we are presently developing at Cambridge. Finally, the concluding chapter discusses some recent developments in LANs which may be important in the near future.

Acknowledgement

We would like to acknowledge the many people at the University of Cambridge Computer Laboratory whose work is directly or indirectly described here. We would particularly acknowledge the influence of M.V. Wilkes, D.J. Wheeler, R.M. Needham, M.A. Johnson, J.J. Gibbons, J. Dion, N.J. Ody, N.H. Garnett and I.M. Leslie.

Andrew Hopper
Steven Temple
Robin Williamson*
University of Cambridge, England

* now at *IBM Zurich Research Laboratory*

Chapter 1 **Introduction**

Many of the concepts which are found in local area networks are taken from earlier generations of computer networks. This introductory chapter attempts to place local networks in the wider context of general computer networks and to explain some of the basic ideas necessary for the understanding of the rest of the book. The features which characterise a local network are described and some of the uses to which they are likely to be applied are illustrated.

1.1 Switching methods for computer networks

Computer networks are made up of communication links which convey data, usually in digital form, between devices connected to the network. The links may be implemented with wires, optical fibres or some other form of communication system. The simplest type of link is known as **simplex**. Data flow on a simplex link is unidirectional, thus if two-way communication is to take place, two cables, one for each direction, must be laid. Fibre-optic transmission systems are normally simplex.

A **half-duplex** link is one which allows transmission in either direction, but not both at once. With this type of link there must be a set of rules or **protocol** to define which of the transmitters may be active at any time. There must also be a procedure for exchanging the capability to transmit between the two devices.

The most sophisticated type of communication link is called **full-duplex**. This permits both of the devices connected to transmit at the same time, thereby doubling the possible line utilisation attainable with a half-duplex link. Telephone lines are an example of a full-duplex system. Computer modems are able to take advantage of this, but human beings normally use such lines in a half-duplex fashion!

The simplest form that a computer network can have is two computers (hosts) connected by a single communication link (Fig. 1.1a). In this case the link would have to be bidirectional (half or full-duplex) so that communication could occur in both directions. A third computer could be added to this network using two more links to join the new computer to the two existing ones (Fig. 1.1b). This latter situation is an example of a fully connected network, there being a direct link between all pairs of communicators. An alternative method of connection would use one new link to join the new computer to one of the existing ones and have that computer forward any messages to the other

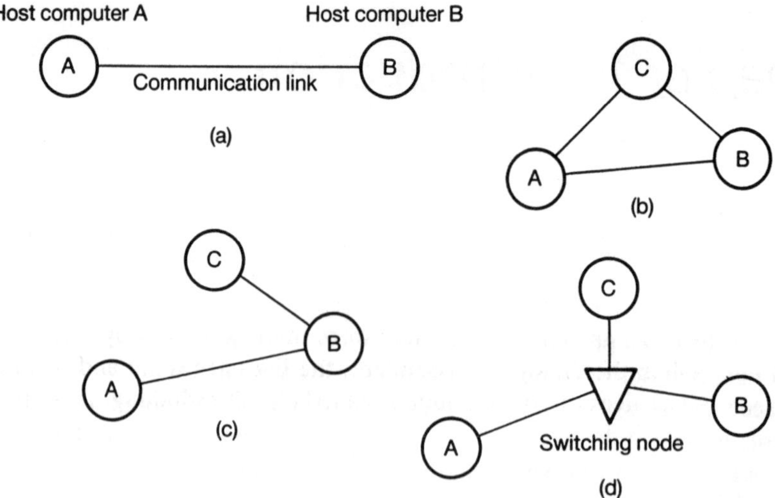

Fig. 1.1   Simple computer networks: (a) two-host network; (b) three-host network (fully connected); (c) three-host network (partially connected); (d) three-host network with switching node

(Fig. 1.1c). This is an example of a partially connected network.

A third solution would be to have a special switching system (a **switching node**) to which the computers are each connected by a single link (Fig. 1.1d). This third solution found favour in the early computer networks because it is relatively easy to add new hosts to the network and it is possible to build in extra links to provide redundancy so that the network can withstand a small number of link failures. Such a network is illustrated in Fig. 1.2.

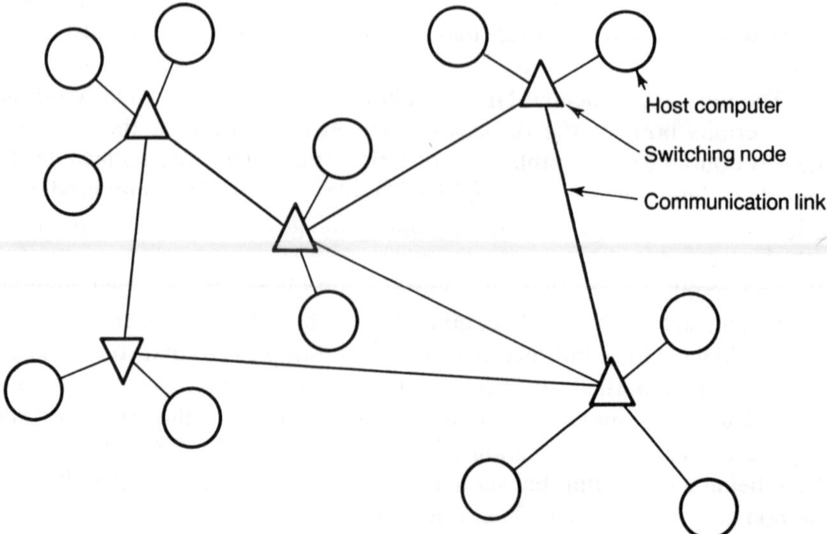

Fig. 1.2   A typical computer network

In this network, data which is sent between two hosts travels along a number of links and through some switching nodes. However, the concept of a simple single communication link between two host devices can still be supported. This can be done by ensuring that all the communication links between the two hosts are reserved for their sole use. The first phase of a dialogue between two host devices is the setting up of this direct link and is achieved by the initiating device transmitting a message describing the identity of the remote host with which it wants to communicate. Each switching node along the way will reserve a line pointing towards the destination host and send the message down it. Once the connection has been made, transmission can begin and proceed as if the two devices were interconnected by a dedicated direct line. When the dialogue is complete, the lines are freed and so can be used by other devices. This technique is called **circuit switching**. In a circuit-switched network the switching nodes act like exchanges in the public telephone service.

As with the telephone system, problems can occur in circuit-switched data networks when a communication line which connects two heavily populated switching nodes is in great demand. Once a connection across the network has been made, this prevents other devices from setting up a link using any of the lines already in use. This is clearly unacceptable if there is a need for multiple dialogues to run concurrently across a single link interconnecting two clusters of switching nodes. A method used to overcome this problem is to attach information describing the location of the remote host to the rest of the data to be sent. The complete set of data is then transmitted on to the network. The switching nodes are able to distinguish between the address and the data in the message. They can also interpret the contents of the address field and so the message can be sent on in the appropriate direction.

The 'dedicated line' problem of circuit-switched networks is therefore solved by not letting host devices reserve the lines. Instead, the switching nodes reserve the lines on a 'hop-by-hop' basis only for the duration of the message. This technique is known as **message switching**. Since there will be data travelling in many directions through the network there will be some inter-message interference, caused by network links being temporarily occupied by messages travelling across the network. This may result in queueing problems at the switching nodes. In an adaptive system it is possible to overcome this congestion by adjusting the routes used by messages so that the traffic load is spread more evenly across the network. The switching nodes of message-switched networks have to be devices with fairly large buffers, since they must be able to buffer several potentially long messages at any one time.

The complexity of these nodes can be reduced by the use of **packet switching**. In a packet-switched network the data to be sent is divided into small chunks called **packets** which are typically a few hundred bits in length. Each packet contains enough addressing information to enable the switching nodes to route it to its destination. It also contains a portion of the message being sent and sufficient information to allow the message to be reconstructed from all the packets. There can still be contention for a link in this scheme and switching nodes must be able to store whole packets while a link is busy and forward them when it becomes free. Networks based on this principle are therefore known as **store and forward** networks.

The user of any network does not need or necessarily want to know the details of how data is transported from one location on the network to another. To the user the most important characteristic of a network is that all the data should arrive error free and within a suitable length of time. If the network splits the data up and reassembles it then it is up to the network hardware and software to do its best to meet the user's demands.

1.2 The spectrum of communication networks

1.2.1 Telecommunications systems

At one end of the spectrum of communications systems lie the telecommunications services provided by national carriers (PTTs). These systems provide densely populated networks which span the entire country and have millions of entry points. The networks were originally installed for voice traffic, but since the need for information exchange between computer systems they have also been used for digital data traffic. Because the frequency range of voice traffic, for which the network was intended, is limited to around 3000 Hz the cost of the network was kept as low as possible by using low-grade cables as the interconnection medium. However, when the need arose for the higher-speed transmission of data the grade of cable used limited the rate at which this type of traffic could be sent. If a higher data rate was essential, this restriction could be partly resolved by the installation of some high grade lines, though the transmission rate was still as low as 50 Kbps.

Organisations that wanted to use the national telecommunications networks as the basis for their private computer network were able to use the service in one of two ways. When a link was required between two computer locations it was possible to attempt to dial up a line in the way that a normal subscriber would when he wanted to make a telephone call. This method of access using circuit switching was particularly suitable when a connection was required on a very irregular basis. If the occasions on which interactions took place were more frequent then the user had the opportunity to lease a line from the PTT. The organisation would then have the sole use of that line and there would never be the possibility of it being engaged.

1.2.2 Wide area networks

As the number of computer systems and the number of prospective users grew there arose a need for a new kind of communications network. The principle of wide area computer networks (WANs, also known as long haul networks) began as a means of connecting remote terminals to computer systems. In such loosely coupled systems the communicating devices can function as independent units and are connected by a network which can span a large area. The communications media used for the networks are either PTT telephony lines or cables laid specifically for the network. The scale of wide area networks is now so large that intercontinental network links have been provided using satellite technology.

The data rate required by such systems can be quite low. Since the size of message is generally large, the time before receiving the acknowledgement of a message can be long. Network speeds in the range 10–50 Kbps, with response times in the order of a few seconds, are typical. These networks are packet-switching networks using switching nodes and the store and forward method of operation. These large systems improved the reliability and availability from the users point of view, but generally made inefficient use off the available computing power and were very costly. A classic example of a wide area network is the ARPA network, which is a sophisticated and geographically distributed network linking machines of many different types (Roberts and Wessler, 1973).

1.2.3 Local area networks

The number of computer-based systems has grown because of advances in microelectronics and this has resulted in the need for a new type of computer network. This has been called the Local Area Network (LAN). Local area networks originated as a way of providing a means for peripheral device sharing within an organisation. Since this first application they have been used for many purposes, including the basis of reliable and sophisticated computer systems where the tasks associated with large computers are distributed over a number of smaller machines. As its name implies, a local network covers a limited geographical area and its design is based on a different set of principles to those of wide area networks. They are normally packet-switching networks but the store and forward approach is not generally used and consequently there are no switching nodes on these networks. Instead, the host is attached directly to the network via a **network node** which performs the functions necessary for the transmission and reception of packets by the host.

In recent years the cost of the devices which use local networks has fallen dramatically. It is therefore desirable that the cost of a network connection should be low. Since the network may be used for sharing file storage devices or for real-time cooperation between processors situated on the network, it should be able to transfer large amounts of data quickly.

As interactions between devices connected to a local area network are normally more frequent than those on a wide area network, the response time experienced by a user must be less than that for the wide area network. The distances that a local network spans are relatively small and so high-grade communications media can be used without influencing too heavily the cost of the complete system. This means that the data rates at which information transfer takes place can be high without needing expensive signal strengthening to be carried out at frequent intervals along the communications path. This also reduces the cost of a LAN connection. The response time in local area networks is also reduced by the fact that the size of data transmitted is typically much smaller than that sent in a wide area network. Most current local area networks operate at speeds of up to 10 Mbps over distances typically less than 10 km.

1.2.4 Tightly coupled systems

At the smaller scale end of the communications spectrum lie the multiprocessor computer systems where individual units are in close proximity to each other and might share common memory. Such multiprocessor systems were initially developed to enable relatively inexpensive processors to share expensive peripherals such as disks. The software did not require alteration, except that the problem of simultaneous access to the shared resource had to be solved. Such systems developed into the very tight multiprocessor configurations where each processor can access a common memory, or set of memory modules, through a complex multiway switch, called a crossbar. However, although this can be considered as a network, crossbar switches quickly become very complex when interconnecting large numbers of modules and thus are only useful for limited numbers of processors and memory units. An example of such a system is the C.mmp multiprocessor (Wulf *et al.*, 1981).

With a tightly coupled multiprocessor network, the size of interaction and the speed at which this takes place are different to the networks described above. A multiprocessor system typically requires that short pieces of data must be transferred between constituent devices at very high data rates. As the devices in such a system are located in very close proximity, the interconnection medium can be well-protected, high-quality cable. Thus, rates of well over 100 Mbps can be supported for the transfer of data from one device to another.

1.3 Network architecture standards

As the importance of computer networks became clear there arose a need for a set of standards to define the way in which such systems were implemented. These standards led to simplification of the task of interconnecting networks produced by different manufacturers to form larger systems. The proposed standards have divided up the architecture of a network into a hierarchy of levels built on top of each other. Each level provides a service for the level above it and in turn uses the service provided by the layer below it. It is important that there is a well-defined interface between each layer in the hierarchy.

To the user, who sits at the top of the network hierarchy, it appears that a conversation with another user takes place across a direct link. In fact, this virtual connection only happens through all the network layers below. At every level in the hierarchy there is a virtual connection with the corresponding layer in the dialogue partner. The only layer at which there is a direct link is the very bottom one, at which there is an actual physical transmission medium connecting the host to the network. The implementations of the protocol layers in different network hosts do not have to be the same, the only requirement is that they agree on the structure of the interfaces between them. They must also agree on the techniques to be used for various network control functions such as error control, flow control and the buffering requirements of network nodes.

1.3.1 Open Systems Interconnection

The most widely publicised step towards the standardisation of computer networks was the definition by the International Standards Organisation (ISO) of its Reference Model for Open Systems Interconnection (OSI). This standard attempts to define the structure of a network as a 7-layer hierarchy, each of which has a well-defined function (Zimmerman, 1980).

The main aim of the OSI standard is to define the way that a network node should look from the outside, i.e. from other network nodes. This enables the interconnection of networks which differ in terms of the implementation, internal organisation and operation. A brief description of the seven layers of the OSI model is given below.

1. The **Physical Layer** is the level at which the interchange of electrical signals which represent data and control information takes place. This layer includes a specification of the electrical and mechanical characteristics of the physical connection. Also defined are the procedures that should be carried out to establish, maintain and release connections between electrical circuits which are linked by the communications medium.

2. The **Data Link Layer** takes the bare bit-level communication system provided by the physical layer and superimposes onto this a means for transmitting data and control information. The protocol used may be character-oriented, where control characters are used to delimit the various fields of the basic transmission block, or may rely upon positional significance. Acknowledgement of receipt of data and error control are both implemented at this level with the facility for retransmission if necessary. Flow control to prevent fast devices swamping slower devices may also be present in this layer.

3. The **Network Layer** of the hierarchy takes the packet-sized data blocks which are handed down from the transport layer and attaches to these the address and routing information which completes the packet. The choice of routing algorithm is arbitrary and so routing can be fixed or adaptive, in which case packets are routed according to current network traffic loads. Routing can be limited to a single network or be extended to transfer packets between interconnected networks.

4. The **Transport Layer** provides a reliable data transmission and reception service for the session layer. The data is transmitted in the most efficient way that is suitable for the needs of the session layer. This may be an error-

free virtual connection with acknowledgements on a per packet basis for secure data exchange. It could also be a transmission service with no guarantee of delivery, which may be suitable for certain types of traffic, digital voice for instance. The transport layer takes data from the session layer and splits it up into pieces the size of the packet data field. It then passes these data blocks to the network layer.

5. The **Session Layer** provides a service to establish, maintain and terminate a connection with a process in a remote host computer. This layer should provide a reliable service to the presentation layer and have the ability to re-establish a connection should one of the lower layers in the hierarchy fail. During the establishment of a connection the session layer must be able to negotiate with the remote machine over certain connection parameters. These may include the type of communication to be employed (e.g. full or half-duplex), how the integrity of the session connection is to be controlled and the 'quality of service' to be expected by the session users.

6. The **Presentation Layer** provides a set of services to the application layer which can be used to process the data exchanged across the session connection. For example, the services may include compression, translation and encryption of the data.

7. The **Application Layer** is the highest layer in the network hierarchy. This layer of the protocol interacts directly with the application software wanting to transfer data across the network. All the other layers in the hierarchy exist for the sole purpose of satisfying the needs of this layer and the physical characteristics of the underlying network are hidden by those layers.

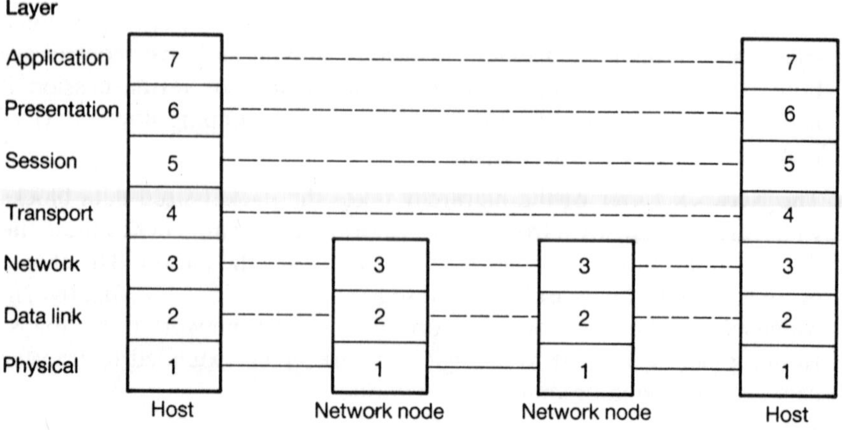

Fig. 1.3   Host-to-host communication using the ISO 7-layer model

It is important to realise that the OSI standard is just a model. Very few local networks adhere strictly to the 7-layer structure. In some instances layers may be missing because they are not needed in the application, in other cases the functions normally associated with a particular layer may be implemented in different layers. Figure 1.3 shows a network connection between two hosts established according to the ISO model. A more extensive description of the ISO model may be found in Tanenbaum (1981).

1.4 Characteristics of LANs

There are a number of characteristics which distinguish LANs from the other types of network mentioned. It is their size which earns them their name but there are other features which can be said to be typical of LANs and the following sections will discuss these.

1.4.1 Size

The size of a LAN is typically that of the organisation which employs it. LANs are normally private networks installed to serve the needs of a single group of people and the range of sizes reflects this. The smallest application might be in a school classroom where a LAN is used for peripheral sharing among many educational microcomputers and in this case the LAN might be no more than 50 m long. A medium-sized application could be in an office building where word processors and microcomputers in rooms on several floors are connected. In this case a few kilometres of cable may be used although no two connections are more than 100 m apart. The largest typical application could be on a distributed site such as a university campus or an industrial plant. Here, many buildings will be connected over an area typically 5 km in diameter. In this case the LAN may be 10 to 20 km in length and this may be regarded as the upper limit for contemporary technology. In the last two cases it is possible that there will be a link from the LAN to a wide area network to allow any user of the LAN to have access to the outside world.

1.4.2 Cost

Because many applications of LANs involve low-cost microprocessor systems, it is desirable that connection of such systems to a LAN should be economic. The hardware cost of a LAN connection presently ranges from around £10 to over £1000. The former sum buys a small number of integrated circuits to build into a microcomputer from the design stage and results in a limited but nonetheless effective LAN for use over small distances and at modest data rates. The latter buys a LAN adaptor box for many computers currently in use and allows connection to a high-speed LAN. The connection cost to a LAN can therefore be appropriate to the type of computer which is being connected and good value in view of the benefits which are obtained.

Another factor which influences the cost of a LAN is the wiring which must be installed. There is both the cost of the wirer and its installation to consider. Many LANs use very inexpensive cable such as twisted-pair telephone wire. The cost of installation will vary with the site, but in many cases it is possible to lay the cables in existing ducting and the cost of this is quite small.

1.4.3 Speed

The data rates of currently available LANs cover a wide range. The slowest transfer data at around 100 Kbps while the fastest have data rates of up to 100 Mbps. There is some overlap at either end with wide area networks and with tightly coupled systems. The data rate of a network is not sufficient to classify it as a LAN and other speed related properties must also be considered. Probably the most important of these is **delay** which is the time between the sending of a packet on a network and its reception. The delay of LANs is small and typically in the range 10–$100\,\mu s$, faster than a wide area network but slower than a tightly coupled system. The main reason for the small delay is that there is generally no buffering performed on the LAN itself. Packets normally travel directly from source to destination without passing through any form of switching node. Another reason is that the data rate is high and the distances travelled are small.

1.4.4 Simplicity

This is a somewhat subjective heading which manifests itself in LANs in a number of ways. The first is the shape of the network. The connection pattern of a LAN is normally a simple topological form such as a ring or a tree and this has implications for the routing of packets on a LAN. Generally, it means that no routing is necessary since every packet transmitted is seen by all devices connected to the network.

The simple topology simplifies another problem, too. In more complex topologies there may be contention for a link within the network. This is normally resolved by providing buffers within the network and some associated intelligence to control access to the link. As already mentioned, this function is provided by devices known as switching nodes. LANs do not have such devices, contention and buffering being performed within the host's LAN adaptor rather than on the network itself.

1.4.5 Error rate

Because the distances covered by LANs are small and cables of reasonable quality can be used without greatly increasing the cost, it is normally the case that the basic bit error rate of LAN cables is low. Short cables mean low attenuation and hence a good signal-to-noise ratio at the receiving circuits. Error rates of 1 bit in 10^9 are considered acceptable and practical measurement of a typical installation has indicated an error rate of 1 in 10^{11} (Dallas, 1980).

The low error rate of LANs has implications for the error recovery aspect of LAN protocols.

1.5 Local network protocols

Local area networks provide a basic transmission system for transporting small amounts of data from one network node to another in packets. The network will do its best to deliver packets to their correct destination, but will rarely guarantee their arrival.

The data transported by packets is normally part of messages which are being transferred between users of the network. Sometimes the messages will be small enough to fit in a single packet and at other times the message will be so large that it must be split between several packets. Quite often messages are passed between pairs of host devices that are engaged in a dialogue. In this case a sequence of packets making up a message will flow from one host to the other and then another message will be passed in the reverse direction. The dialogue continues with the passing of messages back and forwards. The user process in a host will expect to see such transactions as the error-free passing of complete messages. It is the role of the protocol implemented on top of the network transmission system to provide this service.

In order to perform this function, the protocol driver takes complete message buffers from the user process and chops them up into suitable transmission units defined by the network packet size. It then transmits each unit according to the network access method. Normally the protocol driver is implemented in software but implementations in hardware are possible for very simple protocols. When a message has been transmitted, the receiving protocol system must inform the sending protocol system whether or not the transfer was successful. This is done by the remote system transmitting acknowledgements to the source of the message. Normally, the acknowledgement says that the data was received without error but other information may be supplied such as whether the receiver has any free buffers left. In some cases a negative acknowledgement may be given, indicating that the receiver has received some or all of the message and found some sort of error in it. This form of acknowledgement is normally interpreted as a request for the message to be retransmitted.

On some networks the provision of a simple acknowledgement scheme has been included in the basic network transmission system. In particular, packets transmitted on the Cambridge Ring contain two response bits which are marked by the destination of the packet. Since packets always return to their source in this system, the sender can find out if reception was successful at the destination.

A powerful tool, which helps keep the ordering of packets correct when they are liable to be lost by the network, is the use of sequence numbers. Each packet bears a small number and this number is incremented in successive packets. A receiver therefore expects to find incrementing sequence numbers in its incoming packets. If it does not, it is likely that a packet has been lost and the two participants should take action to get into step once more.

Whatever the protocol implemented on a local area network, an important part of it will be an error detection mechanism. This is used to detect various levels of bit errors, depending upon the sophistication of the technique employed. Most networks include some level of error detection at the packet level. This ranges from a single parity bit to a 32-bit checksum field, which is calculated on the contents of the packet. Depending on the error control at the packet level, there will also be error detection mechanisms employed by higher levels of the protocol. If the result of an error check is negative, then the receiving host will not acknowledge receipt of the message. In some protocols the receiving host will not respond in any way, thus waiting for the transmitter to time out and retransmit the data. With others, the receiver will transmit a negative acknowledgement to the source, thus prompting it to repeat the data.

Another important task performed by a protocol is to prevent a high-speed transmitter from swamping a slower receiver. Similarly, other users of the network must be protected from the performance degradation effects of a fast device attempting to do this. This is **flow control** and an important part of this mechanism is for the two corresponding devices to agree on the maximum size of data which can be transmitted before an explicit agreement for further data must be received.

In some networks there are elements of flow control built into the basic transmission system. A packet transmitted on the Cambridge Ring will not be accepted at its destination station, unless its host has given an explicit command allowing data to be received. If this command has not been given, the packet returns to the transmitter with the response bits marked as **busy**. The source host may repeatedly attempt to retransmit the data until the packet returns marked as **accepted**. Furthermore, the Cambridge Ring station attempts to reduce the load on the network by delaying informing the host of the return of packets which repeatedly return with the busy response. Thus the rate at which a host can transmit packets to a destination which frequently gives a busy response is lower than if the packets were accepted.

On the Cambridge Ring, as well as other networks, there will also be flow control at the level of the host buffer size. Here acknowledgements can also be used as a flow control mechanism. By creating two types of acknowledgement and associating a different meaning to each, as well as being informed that the previous data was received successfully, the source host can either be informed that a buffer is available for further data or that there is no spare buffer capacity at the destination. If the latter type of acknowledgement is used, then the destination must explicitly inform the source when it has a free buffer.

As part of the flow control scheme, a protocol can have either a variable or fixed **window size**. A window is the number of acknowledgeable transmission units which can be sent before the receipt of an acknowledgement is required. If both hosts in a dialogue can process data buffers at a high rate, having a window size greater than one can increase the aggregate data rate of a network connection, since the restrictions on the rate at which a host can transmit are reduced. Agreement must be made on a suitable window size during the initialisation of a connection to prevent either of the participating hosts from getting swamped with data.

1.6 Uses of LANs

Local area networks may be used wherever there is a need for the exchange of information between groups of devices over modest distances. This means that they are likely to be useful in most centres of human activity such as industry, business, education, hospitals and the home. A typical application for the local area network is in the 'Electronic Office'. In business, where large quantities of information have traditionally been passed round as paper documents, there is the greatest opportunity for rationalisation. This could occur at every stage in the use of information; its creation, dissemination and its storage. The creation of written information would take place in a similar fashion to the way it was created in the non-automated office, by entry at a keyboard. However, the use of word processors increases the efficiency of error correction and multiple copy generation. Once text has been entered at the word processor console it can be printed or filed away locally, for instance on a floppy disk. However, if the word processor has been integrated into a complete office system it will be possible to transport information throughout an organisation by giving a simple command. Information will therefore be available when and where it is wanted. Traditionally, once paperwork has exhausted its immediate use it is filed away, resulting in large amounts of valuable office space being occupied as storage. The use of high-density storage devices to hold information, once it has been converted into digital form, would be a more effective use of this space.

Local area networks will be applied in industry. The manufacturing industries should adapt rapidly to take advantage of the increase in efficiency that can be experienced when automated production systems, or robots, are installed. Current generation manufacturing robots are closed systems whose repertoire is limited to performing a single task, the welding of a car body panel for instance. As the sophistication of robot systems increases one robot will be capable of performing a whole range of tasks. When this happens there will be a need to be able to interact with the robot so that it can be given instructions or information can be obtained from it. Similarly, within the application area of industry, local area networks can be used in a control role. In an industrial control environment there may be hundreds of devices which must be constantly monitored so that a process may be adapted to suit changing conditions. The local network is ideal for gathering information and providing controlling data in such situations.

1.7 References

Dallas, I.N., 'A Cambridge Ring local area network realisation of a transport service'. In *Proc. IFIP WG6.4 Workshop on Local Networks, Zurich 1980*, eds. A. West and P. Janson, pp. 245–269. Amsterdam: North-Holland.

Roberts, L.G. and Wessler, B.D., 1973. 'The ARPA network'. In *Computer Communication Networks*, eds. N. Abramson and F.F. Kuo, pp. 485–500. Englewood Cliffs, NJ: Prentice-Hall.

Tanenbaum, A.S., 1981. *Computer Networks*. Englewood Cliffs, NJ: Prentice-Hall.

Wulf, W.A., Levin, R. and Harbison, S.P., 1981. *Hydra/C.mmp: An Experimental Computer System*. New York, NY: McGraw-Hill.

Zimmerman, H., 1980. 'OSI Reference Model – The ISO model of architecture for Open Systems Interconnection'. *IEEE Trans. Comm.*, **COM-28** (4), 425–432.

Chapter 2 **Hierarchy in networks**

In this chapter the ISO Reference Model for Open System Interconnection (the OSI model) is used as a framework for the classification of various aspects of LAN design, providing a basis for comparing different LAN architectures. In Section 2.1 those features of a LAN which are present in particular layers of the OSI model are identified and in subsequent sections the layers are examined in more detail.

2.1 LANs and the OSI Reference Model

One of the ways to define a local area network is to identify which layers of the Open Systems Interconnection model it implements. Because a LAN implementation is a mixture of hardware and software this can be a difficult task. The lower layers might be expected to be implemented in hardware and higher layers to be formed in software with some level at which a transition from one to the other occurs. Unfortunately, this is often not the case. This book is mainly concerned with the hardware implementation of LANs, so this chapter will be concerned with the lower two layers of the OSI model. In most LANs, level 1 is implemented in hardware and level 2 is partially implemented in hardware, the remaining loose ends being tied up with software. Levels 3 and above are normally implemented entirely in software. Level 3 is usually the highest layer which must take account of the properties of the particular network on which it is operating. Higher layers are normally network independent and will not be discussed further here.

2.1.1 The physical layer

The physical layer is simple to identify in a LAN, it is the basic transmission system used to transport information. A variety of communications media are used in LAN designs, notable examples are twisted-pair, coaxial and fibre-optic cables. Information injected onto and removed from the communications medium is encoded using modulation/demodulation circuits which convert between the logic values and their corresponding electrical communication signals.

At the physical layer it is possible to place LAN architectures into one of two categories, **baseband** or **broadband**. On a baseband network both data and control information are encoded and the resulting signal is injected directly onto the communications link at its base frequency. Hence, a 10-Mbps data stream will be represented by a waveform of similar frequency. In a broadband LAN, once the data stream has been encoded, it is modulated onto a higher-frequency signal. This enables the simultaneous transmission of a variety of data streams on a single medium. The advantages and disadvantages of these two schemes will be discussed in Section 2.2.

2.1.2 The data link layer

The functions of the OSI data link layer can be divided into two groups. The lower-level functions are involved in taking the bit transmission system of the physical layer and superimposing onto it a scheme for transmitting frames of user data. To do this, sequences of bits are logically grouped together to form **packets**. As well as the data to be transmitted, a packet contains addressing information, typically identifying the source and destination of the packet, and control information. The control information is used by the data link layer to control access to the communications medium, to provide error checking on the packet contents and in some networks, to provide feedback information to the transmitting device. This feedback information might indicate whether the destination is able to accept more packets or pass other control information. The control fields are also used by network management functions to detect certain classes of error conditions, such as failures in the data link layer hardware. The fields present in a typical LAN packet are illustrated in Fig. 2.1.

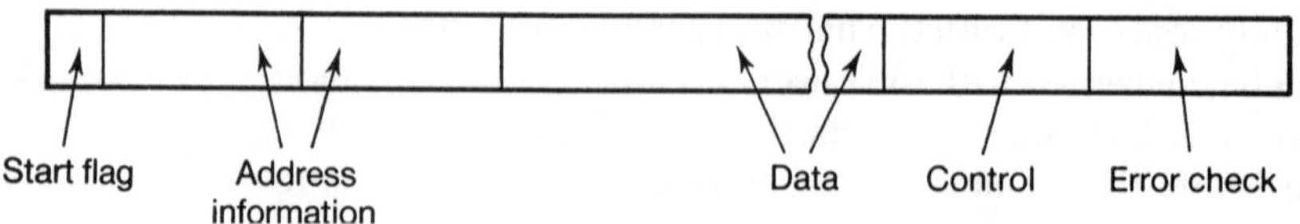

Fig. 2.1   Fields present in a typical LAN packet

The lower sub-layer of the data link layer is referred to as the Media Access Control (MAC) because it provides a transport mechanism for user data and controls the way in which potential transmitters can access the data transport mechanism. In the OSI model, the higher-level data link control functions take the service provided by the MAC sub-layer and add end-to-end flow and error control. This is done by implementing a logical connection between the two ends of a link and providing some mechanism for acknowledging the receipt of error-free packets. This involves the explicit transmission of acknowledgement packets. This higher sub-layer, the Logical Link Control (LLC), is generally not present in LAN architectures and these LANs are therefore said to possess a 'connectionless' data link layer.

The fact that LANs tend to have connectionless link layers reflects some of the characteristics detailed in Chapter 1, especially with respect to speed, cost and low error rates. These considerations are discussed below:

Speed   A LAN should provide a fast and efficient communications facility. Therefore, the additional overhead in providing a connection-based link layer is undesirable.

Cost   Implementing a connection-based link layer would increase the cost of a LAN connection. This additional cost might represent extra hardware and/or software, depending on the LAN implementation.

Error rates   Since LAN transmission systems are designed to possess very good error characteristics (in the order of 1 bit error in 10^{11} is often quoted) it can be argued that a connection-based link layer would be an unnecessary luxury.

2.1.3 The network layer

The network layer of the OSI Reference Model is concerned with the routing and flow control of data packets through a network. The question of whether a LAN adaptor performs ,packet routing depends upon the interconnection pattern, or 'topology', of the network. Topology, a popular way of classifying LANs, is discussed in Chapters 3 and 4. Often local networks have simple topologies making the functions of this layer very simple.

2.2 The physical layer

This section describes the elements of the OSI physical layer which relate to LAN design. The choice of communication medium is a principal consideration at this level, since it affects the final cost of a system and the speed at which data will be transmitted. A topic closely related to the choice of communications medium is determining the type of modulation to be used. A decision must be made as to whether the transmission system is to be baseband or broadband. An excellent treatment of many of the topics discussed in this section may be found in Bylanski and Ingram (1976).

2.2.1 Carrier systems

One of the most important components affecting the operation of a local area network is the transmission medium. There is a wide range of media available to the network designer and the one chosen must suit the environmental and cost requirements as well as the operational requirements of the system. The first measure of a communications medium is whether it will support data transmission at the speeds expected of the local area network, typically from 100 Kbps to 100 Mbps. This is determined by measuring the degree to which a signal injected into one end of a section of the medium is distorted or attenuated before it reaches the other end.

A second consideration in choosing a communication medium is the cost in terms of length and connection. Even though the scale of local area networks is small compared to that of global networks, they may span distances of up to 10 km. So, given that one of the design constraints of this type of network is low cost, this means that the carrier cost must be limited. Traditional media, such as twisted-pair and coaxial cables, are being replaced by newer carriers like fibre-optics, the cost of which is falling as advances in that technology are achieved.

Another important factor in the choice of carrier is the ease of installation and maintenance. A local area network should be modular in structure, implying that it must be easy to extend by the addition of extra lengths of the media. Since it is possible that the network will be inoperative during the extension, the less time that it takes the better. Ease of installation and maintenance will also reduce the overall system costs. The range of communications media which could be considered for use in a LAN design will now be discussed.

Twisted-pair cable

A common type of wire currently used in local area networks is called **twisted-pair**. A length of twisted-pair contains two wires which have been twisted around each other with a pitch calculated to reduce the effects of electro-magnetic interference generated by high-frequency signals being transmitted. This type of communications medium can support data transmission at frequencies of up to 10 MHz without a high degree of attenuation. It is possible to extract the data from the received signal after it has been transmitted through several hundred metres of the cable. At the receiving end an amplifier is used to strengthen the signal. This amplifier may incorporate some hysteresis to reduce erroneous data being introduced by noise. A great advantage of twisted-pair as a medium is that it is both cheap and easy to install. The cost used to be related to the cost of copper which was used as the conductor but now low-cost alloys with good conducting properties are often used. Installation of new lengths of twisted-pair is simple. In general, there will be a standard plug fitting for a given network and each section of the medium will have one attached to each end. Extending the network will therefore involve only the separating and joining of plugs.

Coaxial cable

Coaxial cable is a dual conductor cable in which one of the conductors is enclosed by the other in order to provide a shielded environment. The signal is transmitted down a central wire which is coated in an insulator. This insulating cylinder is then covered in a plait of the second conductor which is used as the ground level. Depending upon the quality of the conductors used in the construction of the cable, the frequency at which this carrier can support a signal with low attenuation can be several hundred MHz. This also means that high-grade coaxial cable can be used for lower-speed network links which span much larger distances than can twisted-pair, without the need for signal regeneration. Coaxial cable has similar properties to those of twisted-pair so far as ease of installation and maintenance are concerned. It is probably the most widely used communications medium in the field of local area networks.

Radio

The use of communication systems based on radio transmission has several advantages. The main one is that there is no physical medium, such as a cable, to be installed. Instead of this the medium is the atmosphere. The cost of installing a link is that of setting up the transmitter and the receiver. A further advantage is that the network nodes may be mobile. The use of the atmosphere as a medium does have some drawbacks. Whereas the attenuation characteristics of a metal conductor will be effectively constant, the characteristics of the atmosphere are certainly not. They are highly dependent upon the weather conditions at any time. The impact of this is that the transmission and reception equipment can be complex and therefore expensive.

The favoured carrier frequencies for local network use are in the UHF or microwave region of the electromagnetic spectrum. Here the signal is directional and reasonably sized 'dishes' may be used for transmission and reception. The Aloha network is an early example of a radio-based system (Abramson, 1973). Packet radio networks have also been constructed for military use where the transmitters and receivers are on vehicles and are therefore mobile. Another application where radio links have been used is in the connecting of more than one local area network. In 'Project Universe' a satellite link is used to connect LANs spread across southern England (Adams *et al.*, 1982).

Waveguide

A waveguide is a tube which has a conducting inner surface and which is filled with a dry inert gas. The transmission component of a waveguide communications system is a transmitter similar to a radio frequency transmitter, but instead of transmitting into the atmosphere transmissions are into the tube. The conduction characteristics of waveguide transmission make it particularly suitable for high-rate data communications. The attenuation encountered by the signal travelling down the waveguide is proportional to the square root of its frequency. This means that increasing the frequency is less of a problem than with other systems where the attenuation is directly proportional to the frequency. Using this type of communications system it is possible to obtain data rates in the region 250–500 Mbps. The drawback of using waveguides as the transmission medium for a local area network is the cost and complexity of installation. At each end of the carrier there would be a need for the high-frequency transmission and reception components. As the carrier itself is a tube, about 5 cm in diameter, its installation is a task of similar magnitude to laying water pipes. If this were undertaken during the construction of a building it would not cause undue problems. However, the ducting in an existing building is unlikely to be able to accommodate a tube of this size and so large-scale alterations would be necessary. This is the prime reason why waveguides are unlikely to be used as a common transmission medium for local area networks.

Optical fibre

The use of very small fibres of glass as a transmission medium was proposed long ago. However, until recently it was not considered suitable for use in local area networks because of its high cost. Advances in the manufacturing processes used for spinning the thin fibres have made the cost comparable to that of coaxial cable.

The transmission characteristics of fibre-optic cables make them especially suitable for use in local area networks. Attenuation of the transmitted signal is very low compared with metal cable conductors. Transmissions can be at rates of up to several hundred Mbps, with the data being extracted after tens of kilometres. Signals are transmitted down the fibres as high-frequency light waves. The cost of the light sources and detectors needed for the complete transmission system has also fallen to a level which makes this type of system competitive. The most common type of light source in use is the light emitting diode (LED) which functions up to around 50 MHz. Above this frequency semiconductor lasers are normally used but these are a good deal more expensive than LEDs.

A great advantage of communications systems based on optical fibre technology is that they can be used in electrically noisy environments without corrupting the data being transmitted. This is because the medium is highly immune to external electromagnetic interference. The installation of fibre-optic cables is of similar complexity to that of coaxial cable or twisted-pair. It may be routed easily through heating or power cable ducts. Connecting lengths of the cable together is more complex than the metal case since each end of the fibre must be polished so that the light signal is not disturbed. This may not be a problem though, since component manufacturers are now producing complete transmission systems which perform data encoding, transmission and decoding at low cost. If an extra long link were necessary the simplest way to do it would be to connect two such transmission systems together.

As the speeds demanded by users of local area networks increase, optical fibres are likely to be one of the main transmission media in use. They are now frequently used in newly designed LANs.

Infra-red

The use of infra-red transmission as a carrier for local area networks has been proposed. This type of transmission is normally limited to the interiors of buildings since the intensity of the solar infra-red source would swamp any exterior transmissions.

Another problem with infra-red transmission is that it suffers from shadowing. If a large object is placed between the transmitter and a receiver then the signal will be effectively cut off. A possible solution to this is to place the transmitter on the ceiling of a room so that the chance of breaking the transmission path is reduced. An advantage of using this type of transmission system is that there is a very small cost of installation because there is no physical link. So far the use of this technology is at an experimental stage and the data rates achieved have been limited.

2.2.2 Modulation and line encoding

One of the ways in which local area networks are categorised is whether they are baseband or broadband. These terms relate to the way in which data is transmitted onto the communications medium.

In a baseband network the encoded electrical values representing the logical 1s and 0s that make up the data are inserted directly onto the communications medium. Most baseband systems use **two-level encoding** in which two signal levels, representing the two logical values, appear on the medium. Line transitions between these two levels are at a frequency similar to, or the same as, the data rate. However, the transmitted signal is generally not a bit-by-bit representation of the data; the reason for this is to simplify the task of receiving the data.

In a broadband system a high-frequency signal is normally transmitted which has the data **modulated** onto it in one of a number of ways. One modulation scheme is to vary the amplitude of the transmitted wave over a fixed number of wavelengths. A logical 0 could be represented as a series of low-amplitude wave periods while a series of high-amplitude periods would represent a logical 1. This technique is known as **amplitude modulation**. Another method is **frequency modulation** in which two different frequencies, normally quite close together, are used to represent the two logical values. These two methods are illustrated in Fig. 2.2.

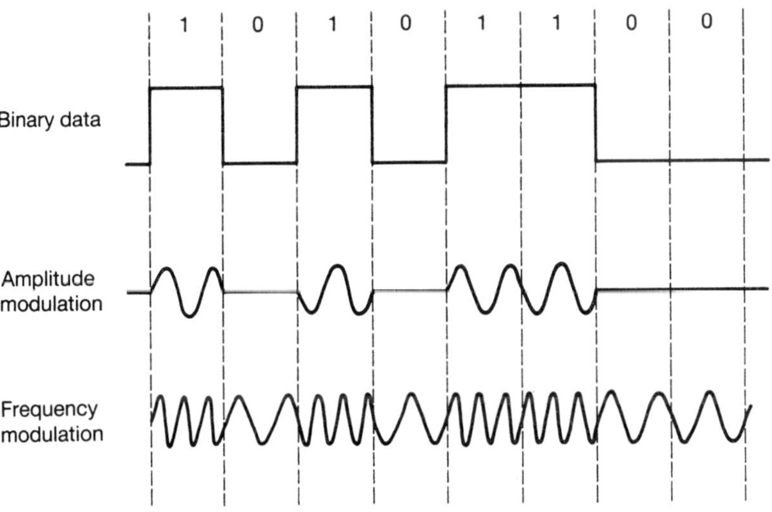

Fig. 2.2   Broadband modulation methods

The major advantage of broadband over baseband methods is that the former allows many channels of information to be sent over a single medium. Each channel has a different carrier frequency and by appropriate filtering techniques, the channels can be separated by the receiving circuits. A broadband network can carry digital signals as well as analogue information such as video and audio. There is a price to be paid for all this flexibility and that is cost and complexity. The analogue filtering circuits and demodulators and modulators are complex and difficult to make cheaply. The majority of LANs use baseband transmission but there are a number of broadband systems in existence such as LocalNet (Biba, 1981).

A problem which is common to both methods is that of extracting timing information from the received data. Both methods allow the injection of logical values onto the medium at the transmitter and the recovery of these values at the receiver. It was mentioned above that the signals sent down the medium are not normally the same as the data itself and this is because timing information is commonly encoded along with the data, to allow the receiver to sample the incoming bit stream at the appropriate time.

The rate at which data is transmitted on a network will be known by all nodes on the network and so they will also know the duration of a bit. In order to receive data it is then necessary to sample the incoming signal once per bit time. Ideally this will be done near the centre of each bit so that its tolerance to frequency shift will be high. However, when the data is transmitted from one point on the network to another there will be a delay while it passes along the communications medium. Even if the receiving device knows the precise length of a bit, it is difficult for it to know when one bit time ends and another begins. This can lead to problems if the receiving node does not know when to sample the line as it could do so at the end of a bit time and so sample a transitory value.

When this problem was experienced in the connection of simple devices, such as teletypes, to computers it was overcome by the use of **asynchronous** transmission techniques. Here each byte of data is preceded by a start bit (a 0) and followed by a stop bit (a 1) as shown in Fig. 2.3. The idle state of the line is logical 1 so that when a byte arrives the receiver uses the start bit to synchronise itself to the bit timing of the incoming signal. To do this a clock running at 16 times the bit rate is used and the alignment can be made to one sixteenth of a bit time. So long as the receiver's clock is roughly the same as the transmitter's it

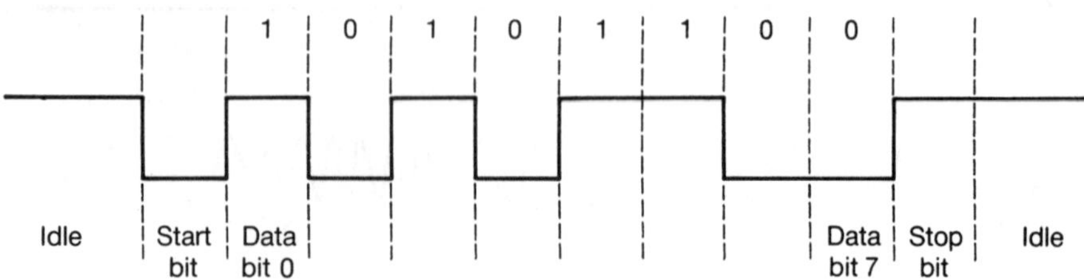

Fig. 2.3   Asynchronous transmission format

will remain aligned with the incoming data long enough to read the 8 bits of data which are arriving. It will then re-align with the start bit of the next byte of data.

This method works well at low speeds but at higher rates providing a 16 times clock can be difficult and having to transmit the start and stop bits with every byte of data means that the line utilisation is only 80% of its maximum. To get around these problems **synchronous** transmission methods are used. Here a clock is maintained in the receiver with the same frequency as the transmitter's clock and the same phase as the incoming data. This can be achieved in a number of ways. One solution is to duplicate each length of the communications medium in the network. The link can then be used to transmit a clock with an identical phase to that of the data signal. This second signal would be subjected to the same delays as the data and the receiving device would then be able to use this clock to sample the incoming data bits. A drawback of this scheme is the extra cost of the communications medium. If the transmission system is baseband then another conducting path will be required and the cost will increase. It may not increase significantly because the cost of installation will be much the same and cables carrying, for example, four conductors are not much more expensive than those carrying two. If the transmission system is broadband then the extra cost will represent the components necessary for a second channel.

The solution to the problem of data delay and frequency shift which is most suitable for local area networks, is to encode the data in such a way that the reference clock can be extracted from the received signal along with the data. A number of methods are available for encoding data. Of these methods only those in which there is at least one transition (low to high or high to low) of the transmitted signal per bit time have the potential for direct clock recovery. In Fig. 2.4 some of the possible ways of representing data during transmission are illustrated. Note that in this figure all the encodings represent the same transmitted data pattern.

The simplest code, in which there is no translation of the data, is called Non-Return-to-Zero (NRZ, Fig. 2.4a). The signal level over the whole bit time corresponds directly to the data value being transmitted. A logical 0 is represented by one signal level while the other signal level represents a logical 1. A sequence of either of the possible data values is therefore represented as an unchanging signal level. As there is only a change in the transmitted signal level if two consecutively transmitted bits are of differing values, there is no opportunity to derive the base clock frequency from the received signal. In order to accurately receive all data it is therefore necessary either to restrict the maximum length of a constant value sequence or to make the clock used for transmission available to the receiver by means of a duplicate channel.

A more practical encoding which is widely used in LAN applications is called Manchester encoding (Fig. 2.4b). In this scheme logical 1 is represented as a square wave cycle with the mark (high level) appearing in the first half cycle and 0 is represented by having the mark in the second half of the cycle. As both data value representations have a transition of the signal level half-way through

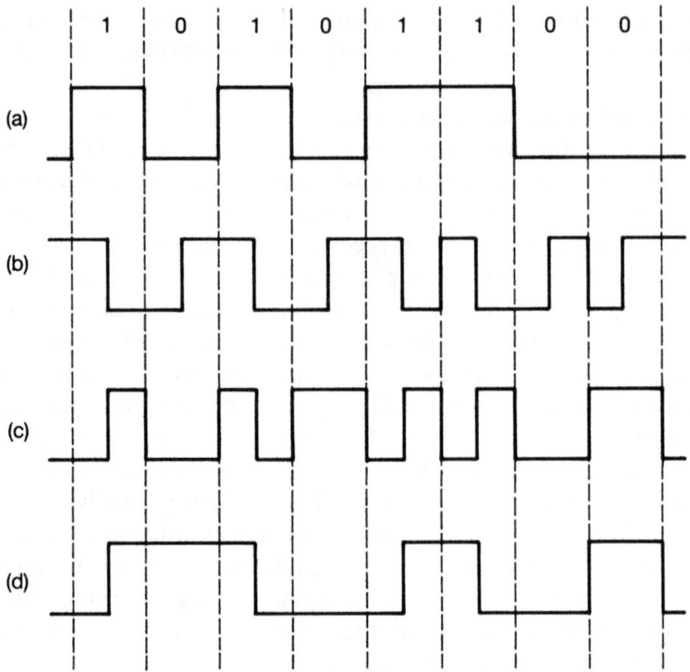

Fig. 2.4   Some encoding schemes suitable for baseband signalling: (a) NRZ encoding;
(b) Manchester encoding; (c) biphase encoding; (d) delay encoding

the bit time this scheme allows the receiving device to regenerate the frequency at which the transmission was made. As the change always takes place at the same time, it is also possible to reproduce the phase of the original clock.

The factor which contributes most to restricting the rate at which data can be transmitted along any communications medium is the way that instantaneous signal level changes are distorted. As the transmission frequency increases, so the length of pulses on the medium will decrease. Since each signal transition is distorted the situation can arise where the true value of the pulse is not achieved. In using an encoding scheme which allows two transitions per bit time the maximum operating frequency is halved compared to that attainable with a scheme where only one transition is permitted. This is the case with Manchester encoding and a similar scheme known as biphase encoding (Fig. 2.4c), in which there is always a transition at the start of each bit time and there is an additional transition in the middle of the bit time if the data is a logical 1.

An encoding scheme which has only half as many line transitions as Manchester or biphase is known as delay encoding (Fig. 2.4d). On a given link this allows transmission at twice the rate of the previous schemes but is rather more complex to encode and decode.

2.2.3 Effects of physical parameters

A common problem to be overcome in digital transmission systems is jitter. This occurs when signal transitions on the line do not take place at the correct point in time, but are spread out around the theoretically correct time. The displacement can be due to a number of factors such as the characteristics of the transmission medium and the driving and receiving logic. In addition, the actual data patterns can influence the amount of jitter, some patterns of 0s and 1s being worse than others. If it is not controlled in some way, jitter tends to accumulate as it passes through successive links in the transmission medium. Ultimately, it becomes impossible to derive a suitable clock from the incoming data and bits can become lost or random bits injected into the data.

Jitter can be controlled by the use of averaging circuits such as phase-locked loops. In a phase-locked loop the frequency of oscillation is controlled by a voltage which is derived from the incoming waveform. If this voltage averages the incoming waveform over a period of time, the rate of change of the resulting oscillation will be reduced. Thus the magnitude of the jitter can be controlled, reducing the chance of inserting or removing bits.

2.2.4 Errors

In the OSI model, errors are normally considered at the physical layer as well as other layers. This is because among carrier systems for all networks one has to consider poor quality systems which result in high error rates on the transmission medium. This is often not the case in local networks, since the design of the network is such that the error rate at this level is very low. This is ensured either by using high-quality transmission systems, or by restricting the domain over which such transmission systems can be used so that it is easier to achieve a low error rate. Alternatively some local network designs which are inherently error prone, have special circuits specific to the design which ensure that the error rate as seen by the higher levels is low.

By making the transmission system relatively error free it is possible to adopt a strategy where errors are only detected at high levels in the system. Providing this happens infrequently there is a gain in simplicity by not having to detect and correct at the lower levels as well.

2.3 The data link layer

The functions of the OSI data link layer (in the case of LANs just the Media Access Control sub-layer) which are relevant to LAN design can be split into two groups. Firstly, this sub-layer takes the basic transmission system provided by the physical layer and superimposes onto it a scheme for transmitting pieces of user data. This involves defining a framework for the transmission of data, commonly referred to as a packet format. The ways in which data are represented on the transmission system are discussed in Section 2.3.1.

The second goal of the MAC sub-layer is to control the way in which devices are permitted to access the facilities provided by the physical layer. These schemes define the protocols to be followed when transmitting packets. The different schemes used for access control are described in Section 2.3.2.

2.3.1 The representation of data

The data link layer transmits blocks of data embedded in structures called packets. The size of packets used by LANs varies from under 30 to over 1000 bits. Some LANs have a constant packet size, others allow it to vary. The evolution of such packets from their origins in early networks is now described.

In early WANs, packets were made up from groups of characters from a character set such as ASCII or EBCDIC. Certain sequences of control characters were used to mark the start and end of the packet and the actual data was placed between these markers. Such packets and the protocols associated with them are said to be **character-oriented**. A typical packet is shown in Fig. 2.5.

This method works well when textual data is sent but is less satisfactory when binary data has to be transmitted. In this latter case there is always the possibility that the data could contain a character sequence which is the same as the end of packet marker. To avoid this the data is scanned on transmission and if such a sequence is found it is modified by the insertion of an extra control character. Thus the offending sequence will be changed and will not be recognised by the receiver as the end marker. The receiver must now scan the received data and remove any control characters which were inserted by the transmitter. This mechanism of character insertion and removal is known as **character stuffing**.

Because character-oriented protocols were dependent on the character set used and all computers did not use the same number of bits to represent a character, a different approach became necessary when more and more computers had to communicate increasing amounts of data. This approach was to make protocols and packets **bit-oriented**, in which a packet may contain an arbitrary number of bits. Several differing standards emerged while these

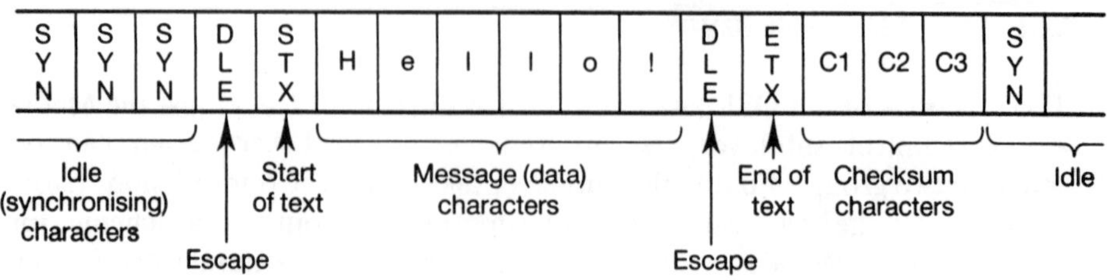

Fig. 2.5   A packet from a character-oriented protocol

protocols evolved and many are still in use. One of them, the High-level Data Link Control protocol (HDLC), was adopted by ISO and this is now the prevailing standard.

As with the character-oriented protocol, this system needs a special mechanism to indicate the start and end of packets. In HDLC, a frame (packet) starts and ends with the bit pattern '01111110'. To prevent the occurrence of this pattern in the data it is scanned during transmission and any sequence of five 1s has a 0 appended to it. Thus the only sequences of six 1s that the receiver will see are the start and end markers. The receiver must then scan the data field and remove any 0 which occurs after a sequence of five 1s. This method of achieving data transparency is known as **bit stuffing**. The format of an HDLC frame is shown in Fig. 2.6.

A protocol for transmitting and receiving HDLC frames is defined as part of the standard and the address, control and checksum fields are used by this protocol. The checksum field is part of the error-checking mechanism. It is formed by taking a cyclic redundancy checksum (CRC) of the address, control and data fields at the transmitter. At the receiver this value is again computed from the arriving frame and compared with the checksum field of the packet. If they are different then an error has occurred on the line. If they are the same then it is probable (but not certain) that the frame is correct. The HDLC frame can carry an arbitrary amount of data but the effectiveness of the checksum diminishes with increasing data. Large-scale integrated circuits are available which will transmit and receive data using the HDLC protocols and they have been used to implement LANs by embedding the LAN packet within the HDLC data field.

The packets used on LANs normally carry two address fields which are usually of fixed size and range which, in practice, are from 8 to 48 bits in length. There is also a data field which may be of fixed size or may be variable. If it is variable then it is likely that there will be a length field in the packet which indicates the size of the data field. Most LAN packets have some form of error-detection field, which can range from a simple parity bit to 16 or more bits of CRC. Most LAN packets also have a small number, generally less than 10, of control bits. These have a variety of uses and examples will be seen in later chapters.

At the physical layer the idea of bit synchronisation was discussed whereby the receiver becomes and remains synchronised to the incoming bit stream. At the data link layer there is the analogous idea of packet synchronisation in

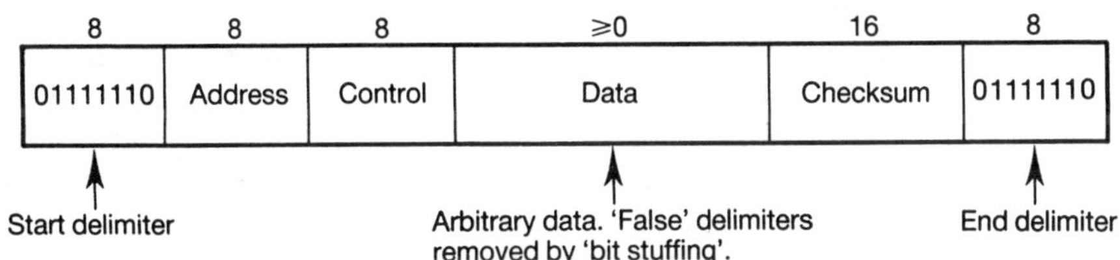

Fig. 2.6   Format of an HDLC frame

which the receiver must synchronise to the start and end of packets. Finding the start is normally harder than finding the end, since the length of the packet is normally fixed or deducible from a length field near the front of the packet. In many cases the LAN medium is idle when no packet is being transmitted and just a few distinctive bits at the start of the packet are sufficient to warn the receiver that a packet is arriving. In such cases it is always possible that a receiver will be switched on and become active part of the way through a packet. When this occurs the receiver could misinterpret the packet. Some networks avoid this by using the HDLC approach of reserving certain bit patterns as the start marker and using bit stuffing to achieve data transparency.

Another method which is used is to violate the line encoding scheme at the start of a packet. This could be done with the Manchester encoding scheme by having a bit time in which no line transition occurred. An error on the line could, of course, cause the same effect and with all such schemes the data link layer must cater for such eventualities.

2.3.2 Access methods – sharing the communication medium

The aim of a local area network is to allow efficient communication between devices which are attached to the network. The method used to share the transmission system can be either static or dynamic in nature. That is, the allocation of the resource can be fixed or it can be dependent upon the needs of the transmitter. The technique of circuit switching is not suitable for sharing the communications medium in general purpose local area networks because there is a minimum length of time required to set up the direct link between the two devices which want to communicate. Data sent over a LAN is typically transmitted at high speed and in bursts. This means that the overhead of setting up the link represents a significant proportion of the total transaction time and therefore renders this scheme impractical.

As previously described, the principle under which almost all local area networks have been designed is that of packet switching. Data is transmitted across the network in small frames which also include addressing and control information. The amount of data which can be held in a single packet varies from network to network. Some networks have a fixed-length packet. A particular example of this type is the Cambridge Ring in which the basic transmission frame contains just two bytes of data. Other networks have a variable-length data field in the packet, an example being the prototype Ethernet which has a maximum data length of 512 bytes.

In wide area packet-switched networks the switching nodes which connect groups of transmission lines are complex devices. Their most important feature is that they have the capacity to buffer complete packets as they arrive. This means that if the line on which they are to be transmitted is busy or if the next node down the line is not ready they can wait. Such a facility makes such nodes expensive because they require a large amount of storage and some processing power to control the retention of packets. So, as the cost of nodes in a local area network must be low, buffers should be minimised and packets forwarded rapidly. Typically, this is achieved by removing the need for switching nodes within the network and incorporating the buffer function into the host interfaces. In **bus**-type networks all the host interfaces connect onto a single medium and in this case the switching nodes have been replaced by a simple connection. This type of network has the important property that only one device can transmit at any time.

Local area networks which share out the communications medium in an adaptive manner are usually designed so that transmission takes place in one of two ways, termed **synchronous access** and **random access**. Local networks use one or other of these methods, not usually both. In the synchronous case, transmission will be synchronised to a time frame dictated by the network. When a device has decided that it wants to transmit, it must listen to the network and wait until a special marker arrives. This marker gives a device permission to transmit and once one arrives the device can send a packet onto the network. In some networks only one of these markers will exist at any time, whereas on other types of network several markers will coexist. A local area network which allows random access does not impose any bounds upon the time when a device can transmit. As soon as a device wants to transmit a packet it will attempt to do so.

It is likely that a single communications link will be used by more than one host device at each end. Similarly, within a single connected device there may be more than one process wishing to communicate with the remote host. In these cases the line is deemed to be shared and there has to be some scheme for deciding when each of the interested parties can transmit. The simplest solution to this problem is to allocate all potential transmitters a short equally-sized segment of the total transmission time of the line. The devices transmit one after another until all of them have used the link, at which point the first device may transmit again. This technique is called **time division multiplexing** (TDM).

One of the problems of TDM is that it can cause the line utilisation to be very low when the devices connected to the communications link are very slow and so generate data too slowly to fill up their time slots. When this happens, dummy data has to be transmitted. Terminals remotely connected to a computer system are examples of slow devices which could cause this problem. If other devices generate data faster than their time slot can consume it then their demand will not be met even though other time slots may be hardly used. LANs normally have a more efficient access scheme than TDM.

A local area network may be a connected set of devices of a diverse nature. The way in which access to the network is granted is a consideration that must be made during the design process. One of the most important questions to be answered is whether there should be a single control node which grants other nodes the permission to make data transmissions. Networks which operate in this way are said to employ **centralised control** and are called master/slave networks. If one of the slave devices wants to transmit then it must wait until the master contacts it. The master will continuously circulate between all its slaves, saying to them 'if you want to transmit, do so now'. Once a slave has received this permission it may transmit to any other device connected to the network.

This type of network has the advantage that transmission collisions never take place, i.e. there is only ever a single transmitting device. However, it also has the disadvantage of being extremely inefficient for a network where few devices want to transmit simultaneously. For example, on a network with 100 connected devices and only one which wishes to transmit repeatedly, the master device would still circulate all 99 dumb devices before allowing the active one to transmit.

Part of the inefficiency of this type of network results from the amount of processing that the master device must perform in switching from one node to another. Some types of local area networks with centralised control reduce this overhead by implementing the control function in the network hardware. For instance, the right to transmit may be linked to possessing a **permission token**. This token can be a unique sequence of bits which is circulated around the network by the network control logic. Obtaining such a token is similar to being told by the master device that the network is available for a transmission. As only one token would exist at any time, there should be no chance of more than one device transmitting simultaneously.

The alternative to centralised control networks are those in which control of access to the network is distributed between all network nodes. In this type of system each network node reserves the right to transmit when its attached device requests this service. The most important drawback of this scheme is that it is particularly prone to transmission collisions, which occur when more than one device wants to transmit. This problem can be alleviated by altering the network node's transmission policy. One solution demands that the node listens to the network to ascertain whether another transmission is already underway. The node only initiates its own transmission if it regards the network as quiet. Another way of reducing the probability of transmission collision is to divide time up into slots of equal length, where all network nodes have a common reference point. When a transmission is required, the network node must wait until the beginning of the next time slice before starting. As there is a chance of a collision taking place during normal operation of a distributed control network, the protocols employed on them must be able to detect such errors and retransmit. The techniques used to provide distributed control in this way are described further in Chapter 3.

The type of service to be provided and the type of traffic to be carried are major factors which influence the design of the access method. In some applications of a computer network the idea of a guaranteed service time is essential, whereas in others the ability to send data for relatively long periods of time is more important. An example of an application requiring some kind of guarantee is the transmission of digital voice traffic. Although in this case it does not matter if some of the data is corrupted or even lost during transmission, there must be a continuous flow of data so that unnatural pauses do not break up the conversation. For this type of traffic a **deterministic** network would be most suitable. This is one in which an attached device is guaranteed a regular opportunity to transmit within a time limit that can be accurately calculated. The main disadvantage of this type of network is that, since the service must also be offered to other users on a regular basis, the length of time for which a device can transmit may be limited. Deterministic networks generally employ synchronous access.

For applications where the ability to transmit bulk data is more important than having a regular service interval, a **probabilistic** type of network may be suitable. Here the only way of estimating the waiting time that a device is likely to encounter before being able to transmit is by calculating the probability that another device is using the network. Although the waiting time is difficult to predict and may be long, once a device has permission to transmit the limit on the amount of data which it can send may be high. Such networks normally use a random access method.

2.4 The network layer

At the network layer the important questions to be considered are the sort of interface the network provides to the higher layers, how packets are routed within the LAN and whether any flow control procedure is provided. When discussing this layer it is also appropriate to consider how networks are connected together. The connection to both like and unlike networks must be considered. In the case of unlike networks, the network layer is the appropriate level for connection, while for like networks the data link layer is often used. For a discussion of LAN interconnection see Leslie (1983).

2.4.1 Routing and flow control

It is a characteristic of many LANs that routing is either very simple or unnecessary. For example, in many ring LANs packets make a complete revolution and thus no routing takes place. In other cases the address space can be partitioned so that it is easy to decide which way a packet should be sent on the basis of the address bits. The user may sometimes wish to have direct access to the routing decisions in order to take advantage of particular performance features.

The devices which an organisation may want to attach to a local area network will range widely in terms of their function, complexity and cost. This has an important impact on network design in two particular areas. Firstly, the amount of data that a device can transmit at one time and, secondly, controlling when it should be allowed to make a transmission. If a network was used solely by sophisticated devices which had a large amount of local storage, for use as buffers for the reception of messages, then the size of data that could be transmitted would not have to be limited. However, it is likely that simple devices, which do not have the capacity to buffer large amounts of data, will also be attached to the network. There must, therefore, be a method of controlling how often a device may transmit.

A device characteristic which is closely related to the size of buffer available is the rate at which it can use the data that it receives. Clearly, a device which can always process the data that it receives faster than the network can provide it, is able to receive large blocks of data without the need for high-capacity buffers. On the other hand, a very slow device can still accept data from the network in large quantities if it has large buffers. So the method used to control the rate at which a device may transmit must take account of the variable nature of how fast a receiving device can consume data as well as the size of its buffers. In an extreme case there could be a slow device with very small buffers which wants to communicate with a device which has very large buffers or which has a very high processing rate. When the slow device is transmitting there is no problem since the fast device can cope with whatever it receives. In the opposite case, however, the fast device must be restrained so that it does not transmit so fast that it swamps the slower device.

This type of control, which is called **flow control**, can be exercised in several ways and it often appears at more than one level in the hierarchy. In one local area network, the Cambridge Ring, it is a function of the network hardware and therefore present in the data link layer. In this case packets are rejected by the network node to which the receiving device is connected until that device has dealt with the last data received and has directly instructed the node to accept more data. The data which is transmitted returns to the source device having been marked by the destination to say whether or not it was rejected. Further flow control must still be provided in higher-level protocols but this low-level flow control serves a useful function in improving the efficiency of packet transmission.

In the majority of local area network architectures it is difficult to perform flow control at this level. In these cases it is necessary for the destination device to explicitly acknowledge the receipt of a piece of data, and thereby say that it is ready for more data, by initiating a completely new transmission. If either of these schemes is to work, then either the network node or all devices connected to the network must be capable of receiving a minimum, predefined-sized piece of data. This ensures that even the most simple device will be able to receive complete messages.

In addition to flow control protecting hosts from over-copious dialogue partners, its presence in the network layer also allows some degree of control over the amount of traffic on the network and hence the level of congestion. This level of control is not strictly necessary in LANs but is very important in store and forward networks. It becomes important in a LAN context when LANs are interconnected by devices which have a store and forward nature.

2.4.2 Level of service

The level of service provided by the network layer generally falls into two categories and the layers above may choose to use one or the other. The data link layer will accept packets from the network layer and attempt to deliver them to the destination. The packets may arrive out of order or not at all. This level of service may be offered to the higher layers by the network layer and is called a **datagram** service. With this level of service there is no concept of an enduring connection between the network layers of the two hosts. A datagram service does not hide some of the characteristics of the data link layer from the layers above the network layer. In particular, the probabilistic or deterministic nature of the data link layer will show through.

Alternatively the network layer may provide a more sophisticated level of service. Each packet of data that is received has its contents and its position in the whole data verified. If the data contains errors or the packet was received out of sequence then it will be rejected and the source will transmit another copy. All the data segmentation, error-checking and retransmissions will take place without the user being aware of them and are thus said to be transparent to the user. This type of connection-based service is called a **virtual circuit**.

2.4.3 Interconnection of LANs

As a local area network grows, its performance will begin to deteriorate and it will become less attractive as a tool for resource sharing. A solution to this problem is to split the network into two or more individual networks and interconnect them in some way. It may be possible to group together devices which frequently communicate, although it may also prove cost effective to perform the splitting on a geographical basis. In this case the connected networks are of the same type and the connection might be performed by simply exchanging packets from the data link layer between the two networks. A device to oversee this operation is required and it is normally a computer with interfaces onto both networks. When connection is performed at this level the device is usually termed a **bridge**.

When dissimilar networks are connected, rather more work must normally be done by the device to match different addressing schemes and packet sizes on the two networks. In this case the interconnection is normally done at a higher level, dealing with packets from the network layer, and the connecting device is termed a **gateway**, a term borrowed from WAN technology. A gateway may provide interconnection in terms of a datagram service or a virtual circuit service. In the latter case the gateway must contain state information regarding the connections currently established through it. The reliability of the gateway is therefore of some importance when used in this way.

Two important issues to be considered in the interconnection of LANs are addressing across a system of networks and the level of packet responses which can be implemented. These problems have also occurred in the past when the need to connect wide area networks arose. However, in the case of LANs the solutions to these problems must be derived differently since the mechanisms for addressing and responses have usually been cast into the network hardware design.

Addresses in a LAN are usually a fixed-length field appearing near the beginning of a packet. The length of the address field defines the number of devices which can be attached to the network, since each device must have a unique address, and the entire field is checked by the node hardware to determine whether it should receive the packet. The address field could be split up into two subfields, one corresponding to the name of the destination network and the other to the destination device connected to that network. However, once the hardware which examines the incoming destination address has been designed and implemented, there is no potential to expand the meaning of the address field into the wider context of a set of connected networks. Transmissions intended for a remote network must therefore be directed at the address of the relevant bridge. When the bridge receives a packet from a network the information in the address field only represents the intended destination network. The address of the destination device has to be placed in the data field of the packet and the protocol in use must define precisely where the bridge can find it.

Depending upon the network access protocol in use on the destination network, the bridge may have to receive the whole packet before it can transfer it onto the destination LAN. The major consideration in this respect is the size of packet on the two networks. If the LANs are the same, then a one to one correspondence can be made between packets received and transmitted by the bridge. If packets on the destination LAN are shorter than those on the source LAN, the bridge can start to forward the data before the entire packet has been received. This could be used as a mechanism for maximising the performance across the bridge. However, it might also have the effect of complicating the protocols implemented above the packet level. This would be necessary, since there would have to be a mechanism for backing out of the situation where an error is detected at the end of a packet being received by the bridge and part of the data field of that packet had already been passed on to the destination LAN. In the case where the source LAN has a shorter packet size than the destination LAN, no such optimisation can be made. Here, sufficient packets to fill a destination LAN packet have to be received from the source LAN before a transmission can be made.

The vital piece of information to be received before the bridge can start transmitting is the destination address. Once the bridge has received the portion of the data field which contains this address it can attempt to forward the packet on to the second network. The delay experienced by the packet depends upon the access method used by the destination network and this delay may cause the whole of the packet to be received from the source network before the transmission starts.

2.5 References

Abramson, N., 1973. 'The Aloha system'. In *Computer Communication Networks*, eds. N. Abramson and F.F. Kuo, pp. 501–17. Englewood Cliffs, NJ: Prentice-Hall.

Adams, G.C., Burren, J.W., Cooper, C.S. and Girard, P.M., 1982. 'The interconnection of local area networks via a satellite network'. In *New Advances in Computer Systems*, ed. K.G. Beauchamp, pp. 201–10. Dordrecht, Holland: Reidel.

Biba, K.J., 1981. 'Packet communication networks for broadband coaxial cable'. *Local Networks and Distributed Office Systems*, Online, May, pp. 611–25.

Bylanski, P. and Ingram, D.G.W., 1976. *Digital Transmission Systems*. Stevenage, England: Peter Peregrinus Ltd.

Leslie, I.M., 1983. 'Extending the local area network'. PhD Thesis, Computer Laboratory, University of Cambridge, February.

Chapter 3   Local area network architectures

A convenient way of classifying LANs is by means of topology and this chapter begins by summarising some of the topologies which are used. Some examples of LANs with differing topologies are also described in this chapter and the next. This chapter deals with LANs having bus, tree and mesh topologies, while Chapter 4 describes the various types of ring LAN which have been devised.

3.1 LAN topologies

The topology of a LAN is usually a description of the wiring which connects the network nodes. However, it does not always describe the route which packets take when they traverse the network. In general, the topologies employed by LANs are simple and include rings, stars and buses. This is in contrast to the topologies of wide area networks which are normally rather more irregular. The most common topologies presently in use for LANs are the bus and the ring, the reason for their prevalence being that they are both very simple to implement. Rings and buses both require only one sort of node on the network. This node serves both to connect hosts to the network and to perform packet routing. The other topologies generally require two types of nodes, network nodes for the attachment of hosts and switching nodes for routing packets. Examples of network topologies are shown in Fig. 3.1.

3.1.1 Bus topology

In this, the simplest of all LAN topologies, a common communication medium is used to which all network nodes are connected. Connection at the physical level is simple in that a device has only to tap onto the medium. The bus is normally 'passive', that is, it contains no active circuitry to amplify signals. This means that buses are inherently reliable but may be limited in size since transmitters must be able to send a signal the full length of the bus. When a packet is placed onto the bus it is seen by all devices which are attached to the bus. In terms of interconnecting devices and installing a network, bus systems are often simpler than other topologies.

    Bus systems have been designed and implemented using a very wide range of communications media. Both cable (coaxial, twisted-pair) and atmospheric

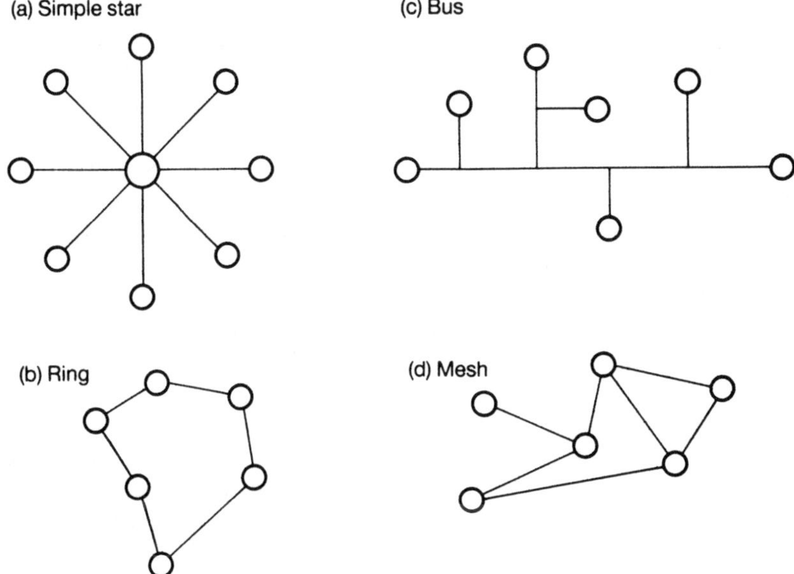

Fig. 3.1   LAN topologies

types (radio) are suitable for use in buses. A bus network using coaxial cable will be described later in this chapter.

A wide variety of access methods are also employed on bus systems. One system is the random broadcast technique, where each device attempts to transmit as soon as it has data available. This is an attractive scheme, since implementation is not difficult. As a result of standardisation in the Institute of Electrical and Electronic Engineers (IEEE) and the European Computer Manufacturer's Association (ECMA), an architecture for a bus system using the permission token access protocol has also been drawn up (IEEE, 1982). This architecture is seen as combining some of the best characteristics of the token ring access protocol (described in Chapter 4, Section 4.1) with the modularity and reliability of bus systems.

3.1.2 Ring topology

A ring network contains a loop of communication medium. Data flows around the ring in one direction only and devices connected to the ring can receive data from it. In order to transmit, it is necessary for a device to interrupt the data on the ring so that it can inject its own. Rings are normally 'active', that is, they include regenerating circuits which must operate continuously. This means that rings can be extended to any size provided sufficient regenerating circuits or **repeaters** are included.

When a packet is transmitted on a ring it will circulate indefinitely unless removed. In some ring systems the packet is removed by the source and in others it is removed at the destination. In common with buses, rings have a broadcast nature. Any packet transmitted may be seen by all nodes on the network and thus it is possible to transmit data to many nodes with only a single packet. This is commonly done by reserving a particular network address which is recognised by all nodes.

Ring systems have advantages over bus systems as far as network access techniques are concerned. On some bus systems there is always a risk that a transmission will have to be aborted because the packet has collided with a packet transmitted by another device. With ring systems there are several ways of controlling the packet transmission so that successful transmission is guaranteed. Such schemes are described in the next chapter. In general, the access methods employed on rings ensure that they have deterministic access times.

A ring system appears to have poor reliability since the failure of any element in the ring will disable the entire network. This can be overcome by incorporating a parallel standby ring, and a number of such schemes have been proposed (Zafiropulo, 1974). Such techniques are not suitable for rings with a small number of nodes since the probability of failure of the reconfiguration units is then likely to be greater than the probability of their improving network reliability. Other schemes have been proposed based on continuous monitoring of the ring for breaks and transient faults (Hopper and Wheeler, 1979). In any case, ring failures are very rare in practice, and will often be less serious than a breakdown in a centralised system in terms of fault location and repair times.

3.1.3 Star and tree networks

While the star topology is commonly referred to when talking about LAN topologies, it is not widely used. A star network employs a central switching node to which all network nodes are connected by bidirectional links. In order to transmit a packet, a network node sends it to the central switch where a number of forwarding schemes are possible. The simplest is to have the switch broadcast the packet on all its links and in this way the packet will reach its destination. However, if several nodes try to transmit at once the switch must arbitrate between them so that only one transmission occurs at any time. The Floodnet network, described later in this chapter, provides the means to implement star networks of this type. An alternative scheme is for the switch to be more complex and look at the destination address of each packet. It can then choose the appropriate link on which to relay the packet, and if another packet arrives it can relay that also, provided that the destination is different. The switch can become very complex if many packets have to be handled simultaneously in this way.

Expanding a star network is a problem if only one switch is employed, since the number of links that it can support is likely to be fixed. Thus, to cater for growth, a switch with more links than is initially required must be purchased. This means that the initial outlay is large and the future requirements of the

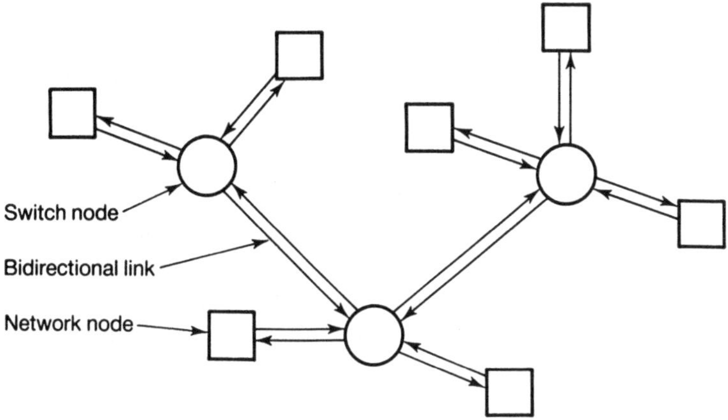

Fig. 3.2 A multi-switch star network

network must be accurately estimated. An alternative scheme is to have switch nodes of limited size and allow them to be connected not only to network nodes but also to other switch nodes as in Fig. 3.2. This configuration is known as a multi-switch star (or tree) and has the additional advantage over the single-switch star that it will use rather less of the communication medium. The multi-switch star configuration has been employed in wide area networks for some time with the switches being used in a store and forward manner. A good example of a multi-switch star LAN is the Datakit system built at Bell Laboratories (Fraser, 1983).

The most common star network in use is the Private Automatic Branch Exchange (PABX) used for office telephone switching. All the telephone cables in an office building normally run to a central switching room and in order to talk to any other extension, the voice signals are routed to the central switch and back out to the destination office. In common with the national telephone networks, PABX systems are starting to be based on digital rather than analogue circuitry and are able to offer a wider range of services. As this range increases the distinction between a LAN and a PABX becomes much less in terms of the facilities which are offered.

While true star LANs are uncommon, there are many LANs of differing types which are made to look like stars. The reason for this is that having the links to individual network nodes come together at a common point is very valuable when maintenance of the network is required. In particular, many ring networks use this scheme because it allows simple removal of a single faulty node by bypassing it at the centre of the star.

3.1.4 Mesh topology

All of the network topologies discussed so far may be viewed as particular cases of the mesh topology. In general, however, the term is reserved for networks which allow for more random interconnection than was described in the preceding sections. Mesh networks allow for redundancy in that more than one route may be provided for packets between two network nodes. Wide area networks are generally based on a mesh for just this reason. For meshes to be applicable to local networks the switching nodes cannot be allowed to operate on the store and forward principle as this would make the network delay too large.

A number of schemes have been devised to reduce the delay through the switching nodes and are described later in this chapter in the sections on Floodnet and Binary Routing Networks. As yet there are no commercially available local networks using the mesh interconnection technique.

3.2 Access methods for bus networks

When a source transmits on a bus network its signals are heard by all other devices on the bus. It follows that only one device must be permitted to transmit at once, since if two devices transmit simultaneously their signals will interfere and be unreadable. The bus need not be a physical medium such as a wire: early bus networks used radio channels as the bus.

The most commonly used access methods for broadcast networks are called **random access**. In this, control of whether a transmission can take place is distributed among the nodes attached to the network. When a device decides to make a transmission it does so in the expectation that it will be the only transmitting device and no others will interrupt it. If the level of traffic on the network is low the probability of another device wanting to transmit at the same time will be small enough to expect a successful transmission. If a node starts a transmission whilst another is in progress then a packet **collision** is said to have taken place and the contents of both packets can be corrupted. When a collision occurs it may be the responsibility of both nodes to detect it and cease transmitting. It is possible that a packet collision is only detectable by the receiving node using error-checking procedures on the incoming packet. In this case it is up to a higher level of the protocol in use, for instance an acknowledgement or timeout, to initiate a retransmission. When a collision is detected at a transmitting node, it may cease transmission and wait for a timeout to expire before attempting retransmission. The length of this timeout should be different for each node on the network to avoid the possibility of a second collision. A reasonable solution is for the timeout period to be generated randomly when a collision occurs. An example of this type of network is the Aloha system (Abramson, 1973).

Broadcast networks with a higher level of traffic, and hence a higher probability of packet collision, employ techniques which are designed to reduce the need for retransmissions. When the propagation delay between the source and destination is small in relation to the packet length, a technique called **Carrier Sense Multiple Access** (CSMA) can be used to increase the line utilisation. With CSMA the broadcast channel (bus) is sensed before a transmission is attempted and if it is already in use, the transmission is deferred until some time later. If the channel is sensed as being idle, then the transmission proceeds. When a transmission is started the packet is vulnerable to collisions for a time equal to the propagation delay between the two most distant points in the network and the transmitter can be sure no collision has taken place in at worst twice the end-to-end propagation time.

In some versions of this access method, a collision is detected by both transmitters and the packets are retransmitted after each node has paused for a back-off delay. This access method, CSMA with collision detection (CSMA/CD), is the basis of transmission on the Ethernet system which is described later in this chapter. Once a transmission has been established it continues without interruption.

The potential multiple transmitter restriction of broadcast networks can lead to poor operating characteristics as the traffic intensity grows. As the number of nodes attempting to transmit increases, the probability of a packet collision rises. When a collision occurs both transmissions are aborted and the channel utilisation, for the period of time between the first of the transmissions commencing and the end of the collision, is zero. Under such heavy load conditions every transmission may have ended in a collision and unless care is taken with sorting out the resulting retransmissions, the line utilisation may fall to an unacceptably low level.

There are a number of broadcast techniques which attempt to resolve the instability problems which occur under network overload conditions (Heitmeyer, *et al.*). These fall into two categories, dynamic control procedures for Aloha-type systems and channel reservation schemes. Dynamic control schemes require each user to take action to prevent channel saturation when the backlog of packets reaches some predetermined level. Reservation schemes involve a prospective transmitter sending a channel reservation packet to a central control device. Since there is a whole packet overhead required for reserving the channel, this scheme is only suitable for systems where typical messages are long enough to occupy several packets.

The permission token scheme, which will be described with reference to ring systems in Chapter 4, is also used as an access method for bus networks. The principle of a token bus network is similar to that of a token ring in that only the device in possession of the token may transmit. However, there are variations on the way that the protocol works and in particular, the way that the token is passed. Since there is no physical loop, like a ring, in which the token can be passed from one node to another, a logical loop must be simulated. This involves passing the token from one node to another logically related node. For instance, the most popular scheme is for a node to pass the token to the node with the next highest address. This continues until the node with the highest address has had the opportunity to transmit, at which point the logical loop wraps round to the node with the lowest address.

The token bus scheme provides the ordered access of a token ring, but at a price. In a ring, the token always passes to the next node round the loop, which will typically be the nearest physical node. However, with the token bus architecture, addresses will be distributed around the network and so the free token will have to travel a greater distance on average before arriving at the next node in the logical loop.

3.3 Ethernet

Ethernet is a baseband mode local area network designed at the Xerox Palo Alto Research Center (Metcalfe and Boggs, 1976). It is a broadcast bus-type of network whose medium is a coaxial cable named the **Ether** after the 'luminiferous ether'. Ethernet was designed as a suitable communications system on which distributed computer systems could be based. The use of a broadcast access method was influenced by its predecessor, Aloha. However, the designers of Ethernet departed from the pure broadcast scheme and attempted to make the network as efficient as possible by reducing the amount of system bandwidth wasted through packet collisions. Hence, carrier sense multiple access with collision detection (CSMA/CD) was used as the access method. In this scheme a potential transmitter listens to the communications medium in order to determine whether there is already a transmission in progress on the network. If the Ether is quiet then the transmission goes ahead, although without any guarantee of success. Since there is a finite probability that a second station initiates a transmission at the same time, a packet collision can occur. The critical time period during which such a collision can occur is equal to the end-to-end propagation delay of the Ether. When a collision does take place, it is detected by a circuit in each of the transmitting nodes and the packets are aborted, leaving the network quiet. In order for this scheme to work it is necessary that the shortest packet is large enough to span the entire network. Thus, as the size of the network increases the minimum packet size must also increase. Since there is only a high probability that a packet will be delivered once a transmission has commenced, Ethernet is referred to as a probabilistic network.

CSMA/CD is an example of an access method with decentralised control. It was intended that the operation of the Ethernet network should not be dependent upon a centralised monitor service which would allocate system bandwidth to other nodes. There is no control structure superimposed onto the Ether, it is a purely passive communication medium. Control of the network is therefore distributed throughout the system. A failure at a single station could bring the system down and since this renders the network inoperable, the hardware and software is designed to minimise this possibility.

The network topology chosen by the designers of the Ethernet was the passive bus structure because of its suitability for modular expansion and for reliability considerations. The amount of hardware that has to be made reliable for the system not to be susceptible to node failures is small. However, in general, a break in the transmission medium will be catastrophic because reflections from the unterminated wires will cause packets to collide with themselves.

An Ethernet is similar to an unrooted tree, from which new branches can extend whenever necessary. During the construction of a building, an Ether could be installed along every corridor. Then, whenever a connection is required in a room, a branch can be attached to the nearest point. The only consideration that must be borne in mind when extending the span of an Ethernet is that no circular return paths may be introduced, i.e. there must be no path from a node, around the Ether and back again. If such loops were to exist, then for every packet transmitted a collision would be detected since the packet would interfere with itself.

The network node of an Ethernet is made up of a number of components as shown in Fig. 3.3. The physical connection to the Ether is made by a **tap**. The only constraint placed on the design of a tap is that it should affect the electrical characteristics of the Ether as little as possible. Connected to a tap is a **transceiver**. It is this component which performs the encoding and decoding of the Ethernet packets. The next component is called an **interface** and its main task is to serialise and deserialise the bit streams which it exchanges with the transceiver. The component onto which the host device connects is called an Ethernet **controller**. The controller is responsible for the correct transmission and reception of packets across the network.

3.3.1 The prototype Ethernet

A prototype Ethernet has been operational at Xerox PARC since 1976. The prototype system was designed to operate at 3 Mbps and support up to 256 stations. The maximum span of the Ether was 1 km.

The communications medium chosen for the prototype system was standard CATV coaxial cable. It possessed suitable electrical characteristics and was available 'off the shelf' at a low price. This meant that the cost of the Ether would not constitute a major proportion of the total cost of connecting onto the network.

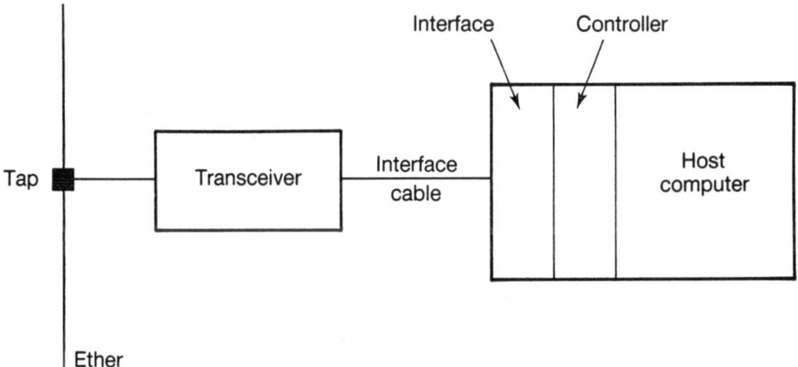

Fig. 3.3 Components of an Ethernet connection

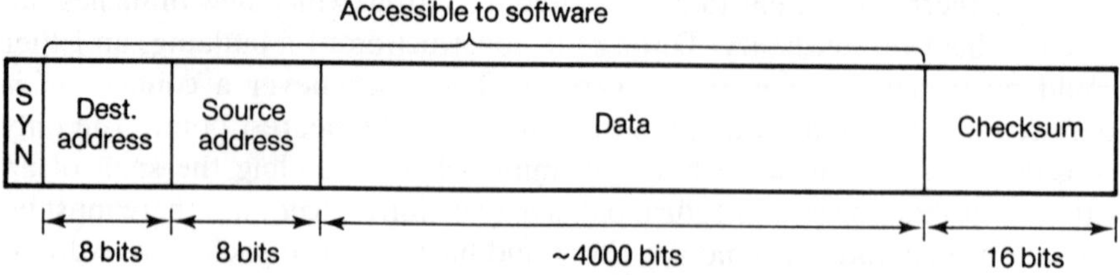

Fig. 3.4   Format of the prototype Ethernet packet

The format of the prototype Ethernet packet is shown in Fig. 3.4. A packet begins with a 1-bit synchronisation field. This is used by the interface hardware to lock onto the bit phase of an incoming packet. The next two fields are addresses, namely the destination address for the packet followed by the source address. Each of these is 8 bits long which allows for addressing of up to 256 devices on a single Ethernet. The next field in the packet is for user data. Up to 4096 bits, in 16-bit multiples, can be accommodated in this field. The final 16 bits of a packet are used to transport a source-generated CRC error check. The implementation of each of the main Ethernet components will now be described.

3.3.2 Transceiver

The point at which the active components of a network connection come into contact with the Ether is in the tranceiver. The transceiver connects onto the Ether via the tap. To connect a tap to the Ether a hole is cut in the casing of the coaxial cable and some of the screening is removed. A needle-like contact then connects to the central conductor; teeth, in the clamp which holds the assembly together, make contact with the outer conductor. The tap is attached to a small box which contains the transceiver. It is the transceiver which contains the line driver and receiver components. In the prototype Ethernet those components were designed to operate with up to 256 devices connected onto an Ether with a span of 1 km. Since it is the transceiver which comes into contact with the Ether and a malfunction in this component could corrupt the whole network, it was designed to be extremely reliable. It includes an internal watchdog circuit which constantly monitors its performance and disconnects it from the Ether if there is any indication of a fault. The line drivers and receivers have also been designed to withstand electrical noise and unstable voltage levels on the Ether.

Apart from the circuits used in the transmission path of packets, the transceiver also performs functions which are important to the access method and collision control. These functions are termed **carrier detection**, **interference detection** and **collision concensus enforcement**. Carrier detection is used prior to transmission to determine whether the Ether is already being used by another station. The Manchester scheme, used to encode packets transmitted onto the Ether, includes at least one transition of the signal level per bit time.

This level change can be detected by the transceiver and its presence prevents a transmission from going ahead. By using carrier detection, packet collisions will only happen on an Ethernet if two or more stations start to transmit within the end-to-end propagation delay of the Ether. Since no delay is forced upon a packet when the Ether is detected as being busy, the majority of collisions will occur because of more than one station waiting for the Ether to become free. In this situation, once the packet on the Ether is completed, all the pending transmitters will start simultaneously and all the packets transmitted will collide. Each transmission will then be rescheduled with a randomly generated delay.

During transmissions, the interference detection circuits of a transceiver compare the value on the Ether with the value of the bit that is currently being transmitted. If there is a difference, then the packet being transmitted is being interfered with. This is known as a packet collision and the action that is taken when one occurs is to halt the transmission. The presence of carrier and interference detection circuits in Ethernet transceivers is a major difference between the network control techniques used in the Ethernet and Aloha systems. With Aloha, transmissions are initiated as soon as there is data to transmit, irrespective of the current state of the network. So if a station were to transmit a packet, the first bit of which were to collide with the last bit of another packet which was already being transmitted, both packets would be corrupted. Hence, the information carried by the network during the time that the two packets were being transmitted is zero. Had carrier detection been possible on Aloha, the second packet would not have been launched until the first was completed. Similarly, if two stations attached to Aloha were to start transmitting simultaneously, then the packets would almost completely overlap. If Aloha stations had been able to detect this collision, as with Ethernet transceivers, both transmissions could be aborted and the transmission medium freed. But, since collision detection is not present on Aloha (or easily implemented because the out stations in general cannot hear each other), the central resource is occupied until both packets are completed and the system bandwidth has been wasted for their duration.

When a packet collision occurs on the Ether there is a finite probability that one of the participating stations does not realise that this has occurred. If all the stations which detect the collision stop transmitting, the ignorant station would just continue. Even though the collision was not detected by that station, there is still the possibility that the packet which it is transmitting has been corrupted. In order to reduce the chance of bandwidth being wasted in this way, a technique called collision concensus enforcement was included in the transceiver design. Having detected packet interference, a transceiver halts the transmission and then attempts to jam the Ether. Hence, even if a station has not noticed the presence of other packets on the network, it will detect the jamming sequence and halt the transmission.

The connection between the transceiver and the interface is made by a five-pair twisted cable. The twisted pairs carry serial transmit and receive data, an 'interference detected' signal and power supply voltages.

3.3.3 Interface

The function of the interface, which is located between the transceiver and the controller, is to serialise and encode data passing through to the Ether and to decode and deserialise data coming from the Ether. In addition, the interface calculates a cyclic redundancy checksum (CRC) of the contents of packets that are transmitted and received.

When a transmission is to be initiated, the interface is passed an address and a word count by the controller. The address is to be used as the start of a buffer, in the host's main memory, which is to be transmitted. The word count represents the size of the buffer. Then, having encoded the 1-bit synchronisation field, the contents of the buffer are loaded in parallel into the interface and the serial bit stream generated is encoded using the Manchester scheme. During the transmission, the interface hardware calculates a 16-bit CRC as each word is read from memory. The final value of the CRC register is encoded and sent to the transceiver once the last word of data has been processed.

The reception side of the interface is similar to the transmit side. The signal received from the Ether is decoded and the serial bit stream is then converted into parallel words. The words are then stored in a buffer in the station's main memory. The value of the CRC calculated during reception is then used, with the last two bytes of the packet, to determine whether the packet contained an error. If the CRC check fails, then the host is not notified that the packet has been received, thereby discarding the packet.

Similarly, the interface discards truncated packets that are received from the Ether. Truncated packets are a by-product of a packet collision and are caused by the participating transmitters aborting. They can arrive at an interface if the destination address field in the corrupted bit stream matches a physical network address. In this event, the destination interface will imagine that what is being received is a valid packet. However, if the number of data bits received before the signal disappears is not divisible by 16 or the CRC check fails then the packet will be discarded.

Since operation of the interface is dependent upon the host's memory word size and control signals, this component of an Ethernet is host-dependent. Thus for a typical distributed computer system based on an Ethernet, a number of different interface designs will be present.

3.3.4 Controller

Like the interface, an Ethernet controller is dependent upon the characteristics of the local host. The function of the controller is to manage the transmission and reception of packets across the network. The controller has been implemented as low-level software in the host and as a firmware attachment to the host. The main task performed by the controller is the generation of the retransmission delay in the event of a transmission being unable to continue. All retransmission delays are calculated in terms of a **slot**, which is the end-to-end propagation delay of the Ether. Each time that a transmission is not possible because the presence of a carrier on the Ether was detected, the retransmission is scheduled for one slot later. Each time that transmission of a packet is aborted due to collision detection, a random delay is calculated. The mean value of the newly generated delay is twice the previous delay experienced by the same packet. Once the delay has expired, retransmission is scheduled, subject, of course, to the CSMA access protocol.

3.3.5 Extending an Ethernet

Two additional components were used in the prototype Ethernet to extend the scope of a single network. These two components are the packet repeater and the packet filter.

A **packet repeater** is a bidirectional transmitter/receiver which operates at the bit level. When the size of the network becomes too great for the components of the Ethernet transceiver, the Ether can be split into two sections with a packet repeater inserted between them. Through regeneration of the signal, the packet repeater provides the extra line driving capacity that eluded the transceivers. It must be remembered that the maximum size of the combined Ethernets must still be small enough to accommodate the minimum packet size. A network consisting of two Ethernet segments is illustrated in Fig. 3.5.

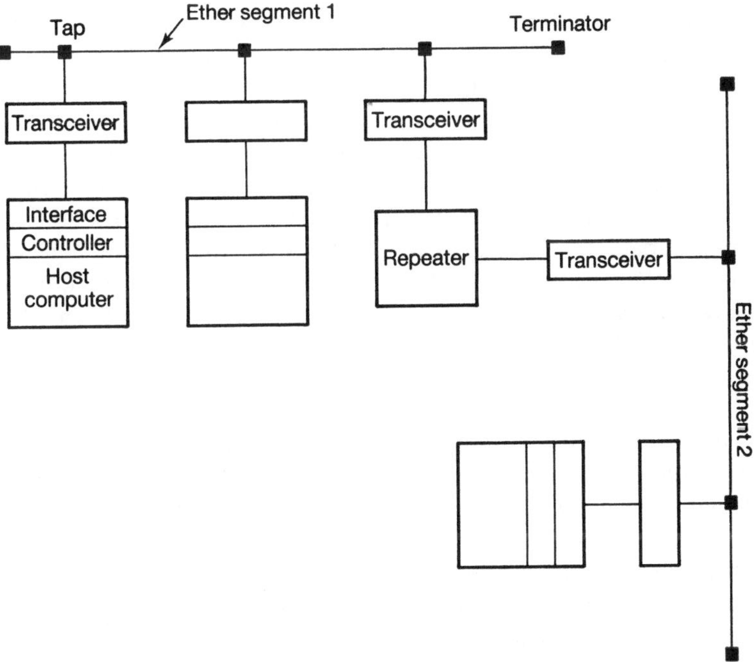

Fig. 3.5   A multiple-segment Ethernet

A **packet filter** was designed for use where the number of stations attached to the network caused too high a traffic demand. As the number of potential transmitters on an Ethernet increases, the line utilisation can fall, due to large numbers of collisions occurring and under these circumstances the access delay increases greatly. The packet filter was designed to overcome this problem by reducing the traffic on different sections of a network. A packet filter is used to join two Ethernet segments in much the same way as the packet repeater. In addition to regenerating the signal, it also forwards only those packets whose destination is on the opposite side to the one on which they were generated. This operation implies that either a list of network addresses is located in the packet filter or that addresses are ordered such that only addresses within a certain range appear on either side of the filter. In order to do this the packet filter must buffer incoming packets in order to see their destination address field before transmitting them on the adjacent Ethernet.

An implication of the use of either the packet repeater or the packet filter in an Ethernet is that the principle of designing a network with no centralised functions has been traded for flexibility. Introducing either of these components renders the network liable to failure through a fault in a single device.

3.3.6 The Ethernet specification

The Ethernet specification is a standard which defines a second-generation Ethernet architecture (Digital, Intel, Xerox, 1980). It was written by a three-company collaboration between Xerox Corporation, Intel Corporation and Digital Equipment Corporation and the standard is referred to as the DIX Ethernet. The intention of this group of companies was to use the lessons learned from the design of the prototype Ethernet to produce a network architecture which was more suited to current communication needs. A prime objective of the specification was to enable a wide variety of manufacturers to design compatible products. A second purpose for the definition of the Ethernet specification was an attempt to have the Ethernet adopted as an industry standard for local area networks. Since the development of such networks is relatively new, no such standards existed and so it was thought that a network with the backing of three large companies would stand a good chance of success. This was the case and the DIX standard, slightly modified, was adopted by the IEEE as part of the IEEE 802 series of local network standards (IEEE, 1982).

The basic philosophies of Ethernet, such as the CSMA/CD access protocol, remain intact in the Ethernet specification. The main differences are a redefinition of network parameters such as speed, network size and the packet format. These were carried out by refining the design of components in the prototype system. The network control components have also been rearranged so that they are now functionally contained in two components, a transceiver and a controller.

In the prototype Ethernet design the data rate was approximately 3 Mbps. At the time of the original design this was considered suitable since it matched the bus speed of the main host device, the Alto computer. Many potential applications requiring very high data rates have since been developed and so it was decided to increase this parameter in the new system. However, as the data rate is increased, the maximum span of the system must be reduced, since the minimum packet size must be kept as low as possible. Increasing the data rate also creates a demand for a higher standard of electronic components in the transceiver, which in turn increases the cost of connection. The data rate chosen for the standard was 10 Mbps. As a result of this tradeoff, the maximum length of a network has been reduced to 500 m, although, by making use of packet repeaters, this length can be extended to 2.5 km.

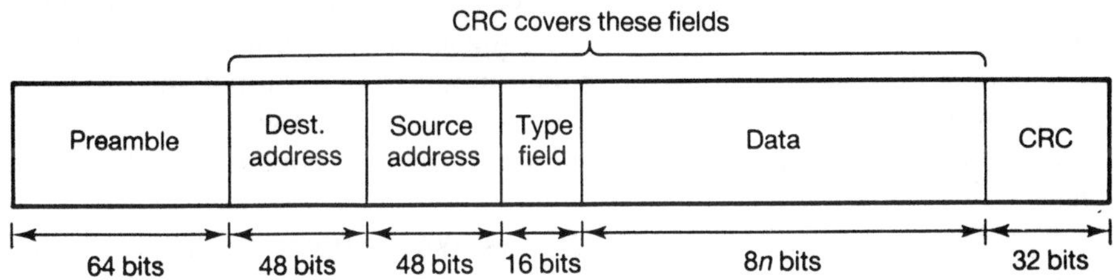

Fig. 3.6 Packet format of the DIX Ethernet

Major changes were made in the packet format for the Ethernet specification. The packet is now made up of a 64-bit preamble, two 48-bit addresses, a 16-bit type field, a data field whose size is in the range 46–1500 bytes and a 32-bit CRC field. The packet format is shown in Fig. 3.6. The 1-bit synchronisation field has been replaced by the 64-bit preamble because of a tendency for some stations in the prototype system to fail to lock onto the first bit of a packet and because of the increase in data rate of the Ethernet specification. It is intended to ensure that all stations will detect every packet on the network. The two address fields were extended from 8 to 48 bits in order to provide for multi-network addressing. By dividing up the field and using the sub-fields hierarchically, sections of the address can be associated with a local network, a neighbouring network and so on. A type field has been introduced into the packet format. This field identifies the higher-level protocols which are implemented in the data field of packets. Finally, the 16-bit CRC has been extended to 32 bits in order to improve error detection.

3.4 Hubnet

Hubnet is a network developed by the Computer Systems Research Group at the University of Toronto (Lee and Boulton, 1983). One of the interesting features of Hubnet is that it is based around fibre-optic links rather than wire. It is also a high-speed network, the links operating at 50 MHz.

3.4.1 Hubnet architecture

Computers and similar devices connect to the network via a **Network Access Controller** (NAC). Each NAC contains a Motorola 68000 microprocessor which implements the upper layers of the protocol architecture supported by the network.

The topology of Hubnet is described by its inventors as a rooted tree. At the leaf nodes of the tree are the NACs and at the branches of the tree are switching units known as **hubs**. There are in fact two trees in every Hubnet, one of which is known as the **selection tree** and the other as the **broadcast tree**. Normally, the two trees are topologically similar and placed on top of each other. The simplest Hubnet is shown in Fig. 3.7 with the trees shown separately. The outgoing link from a NAC goes to a hub on the selection tree and the incoming link comes from the equivalent link on the broadcast tree. Selection hubs pass data from one of their inputs to their output and broadcast hubs copy data from their input to all their outputs. The two hubs on each tree are linked so that data coming into the selection hub is copied to the broadcast hub.

Data is transmitted by a NAC in **frames**. When a frame reaches a hub it will pass through to the output as long as no other frame is passing through the hub, otherwise it will be 'blocked'. In the simple network shown above the frame will pass immediately to the broadcast hub and from there it will be transmitted to the receiver sections of all the NACs. Thus the transmitting NAC will see it, as will all other NACs, and will therefore know that the frame reached its destination.

When a frame is blocked, the hub which is blocking it makes sure that it is blocked in its entirety. Thus, a hub will only ever pass complete frames. A NAC will know that the frame it transmitted had been blocked because it will

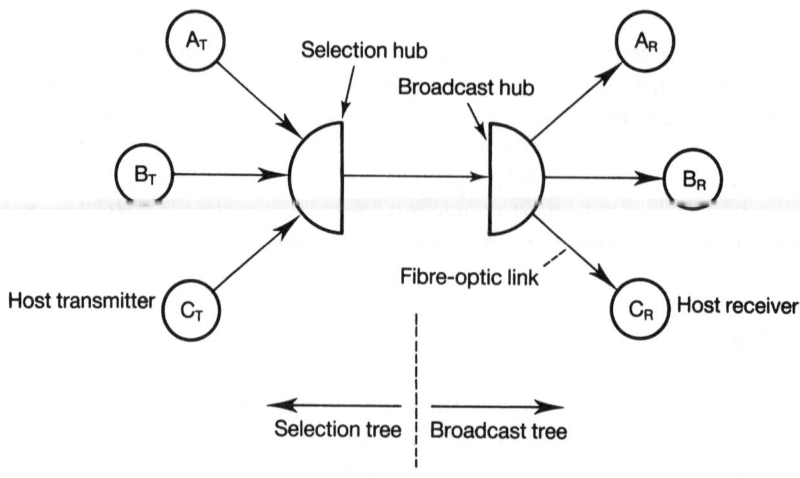

Fig. 3.7   A simple Hubnet

not receive the 'echo' of the frame in its receiver. A timeout is used to detect this and the NAC will then immediately try to retransmit the frame. The hub must arbitrate incoming frames when they arrive simultaneously (within the same bit time) and if it cannot decide which was first then it chooses one at random.

One of the less attractive features of Hubnet is that the timeout which a NAC uses when retrying transmissions is programmed into the NAC by switches, there being no method to calculate an optimum value for it. This means that expanding the network will require changing many of these switches if optimum performance is to be obtained. Alternatively, they can be set to some 'safe' (long) value at the cost of some throughput.

Expansion to make larger networks is quite simple. Each tree is made larger by introducing more hubs. The outputs of selection hubs near the periphery of the tree feed into the inputs of other selection hubs nearer the root of the tree. Both trees are linked at their roots by connecting the output of the selection hub to the input of the broadcast hub as shown in Fig. 3.8.

3.4.2 The Network Access Controller

As already mentioned, the NAC contains a 68000 microprocessor to perform the high-level functions required of it. In addition, the NAC contains transmit and receive buffers for frames and a 'storage pool' to hold the 68000 program and additional frames. There is also an interface to the host which will

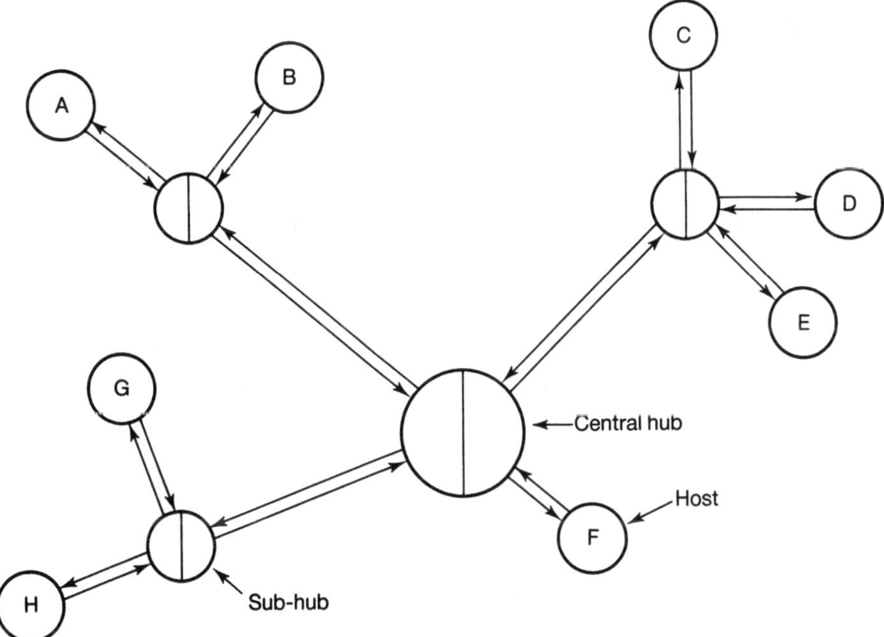

Fig. 3.8 A more complex Hubnet

necessarily be different for different hosts. The prototype Hubnet has interfaces to the DEC Unibus and to clusters of RS-232 (terminal) lines.

The protocol structure of Hubnet is closely modelled on the ISO 7-layer model. The NAC hardware implements the physical and data link layers and part of the network layer. At this point the 68000 takes over and implements the remaining layers up to the presentation layer. The application layer normally resides on the host computer.

3.4.3 The hub

Conceptually, there are two types of hub, those which reside on the selection tree and those which reside on the broadcast tree. In practice, since the trees are nearly always overlaid, the hub hardware contains both hubs in one box and has pairs of links coming out of it. At the central hub the broadcast input is connected to the selection output.

In the prototype implementation it is possible to connect up to 11 NACs or other hubs to any hub. This limit was imposed by the hardware packaging of the devices rather than any other limitation.

3.4.4 Frame format

Each frame begins with a header field which warns receivers that the frame is coming and enables them to synchronise to the bit stream. Then comes a data field and finally there is a CRC. The header field is 8 bits long, the CRC is 16 bits and the data field must be a multiple of 16 bits. NACs discard frames which arrive with an invalid CRC.

Within the frame is embedded a network layer packet. This consists of three 16-bit fields and then a maximum of 2045 fields of user data, each of 16 bits. The first of the 3 fields is the destination address and the second is the address of the NAC which sourced this packet. The third field is a mode field which is a collection of bits used in the higher-level protocols and for extending the addressing scheme to allow the interconnection of Hubnets. The format of the Hubnet frame and the embedded packet is shown in Fig. 3.9.

One of the advantages of Hubnet over some networks is that users are not penalised for sending short packets. On the Ethernet, for example, the sending of many short packets reduces the efficiency of the network and there is a minimum packet size below which the network will not function. With Hubnet, however, sending a short packet simply causes the network to block other packets for less time than if a longer packet had been sent. The transmitter will have to wait the same time for its packets to echo regardless of their length.

3.5 Floodnet

Floodnet is a local area network architecture which comprises an interconnected mesh of switching nodes (Petitpierre, 1984). Devices are attached to

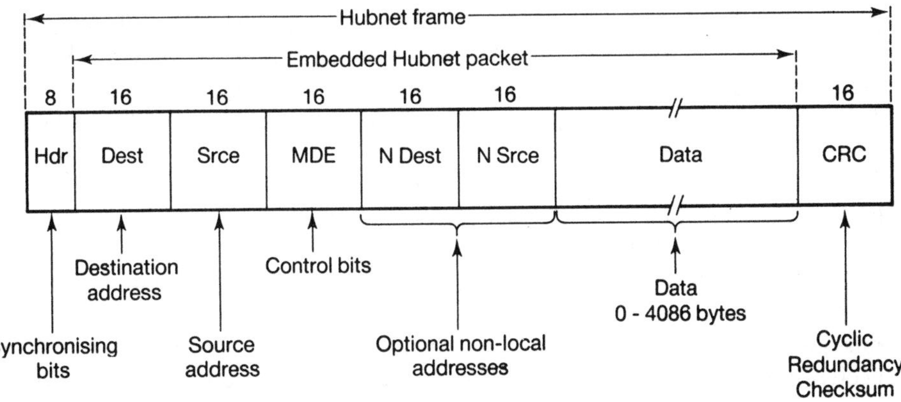

Fig. 3.9   Layout of a Hubnet frame

the switches via terminal nodes. The overhead which routing can impose onto a star network is minimised by routing all the packets using a flooding technique.

A Floodnet switch has an arbitrary number of ports. A port is a duplex communications path by which a switch is connected to another switch or a terminal node. There is no distinction as to which type of device is connected to a port, both generate traffic and respond in the same way.

3.5.1 Switching nodes

The conceptual structure of a switching node is illustrated in Fig. 3.10. Internally a node is arranged such that the input line of each port is connected

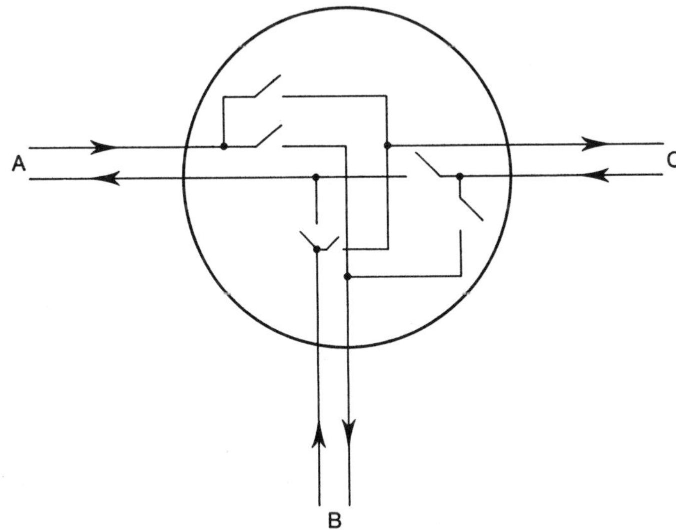

Fig. 3.10   A Floodnet switching node

to the output lines of all other ports via relays. When there is no traffic passing through a node, all of these relays are open. When a packet arrives at an input, this causes the relays which connect that input line to all the other output lines to close. Hence, the packet is routed through the node and towards all attached nodes.

The packet is transmitted on a given output line until a signal is received on the input line of that port. This mechanism is used to provide flow control within the network. At this stage, transmission through that port is terminated. When all the ports being used to transmit a packet have responded in this way, a signal is sent down the output line of the receiving port, indicating that transmission to this node should be ended. When the neighbouring node receives this signal, the packet is terminated and the node under examination returns to the unused state.

3.5.2 A Floodnet network

A network consisting of an arbitrary collection of switching and terminal nodes is illustrated in Fig. 3.11. Consider a packet being transmitted from terminal node A to terminal node B. A sends the packet out on its only port, i.e. that connected to switching node S1. When S1 detects an incoming packet on that line (L1) it makes an internal connection between L1 and the other two ports belonging to S1, i.e. L2 and L3. Thus the packet is propagated in two directions from that node.

When the packet arrives at nodes S2 and S3, the same mechanism routes it on the two output lines of those nodes. In the case of S2, the packet is sent onto terminal node B and switch S3. At S3 the packet is forwarded to S2 and C. Thus the packet is being transmitted in both directions between S2 and S3. As already described, once a reception starts on a port which has already been used for a transmission, the incoming signal is treated as a negative acknow-

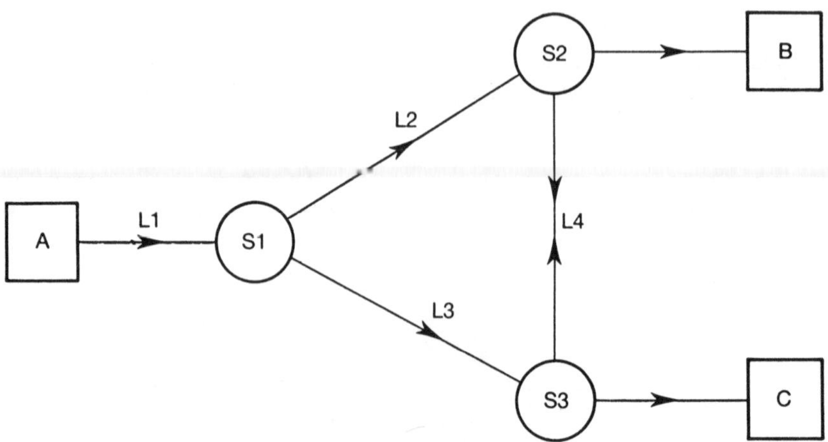

Fig. 3.11 A simple Floodnet

ledgement and that transmission is terminated. Hence, both S2 and S3 stop transmitting on line L4.

Terminal station C, meanwhile, has been receiving the packet and has decided that its destination address does not match its own address. So it sends a negative acknowledgement signal down the line to S3. Now S3 has received negative acknowledgements from both of the paths on which it was forwarding the packet. This causes it to send a similar negative acknowledgement down the line on which it is receiving the packet and enter the idle state. When terminal node B receives the packet, it recognises the destination address as its own and thus continues to accept the packet.

The delay in a switching node should be made as short as possible so that the propagation delay of a packet through a network is also short. In this case the path filtering situation just described, in which a route is selected, will take place during the first few bits of a packet. Switching nodes which are not involved in the final path are isolated from the transmission, which means that several packets can exist on the network simultaneously. There is the limitation that two such paths cannot cross. However, with careful placement of frequent communicators this drawback can be minimised.

A Floodnet architecture includes a low-level acknowledgement scheme. The route filtering will typically be completed by the time only a few bits have been transmitted. The delay across the network must be less than the minimum packet length. A transmitting terminal node will still be sending a packet when the destination starts receiving it. Thus if the destination node does not have sufficient buffer space or does not want to receive the packet, it can reject it by sending a negative acknowledgement to its nearest switching node. This information will then continue making its way back to the source terminal node, which will then cease the transmission.

3.6 Binary routing networks

In this section the design of a network which has a general connection topology is described. The packet format does not need to include the destination address but only the route. This means that each source has to be capable of generating the correct route for each destination. A network of this kind is under construction at the Cambridge University Computer Laboratory (Hopper and Wheeler, 1979).

3.6.1 The binary routing node

To cater for general networks with a single type of switching node, at least two paths must enter and at least two paths must leave a node. The route selection can be set up in advance either by a control path to make a circuit-switching node, or by routing information carried with user data to make a packet-switching node. The latter method leads to control simplicity at the expense of extra switching information carried with each packet. However, each node no longer requires state data and for many purposes the simplicity outweighs the apparent loss of efficiency, and as the paths are more easily multiplexed some of the loss is compensated by the advantages.

The simplest switching node is one which will receive and transmit packets along two paths. To simplify the switching operation, a packet has the steering data in absolute form at the front so that the front bit always indicates which output path should be taken. This kind of node is shown in Fig. 3.12.

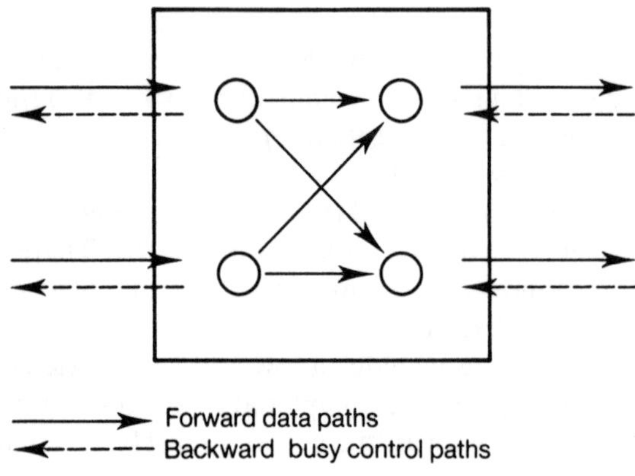

Fig. 3.12   Binary routing node

To minimise the delay through each node the routing bits can be rotated so that the first bit of the route field always indicates the next direction and the used bit is placed at the end of the route field. No translation or directory look up is done so the delay is only one or two bits rather than the entire routing field. The packet format for this scheme is shown in Fig. 3.13.

If a packet can be stopped instantly without loss when it reaches a node then the above system will not lose information even if the output path is already in use. However, practical considerations show that unless the

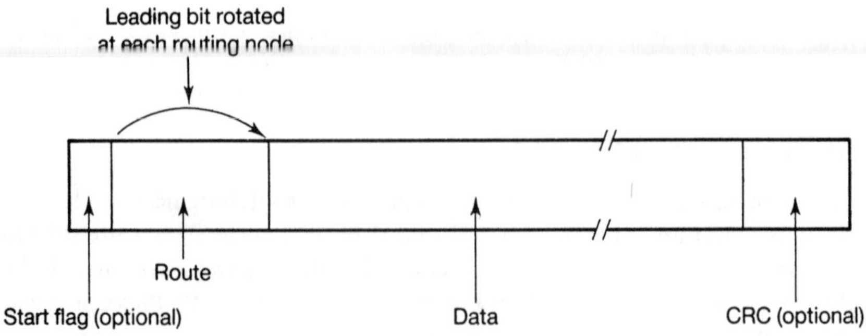

Fig. 3.13   Binary routing node packet format

bandwidth is low, a backward busy traffic control signal cannot reach the previous node in one digit time. Also, a stopped packet would spread across many nodes and obstruct the network. Thus, unless a rather wasteful throw-away protocol is used, each node must be able to buffer some digits (say twice the number in the path) and for simplicity should buffer a whole packet so that a stopped packet does not directly affect the status of more than one node. Hence, a node must be able to buffer one packet and send a busy control signal back to the previous node in time to stop a possible next packet, i.e. every path must be less than one half a packet in length. This is not a severe constraint. A cable of 1000 feet would only contain 50 bits at 50 MHz, and it is possible to ameliorate this by having extra packet buffers for long paths.

Congesting traffic is ultimately delayed outside the network by the backwards propagation of the busy traffic control signal, although occasional blockages are absorbed by the buffers at the nodes. Hogging, that is, one of the inputs inhibiting the other, is avoided by alternating the busy signal between the two inputs. Buffering packets at each node improves the line utilisation and larger buffers would increase this further, but the extra gain becomes smaller as the buffer size increases.

If packets become corrupted they might circulate indefinitely in a network with loops, but this can be avoided by clearing the route bits after use and taking special action for all 0s. Alternatively, the route bits can be made to generate a long pseudo-random sequence of bits, with the first n bits unaltered, where n is the length of the route field. A sequence of $2^n - 1$ bits can be generated, in which all possible groups of n bits appear. Thus the chance of a packet circulating for ever is minimal. This pseudo-random generation is done by replacing the least significant bit by a parity mixture of the first, last and other bits instead of the most significant route bit. The algorithm is reversible so that the destination can work out the entire route by which the packet came simply by examining the route field.

The node has two inputs and two outputs used in routing mode. However, it can also be used for attaching host devices to the network by taking one input and one output and connecting them to the device interface. This means that a single unit can be designed to function as both a routing and a terminal node which makes an LSI implementation attractive. For particular systematic network configurations the routing information can be decoded directly from the destination and source addresses, and can thus be generated rapidly. Otherwise, a simple route table can be kept at each source which may allow alternate routing strategies to be adopted if the network is sufficiently redundant.

3.6.2 Traffic considerations

The delay can be estimated in simple cases. When the traffic is low then the delay will be the total propagation delay plus about 2 bits delay per traversed node. There exist networks with m peripherals in which paths traverse about $\log_2 (m)$ nodes. At medium loads an additional delay is experienced because some outputs of nodes may be blocked. This delay depends on the traffic and packet length. When some links become saturated, their efficiency will be high and the alternation rule will cause sources closer to the saturated link to get a higher share. Many saturated links are difficult to analyse without a network model. It is important to realise that if a peripheral is off, then it must either return packets or else throw them away. If it is inhibited from accepting them, then the blockage will tend to grow and block useful traffic.

An option is the use of timeout counters on buffers within the network. This should be done with care because it may lead to useful data being thrown away. However, it could ensure that under fault conditions a small volume of data can move through the blocked part of the network, thus improving maintenance characteristics.

3.6.3 Extensions

A number of extensions can be made to the basic scheme. Low-level acknowledgement can be provided by allowing the route field to specify the return path as well as the forward path. Then a peripheral station can send a response with minimal logic. An extra control bit is used to indicate when the packet has finally returned to the source. Another approach is to make the node logic more complicated so that the packet is buffered at the destination while more complex operations are performed before it is retransmitted to the source. Variable-length data fields can be implemented by using a control bit as a continuation marker or having a length field in the packet.

Any link could include a translator, to change destinations into bits for steering, at the expense of a route field delay since the entire field has to be absorbed before emitting. In such a case dynamic routing is easily implemented.

A broadcast facility can be provided in the binary routing scheme by 'flooding', i.e. transmitting the broadcast packet on both outputs. For some topologies care has to be taken to ensure that the broadcast messages do not propagate indefinitely. If a broadcast termination facility is required at the lowest level this can be done in the following way. Broadcast messages are identified by a control bit at the front of the packet. On transmission, the route field is filled with 0s except for the last routing bit. As the packet is broadcast through the network this bit is shifted one place forward at each node. When it finally reaches the front of the routing field the packet is deleted. Since the route field is wide enough to steer packets to every part of the system, the broadcast message will reach every node with little propagation delay and it is likely that the number of packets in transition will be small.

3.6.4 Other routing node structures

The basic routing node described above is one of a spectrum of similar nodes of varying complexity. It can be considered as consisting of two sub-nodes, performing the fork and join operations. These can be used separately or can be combined to form a single unit. The advantage of this approach is that the join node does not consume a routing bit and can thus be used without lengthening the route field. This can be done in the same way as with a telephone concentrator to avoid bandwidth being wasted, or where an extra path catering for uneven traffic is required. However, if traffic is heavy, use of the join node in unsuitable positions may lead to congestion.

The simple basic node has separate connections from node to node, one forward for data and one backward for the busy signal used to inhibit incoming traffic. The control signal requires little bandwidth as at most there will be one change per packet duration. Thus it can be implemented more easily than the high-bandwidth data path. However, if the network is symmetrical, then it is natural to multiplex the forward data and the busy for the backward data, saving half the connections at the expense of an extra decoding delay at the node and some extra logic in the node.

Binary routing is the simplest of a set of base-n routing schemes and is chosen as it is the most straightforward to implement in hardware. A more complex scheme would be a four-way switch with two routing bits being used at each node so that the number of traversed nodes could be halved, but the delay at each node increased by one bit. The binary system could, of course, include some base-4 nodes, a simple one of which is equivalent to four base-2 nodes. Another way of using two routing bits per node would be to assign them to mean steer left, steer right, broadcast, or stop. This would allow packets to be routed to some region of the system, then broadcast for a number of links, before being terminated using the stop facility. The penalty in terms of delay through a node is about one third and the scheme has the advantages that lost and broadcast packets terminate and erroneous packets have shorter life times. However, the overhead of routing information for each packet has doubled.

3.7 References

Abramson, N., 1973. 'The Aloha System'. In *Computer Communication Networks*, eds. N. Abramson and F.F. Kuo, pp. 501–17. Englewood Cliffs, NJ: Prentice-Hall.

Digital, Intel and Xerox, 1980. 'The Ethernet – A local area network data link layer and physical layer specifications'. Digital, Intel and Xerox Corporations.

Fraser, A.G., 1983. 'Towards a universal data transport system'. *IEEE Journal on Selected Areas in Communications*, **SAC-1 (5)**, 803–16.

Heitmeyer, C.L., Kullback, J.H. and Shore, J.E., 1976. 'A survey of packet-switching techniques for broadcast media'. Naval Research Laboratory Rep. No. 8035, Washington DC.

Hopper, A. and Wheeler, D.J., 1979. 'Maintenance of ring communication systems'. *IEEE Trans. Comm.* **COM-27 (4)**, 760–61.

Hopper, A. and Wheeler, D.J., 1979. 'Binary routing networks'. *IEEE Trans. Comput.*, **COM-28 (10)**, 699–703.

IEEE, 1982. 'Token-passing bus access method and physical layer specifications'. Draft IEEE 802.4.

IEEE, 1982. 'CSMA/CD access method and physical layer specifications'. Draft IEEE 802.3.

Lee, E.S. and Boulton, P.I.P., 1983. 'The principles and performance of Hubnet'. *IEEE Journal on Selected Areas in Communication*. **SAC-1 (5)**, 711–20.

Metcalfe, R.M. and Boggs, D.R., 1976. 'Ethernet: distributed packet-switching for local computer networks'. *Comm. Ass. Computing Machinery*, **19**(7), 395–403.

Petitpierre, C., 1984. 'Meshed local computer networks'. *IEEE Comm. Mag.*, **22**(8), 36–40.

Zafiropulo, P., 1974. 'Performance evaluation of reliability improvement techniques for single-loop communications systems'. *IEEE Trans. Comm.*, **COM-22 (6)**, 742–51.

Chapter 4 Ring networks

In this chapter the design of ring-based LANs is discussed. A general discussion of ring access methods is followed by examples of some notable systems.

4.1 Access methods for ring systems

An early example of a ring system is the permission token ring proposed by Farmer and Newhall (1969). Each station is allowed to transmit an arbitrary length message when in possession of a token. The token (a distinctive bit pattern) circulates the ring until a station removes it. That station may now transmit a message and when it has finished will place the token back onto the ring. Such a scheme is particularly suited to sources of a bursty nature, that is, where stations want to transmit large amounts (bursts) of data at irregular intervals. The Farmer and Newhall token was implemented using an encoding violation technique. A digit was transmitted as a pair of pulses with opposite polarities and a violation of this principle indicated start-of-message or end-of-message. The single bit which followed the end-of-message marker was the token and was either taken off by the next node, which then transmitted its data, or was passed on unaltered. A ring monitor was required to detect when the token became corrupted or when more than one token existed.

A more recent implementation of a ring system based on the token passing scheme is the IBM token ring. This network was designed to support the sharing of resources and distributed processing and is described later in this chapter.

Further work on rings was done by Pierce (1971), who proposed that a ring be divided into a number of fixed-size slots. Each slot (or packet) contains a control bit which says whether it is full or empty. Stations wanting to transmit wait for an empty slot to arrive and change the control bit to full before placing their data and the destination address in it. The slot travels around the ring until it reaches its destination, where the data is copied to a receive buffer and the control bit is marked empty. Such a scheme allows an arbitrary amount of parallelism since there may be many slots on the ring at once and hence many transmissions taking place simultaneously. It has the disadvantage that a transmitter may use every empty slot which it receives and thereby starve potential transmitters which are downstream of it. This phenomenon, where one transmitter may use more than its fair share of the bandwidth, is known as

hogging. Also, if messages are longer than the slot size, elaborate disassembly, sequencing and reassembling facilities have to be provided. Pierce further proposed a hierarchy of rings with buffering devices transferring messages between neighbouring rings. A single supervisor monitors each ring to ensure that it does not become blocked by undeliverable data. The structure of a Pierce loop is illustrated in Fig. 4.1. A single Pierce loop was implemented at Bell Laboratories and used to connect two laboratory computers. A maximum transmission rate of 50 Kbps was achieved between these two machines (Kropfl, 1972; Coker, 1972).

A further example of a slotted ring is the Cambridge Ring. A Cambridge Ring is divided up into a fixed number of 38-bit slots, each containing two bytes of data. The access protocol implemented in the Cambridge Ring is similar to that of the Pierce loop, except that a mechanism to prevent slot hogging is included. The design and use of the Cambridge Ring will be described fully in this book.

A system where the controller is much more sophisticated and performs error control functions and coordinates stations operating at different speeds is the Bell Laboratories Spider network (Fraser, 1974). This network can handle up to 64 duplex data transmissions at the same time and makes use of two packet types. Large packets are used for data and small packets for network control signals. The ring is divided into a number of slots, each slot being able

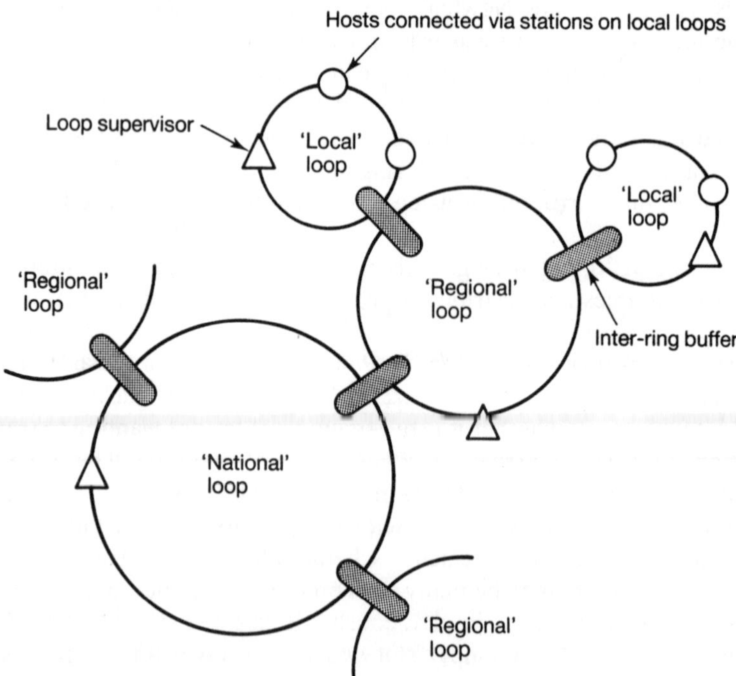

Fig. 4.1   Structure of the Pierce loop

to hold one packet of each type. The Spider network determines the route for all packets in a message in advance, which allows the number of bits in the address field to be reduced. This has the advantage that there are fewer special error and control states, but there is an overhead in changing the communication path. The Spider network is illustrated in Fig. 4.2.

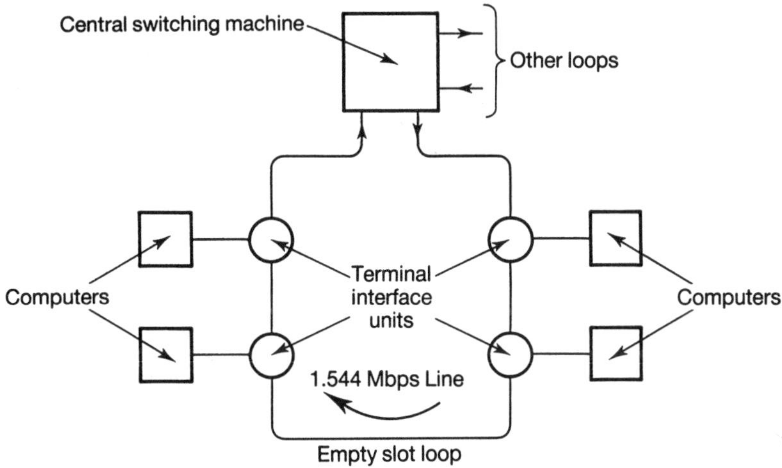

Fig. 4.2 The Spider network

There is a ring scheme, independently proposed by Hafner *et al.* (1974) and by Reames and Liu (1975), based on inserting a shift register into the communication path. The packet to be transmitted is placed in the shift register before being transmitted to the next station. A packet can thus be inserted between two other packets on the ring. This means that bandwidth is distributed evenly between all users, and that the delay round the ring is proportional to the amount of traffic. The SILK register insertion ring is described in this chapter.

Several hybrid combinations of access methods have also been proposed and implemented. One such combination is that of a slotted ring and a register insertion ring. The concept behind this network, called Tornet, is that only stations in possession of a slot can expand the ring for the transmission of data. Tornet is described later in this chapter.

4.2 Multi-ring systems

The maximum size of a single ring communication system is limited for a number of reasons. Probably the most important is the effect on ring performance of an excessively long network. The greatest degradation in service occurs when a ring is populated with many devices which generate packets at a high rate. This extra competition for the network resource causes the level of service to drop since a high network load leads to an increase in the access delay. Another factor which affects the performance is the increase in the round trip delay experienced by packets on a physically large ring.

Reliability is also an important consideration in determining the maximum practical size of a ring. As the ring length increases, so must the number of active repeaters since the distance between signal regeneration devices is normally limited. The increase in the number of ring components, plus the additional length of the transmission medium, makes the system more prone to failure.

An alternative to large-scale rings is a collection of smaller rings interconnected by bridges. This has the advantage that the overall system size need not be reduced and communication between devices on the individual rings can proceed in parallel. When a dialogue with a device connected to a different ring is required then packets are directed to the local bridges. The bridge will then proceed to forward packets onto the adjoining ring, as was proposed by Pierce.

Complex structures of multi-ring systems can be built and in such a network a dialogue may take place across several bridges. The allocation of devices to a particular ring can be arranged on the basis of frequent communication or geographical proximity. As the number of stations on each individual ring is reduced their reliability is increased. In addition, the reliability of the whole system is increased since a failure of one of the constituent rings will not result in failure of the whole network.

4.3 Ring failure modes

The worst type of error experienced by any network is a break in the communications medium. Unless provision has been made to counter this problem then the network will be unusable. Ring networks can be disabled in this way, but the loop topology makes such errors simple to locate. If it is possible for each node on the ring to detect the lack of a coherent bit stream coming from its upstream neighbour then, when such a condition arises, it should be possible for the node to identify the stretch of cable at fault. The error can be reported by signalling the host device or by spontaneously transmitting a packet to an error logging node on the ring.

The ring as a network topology is particularly prone to the effects of bit corruptions in packets. As the network is a loop, a packet which has a faulty control field might circulate indefinitely. This could not happen on a bus network since the erroneous packet would eventually 'disappear over the edge'. An example of this type of error is the full/empty bit of a slotted ring being changed to read full when it should read empty. This will prevent any ring station from using that slot and no station would attempt to empty it. A similar case is a permission token being changed from free to busy by a ring error. It is impossible for a standard ring node to recognise this situation since the access protocol appears to be operating correctly. This class of error must be detected either by a central control node on the ring or by a distributed algorithm running in the nodes attached to the ring. Normally, a distributed algorithm is complicated and adds significantly to the hardware at each node.

4.4 A slotted ring – the Cambridge Ring

The data ring at the University of Cambridge Computer Laboratory was designed to provide a high-speed, low error rate communication path between computers and other devices. The primary uses of the ring were intended to be equipment-sharing and file-dumping (Wilkes, 1975; Hopper, 1978). A detailed discussion of the design and operation of the Cambridge Ring can be found in Chapter 5 and just a brief introduction is given here.

The Cambridge Ring is based on the empty slot principle. The empty slot system, as originally proposed by Pierce, suffers from hogging. This occurs when a single transmitter is allowed to transmit in every empty slot and thus prevents other stations from using them. It can be overcome if each full packet makes a complete revolution of the ring and is marked empty by the transmitter before being passed on. This is the scheme that is used in the Cambridge Ring with the additional constraint that only one slot at a time may be used by the transmitter.

The Cambridge Ring is built using TTL logic and operates at 10 MHz, with a maximum distance of 100 m between nodes. To improve reliability, the logic for repeating the signal at each node is powered via the ring cables rather than from the host devices.

A fixed packet length system is used in the Cambridge Ring and thus an additional mechanism has to be provided to cater for variable-length data. This involves grouping packets together into **blocks**. An advantage of the small packet size is that the buffering requirements of the receiver are minimal since the reception of a block is suspendable at the packet level.

4.5 A permission token ring – the IBM token ring

This section describes a prototype local area network developed at the IBM Zurich Research Laboratory. It was designed to provide a reliable communications facility for a wide range of equipment, including host computers and peripheral devices (Bux *et al.*, 1982).

The IBM ring is based on the permission token principle. The ring consists of a collection of distribution panels which are connected by the communication medium in use, either coaxial or fibre-optic cable. These distribution panels have a number of taps which provide a bidirectional link for the connection of **ring adaptors** (Fig. 4.3). When a device connected to an adaptor wants to be inserted into the ring a relay in the distribution panel is activated to make the link. When this switch takes place the physical length of the ring is increased. An adaptor contains the digital and analogue circuits necessary to

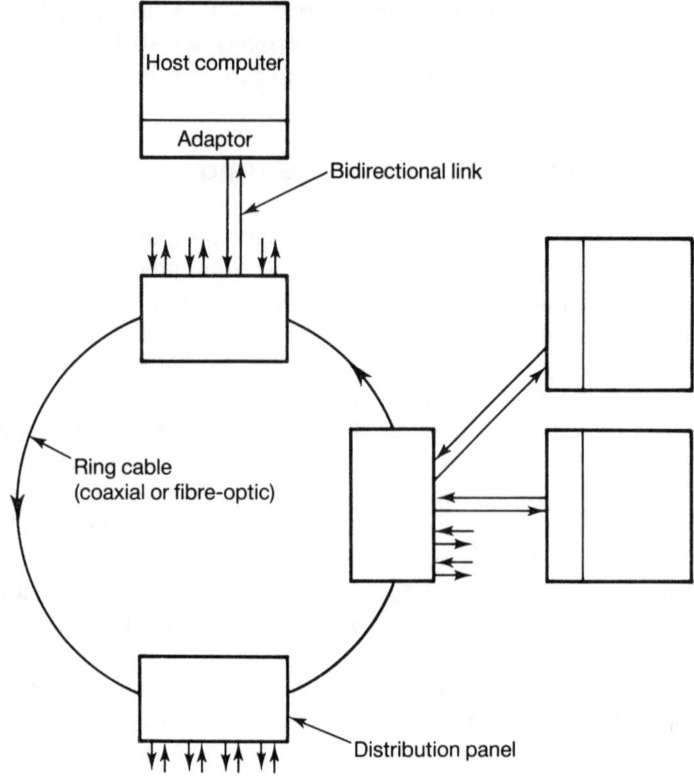

Fig. 4.3   Structure of the IBM token ring

control the transmission and reception of data. This includes manipulation of
the low-level token protocol. Transmission, which only takes place when the
adaptor is in possession of the token, is performed by breaking the ring and
transmitting in one direction down the cable. Reception, which takes place
when the adaptor recognises its own ring address in the address field of a
passing packet, involves copying from the data and control fields of the packet.

At any one time an IBM ring has a single monitor station which has overall
control of the ring and the token. However, the monitor station architecture is
not unique to a particular device, it is present in every adaptor. When the ring
loses the monitor station, i.e. when the device connected to the adaptor which
had assumed the monitor station role is removed from the ring, a period of
arbitration between the remaining adaptors follows. The result of this
competition is that the adaptor with the highest ring address takes over as the
new monitor station. The adaptor hardware also includes an internal monitor
system which can detect errors that may degrade the service experienced by
other ring users. When this happens the adaptor automatically removes itself
from the ring by deactivating the relay in the distribution panel. When an
adaptor is not inserted into the ring it is looped back onto itself at the

distribution panel. This enables a sequence of pre-insertion checks of adaptor functions and of the cable between the adaptor and the panel to be carried out.

4.5.1 Packet format

Data is transmitted on the IBM ring in variable-sized packets. The packet format is shown in Fig. 4.4. The beginning and end of a packet are marked by a 1-byte delimiter. The first 4 bits of a delimiter violate the Manchester encoding scheme used on the ring. Of the remaining 4 bits of the field, only the last two are used and these identify the byte as being a start-of-packet delimiter (DELs) or end-of-packet delimiter (DELe). There is also a third type of delimiter, called the shut-off delimiter, which is transmitted by the monitor station under certain error conditions to deactivate the ring.

	Frame header				Frame trailer	
8	8	32	32		16	8
D E L$_s$	Trans-port Control (TC)	TO-ADDR (A$_T$)	FROM-ADDR (A$_F$)	Transport Information (TI)	Frame Check Sequence (FCS)	D E L$_e$

Fig. 4.4 Packet structure of the IBM token ring

Between the start and end delimiters are three types of field: control fields, which are used for network operation and maintenance, addressing fields and a data field. The transport control field at the front of the packet is an 8-bit field which is used for access control, multiplexing of asynchronous and synchronous packets, ring maintenance and recovery from errors.

The addressing field contains two addresses indicating the destination and source of the packet. The destination address (TO-ADDR) and the source address (FROM-ADDR) are two-level hierarchical addresses. The length of each address is 32 bits. The structure of these addresses corresponds to the notion of a group of rings connected to form a large-scale network. The first two bytes of an address represent the ring number, their contents being used for routing purposes by the devices which form the bridge between two rings. The remaining two bytes of the address correspond to the address of an adaptor on the ring defined by the first two bytes.

The transport information field is a variable-length data field. It is used by host devices to implement the higher-level protocols which perform the establishment, execution and termination of dialogues across the network.

At the end of each packet is a frame check sequence field which is used for error detection using the standard HDLC generating polynomial. The value occupying this field is calculated from the contents of the TO-ADDR and FROM-ADDR address fields and the transport information field.

4.5.2 Transmission modes

A potential transmitter must wait until it has possession of the token before attempting to send a packet. As mentioned previously, the token is simply a bit in a packet which continually circulates the ring. The state of this bit signifies whether or not the packet is in use. If the packet is in use then the contents of the packet are valid and a transmission should not be attempted. If, however, the token indicates that the packet is free then all fields of the packet are invalid. On receiving such a token an adaptor may transmit. There is an analogy here between a token ring operating in this way and a slotted ring which contains only one slot. The only significant difference between the two is that the token ring may have a variable packet size while the slotted ring must have a fixed packet size.

The IBM ring design recognises two distinct types of traffic – synchronous and asynchronous. Synchronous traffic is seen as needing a regular service from the ring with a guaranteed service time. For example, in order to provide a high-quality voice service it must be possible to transmit regularly to prevent pauses appearing in mid-sentence. Conversely, asynchronous traffic has a bursty nature and it is impossible to predict when a transmission will be required. Typical examples of this kind of traffic are packet transmissions resulting from user interaction at a host computer, such as the request to print the contents of a file. These two types of traffic are intended to coexist on an IBM ring by time-sharing the use of the ring between them. There is a **traffic mode** bit in the transport control field which indicates which type of traffic is allowed to use the packet.

The ring access protocol for asynchronous transmission operates as follows. When an adaptor, which is waiting to transmit, receives a free token it breaks the ring by activating an internal switch. It then reserves the packet by setting the token bit. Having updated the transport control field, the adaptor then transmits the source and destination addresses, the contents of the transport information field and the packet trailer. Meanwhile, all other inserted adaptors inspect the destination address of passing packets. On recognising its own address, the adaptor will copy the contents of the source address and data fields. The transmitting adaptor waits for the packet header to return. When the packet has completed its revolution of the ring, the adaptor inspects the contents of the transport control field and the two addresses. A successful transmission is deemed to have taken place if the FROM-ADDR matches the local address, indicating that a breakdown of the token protocol has not taken place. All of the adaptor-definable bits of the transport control field are then cleared, thus freeing the token. When the end-of-packet delimiter is received, the internal switch is closed and the adaptor acts as a passive repeater.

During the passage of the packet header round the ring, the monitor station can update the value of the traffic mode bit in the transport control field. When this bit is set to one it indicates that the monitor station has initiated a period of synchronous operation of the ring. When the synchronous mode is to be entered, the precise action of the monitor station depends upon the current state of the token.

If the token is free, the monitor station sets the traffic mode bit in the header. The token cannot now be used for transmission by any adaptor which has not been selected for synchronous transmission. If the token is not free when the monitor station wants to change mode, then it leaves the traffic mode bit untouched but sets the **priority indicator** bit. As the token is not free this implies that an adaptor is awaiting the return of the header to complete its transmission sequence. When the token returns to an adaptor during transmission, the adaptor must inspect the priority indicator bit. If it is set, the adaptor must not free the token when the current transmission is completed. Therefore, no other adaptors can claim the token and it returns to the monitor station. As the token is received by the monitor station it is removed from the ring and once the end-of-packet delimiter is discarded, a new synchronous token is issued.

The synchronous transmission mode of the IBM ring enables two-way communication between host devices within a single packet revolution. When an adaptor operating in synchronous mode receives a free synchronous token, it marks it busy and attaches the address and data fields as in asynchronous mode. However, when the destination adaptor recognises its address, instead of just copying the contents of the data field, it also updates its contents. So when the packet is on its return path it contains data for the device attached to the source adaptor. When it returns to the original adaptor the contents of the control and address fields are checked and the new data field is copied. If the transmission was successful then the token is freed and the opportunity to transmit is passed on to the next adaptor downstream. When a free token is received by the monitor station all the synchronous mode adaptors on the ring have had the chance to transmit. The monitor station then clears the traffic mode bit and asynchronous mode is resumed.

When the monitor station uses the priority indicator bit to initiate a period of synchronous transmission, it introduces an element of bias to the sharing of the token. When this occurs it will always be adaptors immediately upstream of the monitor station which are denied access to the token when the mode change occurs. However, it is possible to reintroduce a free asynchronous token at the position on the ring at which the last token was removed. This prevents the service experienced by host devices from being unbalanced.

4.5.3 Ring maintenance

The IBM ring was designed with an emphasis on reliable operation and non-interventional recovery from error conditions. The ring contains a number of distribution panels (Fig. 4.5) to which ring adaptors connect using a bidirectional link. As previously described, the insertion of an adaptor into the ring is effected by opening a bypass relay in the distribution panel to which it is physically connected. This means that if an error, such as a faulty adaptor or a break in the cable attaching an adaptor to the distribution panel, is detected

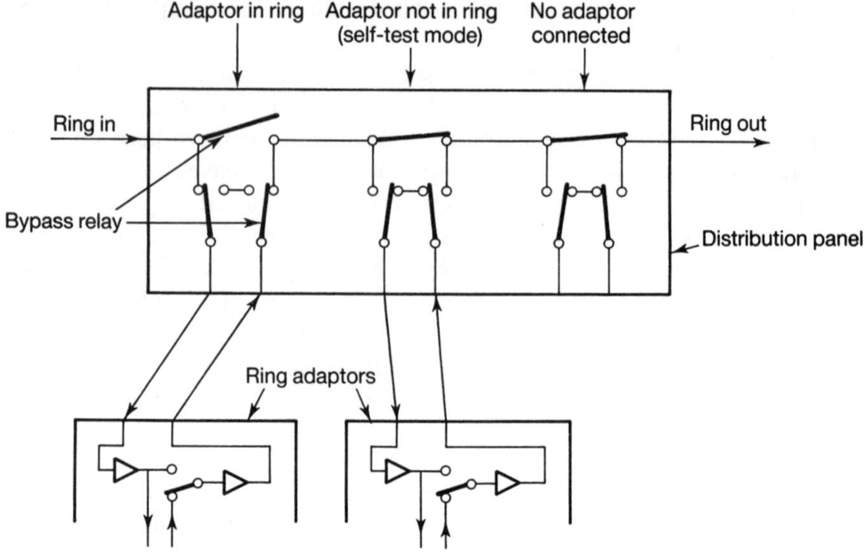

Fig. 4.5   Distribution panel of the IBM ring

then the relevant relay can be closed, thereby cutting out the erroneous section of the ring.

One of the most important reliability factors of a token ring is the integrity of the token. Its importance arises from it being regarded as a guarantee of undisturbed service. There are three distinct token error conditions which the network must be able to detect and correct. Each of these error conditions and the way in which they are dealt with by the IBM ring are described below:

1. **Lost token**   The token can be removed by corruption of the start-of-frame delimiter due to noise or during ring initialisation. This condition can be detected by a timeout being applied by the active monitor station. Once a valid token has passed the monitor station, a timer will be set to a value greater than the round trip delay of the ring. If the timer expires before the token returns then it is deemed lost. Recovery is executed by the monitor station issuing a shut-off delimiter, thus instructing any active adaptor to cease transmitting and enter repeater mode by closing their internal switch. The monitor then clears the ring and when it is known to be free of spurious bit patterns a new free token is issued.

2. **Circulating busy token**   A permission token can be corrupted in such a way as to cause the token bit to be changed from 0 to 1, thus marking it as busy. As there is no transmission under way it will not be cleared and all adaptors are therefore prevented from using it. This problem is detected by using the **monitor count** bit of the transport control field. When an adaptor transmits a packet, the monitor count bit is cleared. During its journey

round the ring the packet will pass the monitor station, at which point the monitor count bit is set to 1. It is therefore possible for the monitor station to detect whether or not a token has passed by before by comparing the value of this bit. If this error is detected the same procedure for recovery as in the lost token case is initiated, clearing the ring and issuing a new free token.

3. **Token duplication** The permission token which circulates the ring must be unique, thereby allowing only one adaptor to transmit at any time. If a busy token were corrupted and changed into a free token this would enable a second adaptor to start transmitting. This error can be detected in two ways. As a packet returns to the source adaptor, its FROM-ADDR field is compared with the local address. If a match does not occur then a duplicate token may have been created allowing a second adaptor to transmit. The second way in which the existence of multiple tokens is detected is if an adaptor which is waiting for the return of its packet receives a free token. Whenever this error condition arises, the adaptor which detected it enters repeater mode without issuing a free token. This causes the token duplication error to be translated into a lost token error which is detected and corrected by the monitor station.

A potential weak point of networks which have a centralised control function is the failure state of the network that can arise if the central controller malfunctions. If there is no backup facility, total network failure can ensue. The IBM ring is such a network, the monitor station representing the centralised control function. However, the monitor station function of the IBM ring has been designed to be a dynamic feature that is present in all adaptors, although only one adaptor will be in the active monitor station mode at any time. At ring startup or when the current monitor station is removed from the ring or if it malfunctions, a period of monitor station contention begins. At this time any adaptor which has noticed the lack of a monitor station will attempt to take over that role by entering **competition mode**. The criterion for entering competition mode is that a valid token has not been observed for a length of time greater than the round trip delay of the ring multiplied by the number of attached adaptors. When this mode is entered, the adaptor continuously transmits special monitor recovery broadcast packets. On receiving such a packet, an adaptor inspects the FROM-ADDR address and if it numerically exceeds its own, it immediately enters repeater mode, thereby terminating its attempt to become the monitor station. This process reduces the potentially high number of contending adaptors to just one. The ring adaptor with the highest address will be the only one to receive back a packet with a matching FROM-ADDR address. When this occurs, all other adaptors must have submitted and so the adaptor assumes the role of monitor station. When the contention procedure is completed the new monitor station clears the ring and issues a new free token.

4.5.4 Multi-ring architectures

The architecture of a local area network envisaged by the designers of the IBM ring was that of a collection of interconnected rings. These subnetworks are connected together by a backbone network, the main component of which is a high-speed data switch called a **block switch**. The role of the block switch is to route data packets between rings at high speed. Between the block switch and the rings are located **bridges**.

Bridges

The bridge acts as a queueing buffer between a ring adaptor and a block switch. Routing is not performed by the bridge, but is done by the adaptor, which accepts the packet, and the block switch. The bridge also acts to interface the speed requirements of the devices connected to it, since the rate of data transfer across the block switch is an order of magnitude greater than that of the ring. A critical factor in the design of such an interface is the size of buffer. Peaks in demand for buffer allocation are usually due to the inability of the destination ring to accept packets because of high traffic levels. If the size of available buffer in the bridge is too small this can result in packets being discarded by the adaptor and hence queues of packets can build up across the network. An over-estimate in the size of buffer needed increases cost and power requirements. It has been calculated that buffers ten times the maximum packet length will satisfy all but the highest traffic demands and will reduce the probability of buffer overflow to an acceptable level.

Packets of either class of traffic, synchronous or asynchronous, are kept in order as they are received by the bridge. However, to provide a guaranteed service for synchronous traffic this type of packet is allowed to jump the queue.

Remote bridges are intended for use where a ring is located well away from the nearest block switch. A remote bridge and a block switch are connected by a full-duplex serial link which operates at a similar speed to the ring and about one tenth of the speed of the block switch. Speed equalisation is performed by also incorporating a single packet buffer per physical connection within the block switch and implementing a simple flow control scheme to control the filling and emptying of it.

Block switch

The block switch performs high-speed routing of packets between bridges. By using parallel internal data paths and pipelining of transfer requests, the data rate attainable by the block switch is 100 Mbps. There are four major components of a block switch, the structure of which is shown in Fig. 4.6.

A bridge is connected to a block switch via a **port**. There are two types of port, input and output, although their operation is symmetrical. An input port signifies the recognition of the arrival of a packet by placing the TO-ADDR address of the packet into an internal register. It then awaits permission to start transferring the contents of the packet across the internal data bus. The **access control** function of the block switch scans the ports until it sees that one of them

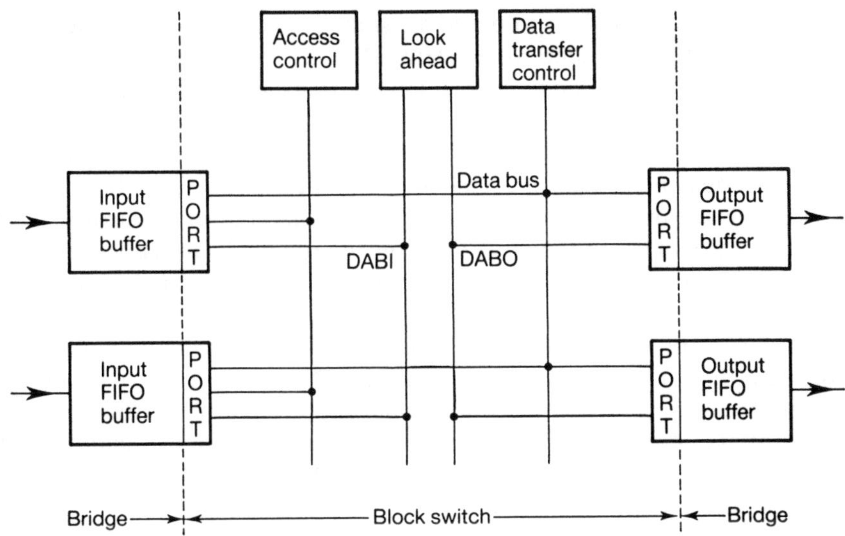

Fig. 4.6   Structure of the block switch

is requesting a packet transfer. The identity of the active port is then passed to the **look ahead** function. The role of the look ahead function is to match an output port to the TO-ADDR address provided by the input port. This is done by telling the input port to place the ring part of its TO-ADDR address onto the Destination-Address-Bus-In (DABI). The look ahead function then maps this onto a routing table in order to determine the identity of the appropriate output port. The output port is then activated by recognising its number which is placed on the Destination-Address-Bus-Out (DABO) by the look ahead function. If the output port does not respond, this indicates that it is prepared to accept the packet from the input port. The receipt of a not-ready signal from the output port means that the port is not available and causes the attempted transfer to be abandoned. Control is then passed back to the access control function which searches for the next waiting input port. If there are no other input ports active then the failed transfer will be reinitiated. If the output port is able to accept a packet then the **data control** function, which performs the transfer of the data across the internal data bus, is invoked. In order to maintain a low interframe pause, as soon as an internal data transfer is underway the access control and look ahead functions attempt to identify the next input port with a pending request.

4.6 A register insertion ring – the SILK ring

A local area network based on the insertion of a shift register section into a communications loop was suggested by Hafner and colleagues of Hasler AG

(1974). The system that they proposed has since been developed commercially and is sold under the name SILK (Huber *et al.*, 1983). The SILK ring is intended to be an integrated network for the transmission of both data and digitised voice traffic.

The size of traffic transmitted in such systems can be expected to be wide ranging. At one end is the single-character type of transmission which can be sent between a terminal and a computer or as a special code in a control system. At the other end of the traffic spectrum is the file-oriented data associated with sending text across the network. The size of such transmissions can be of the order of 100 Kbytes or more.

An important feature of the SILK ring is the concept of integrating voice traffic with the traditional data transmissions. The requirements imposed by digitised voice transmission is for a regular opportunity to transmit a small amount of ata. As a conversation will only require an average data rate of 64 Kbps there is the potential for many such dialogues to take place across a local area network.

4.6.1 The principle of register insertion

When a station wishes to transmit a packet on a register insertion ring it must wait for a suitable break in the packets already on the ring and then insert a shift register, containing the packet to be transmitted, into the ring. The logical length of the ring and therefore its delay is increased when this occurs. The maximum time delay before insertion is possible will be less than one revolution of the current ring length and will depend upon the points of access that are permitted by the access protocol. This may allow a node to insert between packets or may restrict the point of access to the end of the series of blocks that are currently passing the ring node. When a node transmits onto an otherwise empty ring, the round trip delay experienced by the block is small since no other stations have registers inserted into the ring. In this respect a register insertion ring compares well against a slotted ring with more than one slot since, if only one station were transmitting on such a network, the rest of the ring length would be padded out by empty slots and therefore wasted. As a result of this the proportion of the system bandwidth that can be exploited by the user of a register insertion ring is potentially greater.

Exponents of register insertion rings also claim that they have characteristics that make them more attractive than permission token rings. On a register insertion ring more than one station may transmit simultaneously, whereas on a token ring the number is limited to one. However, the performance of register insertion rings deteriorates as the demand for data transmissions increases. As there is no means by which a station can be restricted in its attempt to enter the ring, the only limit to the length of the ring is the number of stations. The round trip delay experienced by transmitted blocks can therefore be very large. The design of a local area network based on the principle of register insertion implies that either the traffic level of the expected applications will be low or the typical block length will be short. The designers of the SILK ring considered it too be a suitable basis for the architecture of a network on which digitised voice in short packets would form a significant part of the traffic. Many simultaneous conversations would be possible across the network without causing a large ring delay.

4.6.2 SILK architecture

The architecture of the SILK ring is a hierarchy of three **planes**. These are the transport plane, the connection plane and the peripheral plane. The transport plane is the system for transporting data between users: in other words it is the LAN hardware. It includes the logic which implements the register insertion access method, thereby controlling the transmission and reception of data by the attached devices. The connection plane consists of devices which interface the transport plane to particular types of host devices. Finally, the peripheral plane consists of the host devices themselves. Only the transport plane will be discussed here.

A SILK ring is made up of a collection of nodes interconnected by links of varying lengths. The transmission of data over each link is treated separately, the signal being decoded and regenerated by each node. Each node is independently synchronised by the reception of special synchronisation bytes from the upstream node. There is one special node in the ring which provides a master clock reference for all other nodes.

The structure of a SILK node is shown in Fig. 4.7. Each node provides for

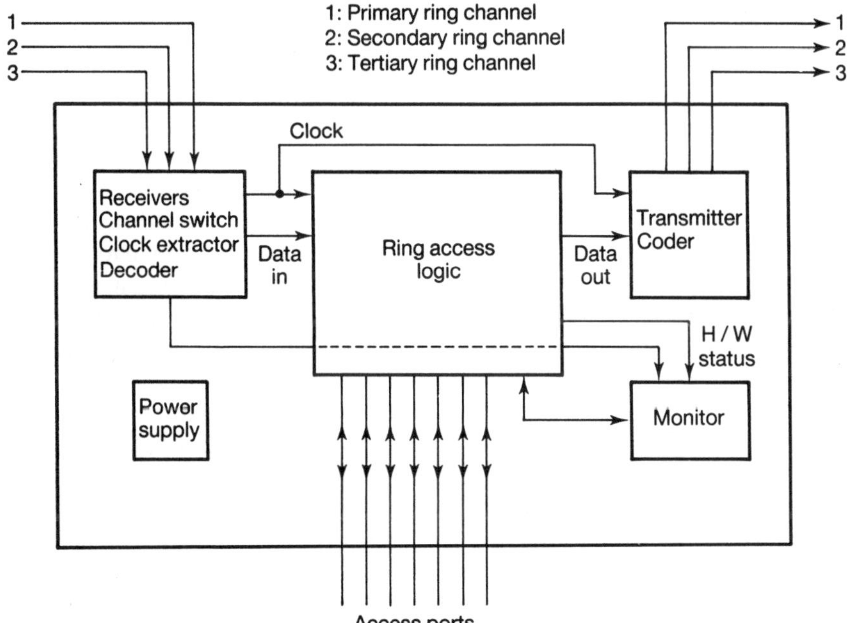

Fig. 4.7   Structure of a SILK node

the attachment of up to 7 peripheral devices, each of which is associated with its own **access port**. There is an eighth access port, internally connected to a **monitor** which is used for observing the error rate of the ring and dealing with certain types of failures.

Data is encoded using the Manchester scheme, with the serial bit rate being approximately 17 Mbps. The ring has been implemented using coaxial cable and link lengths of up to 500 m are possible. Fibre-optic links may also be employed for links of up to 2000 m. The bit error rate experienced on SILK rings is less than 1 in 10^9. Data is transmitted on the ring in variable-length packets each containing up to 13 bytes of user data. As with other networks, the packet format includes control and addressing fields in addition to the data. The basic forms of a SILK packet are shown in Fig. 4.8.

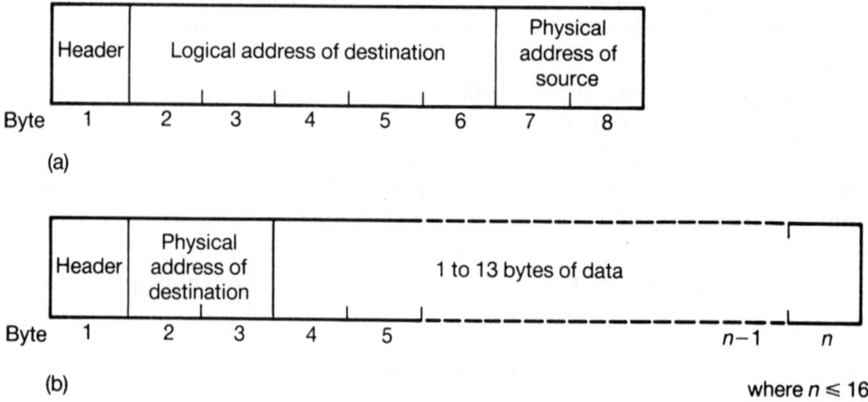

Fig. 4.8   Formats of SILK packets: (a) Format A; (b) Format B

The transmission of data takes place over virtual circuits which are established by a transmission using packet format A (see Fig. 4.8). Two levels of network addresses are recognised, local and physical. A 5-byte long logical address corresponds to a user of the network. Hence, there might be several logical addresses recognised by a single network node. However, a node only responds to a single physical address. The physical address is two bytes long, one byte identifying the node and the other referring to one of the access ports within the node. A virtual circuit is established by the initiator transmitting a broadcast packet containing the logical address of its intended dialogue partner and its own physical address. The use of a broadcast packet means that the partner can be dynamically located. The process is completed when the partner accepts the virtual circuit by transmitting a packet containing its own physical address. This mechanism allows for a flexible policy in physically relocating equipment. Once a virtual circuit has been established data transmission takes place using packets of format B (Fig. 4.8).

The control byte at the head of the packet is used to indicate the packet type. It distinguishes broadcast from non-broadcast packets and format A packets from format B. Broadcast packets operate as follows. When the broadcast packet is transmitted, a bit in the header is set which prevents nodes from receiving it. When the packet passes the master clock node for the first time the bit is cleared and the packet will then be received by all nodes. When the packet reaches the master clock for the second time it is removed from the ring. Thus, broadcast packets will be received once only by each access port. This mechanism is also used to remove corrupt packets from the ring which might otherwise circulate indefinitely.

The reliability of a SILK installation is enhanced by a multiple wiring scheme known as **braiding**. Each SILK node has thre parallel connections along which data can be sent. The primary channels are used to connect the nodes as a ring. The secondary channels bypass a node by interconnecting the two nodes adjacent to it. Groups of nodes can be selectively bypassed by interconnecting areas of the ring using the tertiary channels.

In normal operation, transmission of data takes place around the ring using the primary channels. The integrity of transmissions is monitored by the master clock node regularly transmitting test packets to the monitor within each node. When a node detects an error rate above a predetermined threshold, it switches to another transmission section and signals an alarm on a central alarm unit.

4.6.3 Implementation of the register insertion access method

The structure of the access method logic is shown in Fig. 4.9. There are three registers in each node, which are implemented as FIFO buffers. Two of the registers, the insertion buffer and the transmission buffer, operate together. When the transmission buffer has been loaded and there is no packet currently passing the node, the insertion buffer is placed in the ring so that data from the ring flows into it. The node output switch is simultaneously connected to the transmission buffer and the packet in it is copied onto the ring. Because the packet size is variable, the length of the insertion buffer must be controlled to match. The amount of the insertion buffer which is inserted in the ring can be reduced when the node receives a packet or when empty or synchronisation bytes are arriving. When a packet arrives at a destination node which does not have any buffer inserted in the ring, it is not possible to remove the entire packet as it is received. This is because it is not until the whole of the destination address has been seen that the node knows whether or not to receive the packet. If the packet is received, then its tail is removed from the ring by the receiver but the first three bytes continue to circulate as a truncated packet. Such packets are deleted at nodes further round the ring.

The logic of the SILK nodes is sufficiently sophisticated to allow the queueing of up to 32 packet buffers within the transmission buffer. Each of these buffers can be allocated to one of the eight access ports which are recognised at the node. Even though the transmission buffer has such a large storage capacity, the number of packets which can be transmitted at any one time is limited by the size of the insertion buffer which is only capable of

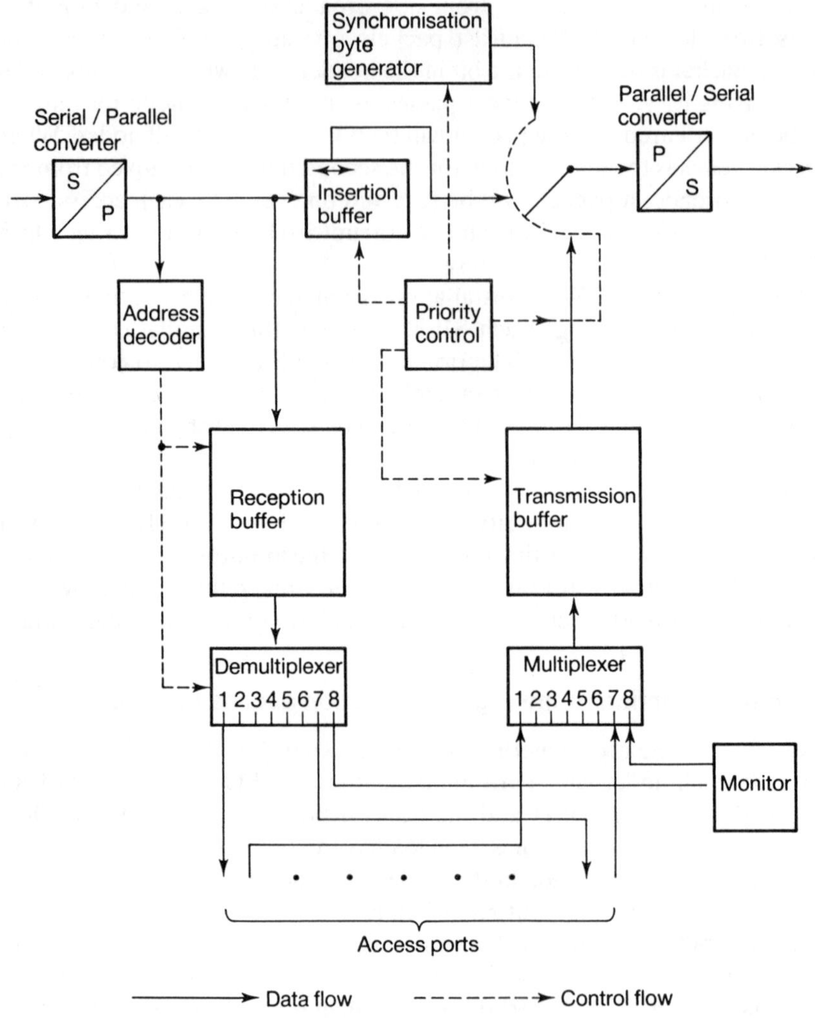

Fig. 4.9   Structure of the SILK access method logic

buffering two maximum size packets. The transmission of a sequence of packets will only be halted when the insertion buffer does not have enough reserve to accommodate the transmission of a maximum size packet.

Reception of a packet occurs when the node hardware recognises the physical address. The packet is then copied into the receive buffer. The contents of the packet can then be accessed by the access port to which it is addressed. The receive buffer has the capacity to accommodate up to 16 full-size packets.

4.7 A multimode ring – Tornet

Tornet is a local area network which has been designed to possess benefits of both slotted and register insertion rings. It was designed and built at the Computer Group Laboratory of the Department of Electrical Engineering in the University of Toronto (Vranesic *et al.*, 1981). A Tornet is a hierarchy of rings, there being a central ring which interconnects many local rings. The local rings are intended to support many different devices, ranging from simple terminals and data collection devices to sophisticated computers, and to satisfy the majority of their communication needs. The central ring provides communication between local rings and also provides specialist services to devices located on the outer rings, such as a high-power computation service. One of the major constraints on the design of Tornet was cost. It was realised by the designers that, since the devices to be interconnected by local area networks are inexpensive, the cost of providing a communications facility to those devices should also be low. In addition, the network must be highly modular so that the cost of an initial installation is low and at the same time providing greater flexibility and ease of expansion.

The structure of a Tornet installation is shown in Fig. 4.10. A local ring is made up of ports which are connected in a loop. Each port provides the signal regeneration for the ring and the access protocol for the host device which is attached to it. Apart from the ports, a local ring also contains a ring controller and a bridge to the central ring. The role of the controller is to synchronise the local ring and to monitor operation of the ring, looking out for error conditions which arise. The bridge is like a pair of back-to-back ports, one of which is located on a local ring and the other of which resides on the central ring. Packets are received at a bridge and routed between the rings in a similar way to the passage of a packet through a normal port to the local host device.

Access to both the local and central rings is by a limited insertion technique. Each ring has a series of circulating slots. The difference between Tornet and a slotted ring is that in the former the structure of a slot does not include a data field. When a slot is acquired by a port which intends to make a transmission, the port inserts a register in series with the ring. The length of the register that is inserted represents the amount of data transported in the packet. On a local ring there are two possible values for the length of the data field, 1 byte and 128 bytes. The short data packets are intended for byte-oriented traffic. These may include terminal traffic, protocol control packets and digitised voice transmissions. The long packets are to be used for the transmission of larger amounts of data such as file transfer traffic. The central ring only supports transmissions using long packets. By adopting the dual packet sizes, Tornet is intended to be efficient as a transmission system for byte-oriented traffic by keeping the delay around the ring as short as possible. At the same time, it also provides the opportunity for devices which require the transmission of bulk data to share the ring.

The similarity between Tornet and a slotted ring has already been

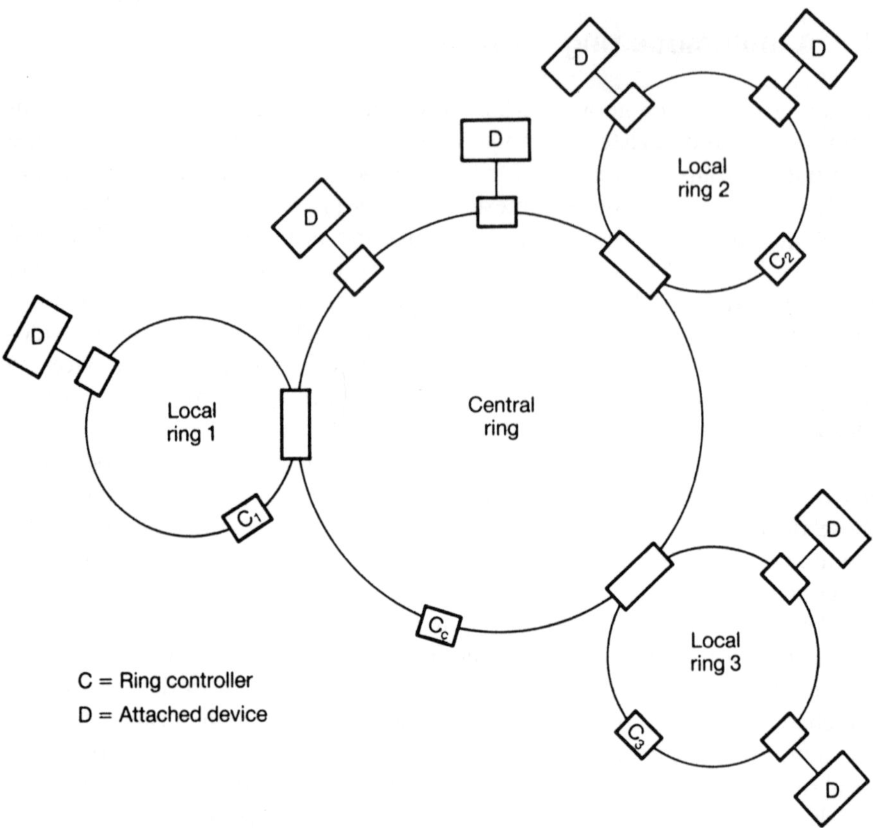

Fig. 4.10   Structure of the Tornet local network

recognised. The structure of packets transmitted on Tornet is very similar to the packet structure of the Cambridge Ring. This structure is illustrated in Fig. 4.11. An empty slot is 24 bits long. The first bit of an empty slot is always a 0. When a slot is reserved by a port, this bit is inverted to a 1. The first bit can therefore be seen as a full/empty bit. When a port marks a slot as being full, it must also set the value of the second bit depending upon the length of the packet to be transmitted. This long/short bit therefore defines how the remaining bits of the packet are to be interpreted. Then follow two 8-bit address fields, representing the source and destination ports respectively. The next field is the data field and then the final field consists of six control bits. The first of these is used by the protocol software to distinguish packets carrying data from those carrying control information. The second is a monitor-passed bit similar to that used in other ring networks. The next three are response bits which are altered by the destination of the packet and the last bit is a parity bit which is calculated from all the preceding bits in the packet. The response bits are set by the destination port during the passage of the packet round the ring.

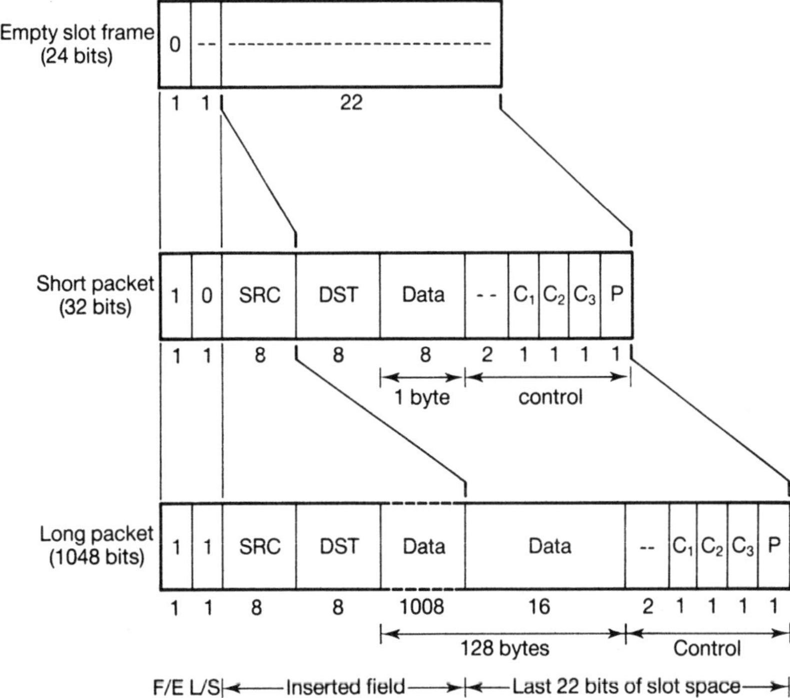

Fig. 4.11   Tornet packet structure

They are used by the source port to determine whether or not the packet was received successfully, and if not, for what reason.

The structure and operation of a Tornet port will now be described. Ports on the local and central rings are identical, except for structural implications of the limit of one packet size on the central ring. The internal structure of a port is shown in Fig. 4.12. A port can be divided up into two sections, one representing the logic which performs the transmission of packets and the other performing the reception of data.

The transmit section can be characterised as a three-input multiplexer, MX1, which feeds the line-driving circuits at the output of the port. The three possible sources of bit streams which can be selected by MX1 are the contents of the ring currently being received, the contents of a short shift register or the contents of a long shift register. When a transmission is not underway, a port is described as being in a passive state. At this time all three multiplexers in the transmit logic have input 1 selected and therefore bits received from the ring are routed straight through the port. The delay through the port in the passive state is 2 bits. When a host device wishes to transmit a packet, it first completes the address and data fields enclosed in the head and tail shift registers of the appropriate size. When the port has been informed of the host's wish to transmit, it starts to search for a passing empty slot by inspecting the first bit of

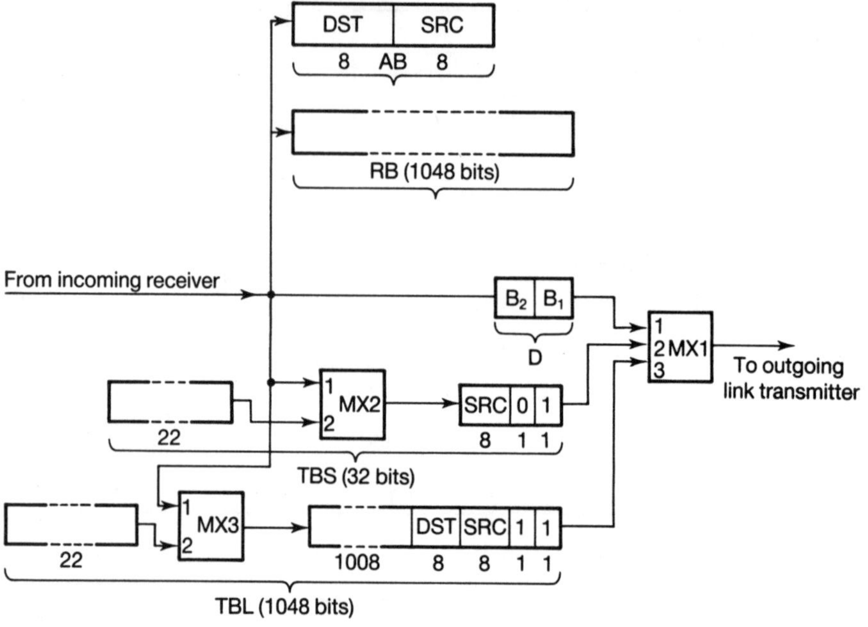

Fig. 4.12   Internal structure of a Tornet port

each slot as it arrives in latch B_1. When B_1 is found to be zero at the beginning of a slot, the port enters its active state. The output multiplexer, MX1, then switches to select a bit stream from either the long or short shift register depending upon the size of packet which is to be transmitted. In the case of a short packet MX1, and also MX2, switch to select input number 2 and the contents of the short transmit shift register are sent serially out onto the ring. The multiplexer switching is synchronised such that the first bit of the shift register appears on the ring at the same time that the full/empty bit in latch B_1 would have done. At this stage the ring has been broken by MX2 to enable the transmission of the contents of the tail shift register segment. The delay of the port is now increased to 10 bits. When the 22 bits of the tail shift register segment have been shifted through to the head section, MX2 reselects input 1 and the ring is closed again. As the response bits in the control field at the end of the packet are transmitted, their values are cleared to 0. The transmitted packet now works its way around the ring and the port waits to detect its return. This is deemed to have taken place when the SRC field of the short transmit buffer (TBS) holds the local port address. Multiplexer MX1 is then switched to select input 1 and latch B_1 is forced to value 0. Hence the 24-bit empty slot is returned to the ring. The response field and parity bit at the end of the packet are now recognised and copied from B_1 and B_2 when they appear. The port has now returned to the passive state. The transmission of a long packet is identical to the operation just described, except that the length of the head segment shift register inserted into the ring is 1026 bits in length instead of the 10 bits for short packet transmissions.

Reception of packets requires considerably less complex logic than the transmission of packets. Two shift registers, one an address buffer (AB) and the other a data buffer (RB), tap the data stream coming from the ring. The contents of full packets are copied into the shift registers as they arrive. The first two bytes, the source and destination addresses, are copied into AB and the rest of the packet is copied in RB. When the contents of the destination address field are recognised as belonging to the local port the contents of RB are retained for reading by the host device. Assuming that the parity bit matches the value calculated as the packet arrived, the control bits are set to indicate that the packet has been successfully received.

A number of situations can arise at the destination port of a packet. Each situation is allocated a code which is inserted into the control field at the end of the packet. If, having calculated the parity of an incoming packet, a port detects an error on comparing it with the received parity bit, control bit C_3 is set to 1 and the packet is ignored. The reason for the 2-bit latency of a passive port is that the contents of the parity bit must be inspected before the contents of C_3 can be set. C_1 and C_2 are used to indicate the state of the receive buffer at the destination port when the packet arrived. The first of the four states indicates that the packet was recognised by the destination and was received by it. The second state indicates that the packet was recognised but could not be received because the destination had no room to buffer it. The third state arises when the destination recognised the packet but was currently listening to only one (different) port. The fourth state, in which C_1 and C_2 are unchanged, indicates that the packet was not recognised.

4.8 References

Bux, W., Closs, F., Janson, P.A., Kummerle, K., Muller, H.R. and Rothauser, E.H., 1982. 'A local area communication network based on a reliable token ring system'. In *Proc. IFIP TC6 Symp. on Local Area Networks, Florence, Italy*, eds. P.C. Ravasio, G. Hopkins and N. Naffah, pp. 69–82. Amsterdam: North-Holland.

Coker, C.H., 1972. 'An experimental interconnection of computers through a loop transmission system'. *Bell Systems Tech. J.*, **51 (6)**, 1167–75.

Farmer, W.D. and Newhall, E.E., 1969. 'An experimental distributed switching system to handle bursty computer traffic'. Proc. of ACM Symp. on Problems in the Optimisation of Data Communications Systems, October, 1–33.

Fraser, A.G., 1974. 'Spider – a data communications experiment'. Computer Science Tech. Rep. No. 23, Bell Laboratories, NJ.

Hafner, E.R., Nendal, Z. and Tschantz, M., 1974. 'A digital loop communication system'. *IEEE Trans. Comm.*, **COM–22 (6)**, 877–81.

Hopper, A., 1978. 'Local area computer communication networks'. Tech. Rep. No. 7, University of Cambridge Computer Laboratory.

Huber, D.E., Steinlin, W. and Wild, P.J., 1983. 'SILK: an implementation of a buffer insertion ring'. *IEEE Journal on Selected Areas in Communications*, **SAC-1 (5)**, 766–74.

Kropfl, W.J., 1972. 'An experimental data block switching system'. *Bell Systems Tech. J.*, **51 (6)**, 1147–65.

Pierce, J.R., 1972. 'Network for block switching of data'. *Bell Systems Tech. J.*, **51 (6)**, 1133–45.

Reames, C.C. and Liu, M.T., 1975. 'A loop network for simultaneous transmission of variable-length messages'. Proc. of the 3rd Annual Symp. on Computer Architecture, Houston, January.

Vranesic, Z.G., Hamacher, V.C., Loucks, W.M. and Zaky, S.G., 1981. 'Tornet – a local area network'. *Computer Comm. Rev.*, **11 (4)**, 180–187.

Wilkes, M.V., 1975. 'Communication using a digital ring'. Proc. of the PACNET Symposium, Sendai, Japan, August, 47–56.

Chapter 5   **The Cambridge Ring**

This chapter describes a typical local network – the Cambridge Ring. This network is widely used within the UK, particularly within the academic community. It is available on a commercial basis from several vendors. The topics covered in this chapter are the network hardware and its principles of operation, the protocols which have been implemented for it and an attempt at integrating the network hardware in order to reduce its cost.

5.1 The design of the Cambridge Ring

The first prototype Cambridge Ring network was commissioned in 1975 in the Computer Laboratory in the University of Cambridge. It was designed using the most advanced components of the day, MSI and SSI TTL circuits. This first generation of the Cambridge Ring was the precursor to future ring development projects in Cambridge (Wilkes and Wheeler, 1979). Two such projects are described later in this book.

The design of the Cambridge Ring was undertaken because of a need for a system that would allow the interconnection of computers and similar devices within a building and be capable of operating at a data rate substantially greater than that provided by conventional telecommunications techniques. A ring had the advantage of conceptual simplicity and it was felt that this simplicity could be preserved in a practical design.

A system was proposed in which information would be sent in very small fixed-length packets. Due to their small size it was felt more appropriate to refer to them as **minipackets** rather than packets. The acceptance at the destination of each minipacket would be verified independently of other minipackets and there would be a minimum of protocol built in at the hardware level. Importance was, however, attached to choosing a system that would be intrinsically safe from the hogging of the ring by one station. Since it was felt that the bandwidth attainable over short distances was more than ample for the purpose, making best possible use of a given bandwidth was not felt to be of overriding importance.

Following a design study it was decided to use a minipacket containing a destination address of 8 bits, a source address of the same size and 16 bits of data. There were also a small number of bits in the minipacket for control purposes. The original design was based on the register insertion principle, described in Chapter 4, where the minipacket to be transmitted is placed in a shift register which is inserted in series with the ring at an appropriate moment. As the delay in inserting a register and thus transmitting is at most one minipacket time, hogging does not occur and bandwidth is distributed to all nodes symmetrically.

In due course it was realised that a more attractive system would be one based on the empty slot principle. In this scheme minipacket frames, or slots, continuously circulate around the ring. Each slot carries a leading bit, the **full/empty bit**, to indicate whether it is full or empty. A station assembles a minipacket it wishes to transmit in a shift register and shifts the information into the first available empty slot that comes along, marking it full as it does so. The minipacket travels round the ring to the destination, where the information in it is copied into the receiving station and it then returns to the source where it is marked as empty. The sending station is not allowed to refill the returning slot, but must pass it on to the next station on the ring. This gives a round robin type of distributed control and prevents hogging of the ring by any station. The service provided to all stations is the same and no station can prevent another station from using the ring.

It was realised that there would be no need for the returning minipacket to be recognised by its source address, since the number of minipackets circulating in the ring is fixed and a station has only to count minipackets as they go by to know when its own minipacket has returned. Thus, it is not necessary to have an additional shift register permanently connected in series with the ring at each station in order that the full/empty bit will not have left the station by the time the source address is recognised. There need, in fact, be no more delay at each station than is necessary to regenerate the signals on the ring. Thus the amount of logic in series with the ring is reduced to a minimum and the reliability may be expected to increase accordingly. A fault developing in a shift register at a particular station will affect transmission from that station, but will not affect the operation of the ring as a whole.

The fact that minipackets always make a complete circuit of the ring would appear at first sight to imply that half the transmission capacity is wasted. However, this is not the case, since the returning minipacket can convey information as to whether the minipacket was successfully received by its destination. Special measures would otherwise have to be taken to indicate this, such as the launching from the destination of a separate minipacket addressed to the original source. Allowing minipackets to make a full circuit of the ring enables a very simple hardware protocol to be implemented, in which the transmission of each minipacket and verification of the fact that it has been received is independent of the transmission of other minipackets.

It is necessary to provide a **monitor station** whose function is to remove from the ring minipackets that circulate indefinitely as a consequence of the full/empty bit in an empty minipacket being set to full due to an error on the line. To detect this happening it is necessary to include a bit in the minipacket called the **monitor-passed bit** which is cleared when the minipacket is marked full and is set when it passes the monitor station. The monitor station marks as empty any minipacket which reaches it with the monitor bit already set. Corruption of the source address byte in a minipacket would not cause the minipacket to circulate indefinitely since, as explained above, this byte plays no part in the recognition by the source of the returning minipacket. The monitor station may also conveniently provide the means whereby the ring is initialised when it is switched on or suffers a failure. It can also be designed to keep statistics of ring performance and loading.

It is desirable that there should be some feature whereby a station may render itself deaf to stations from which it does not wish to receive minipackets. It was decided to incorporate in the station unit an 8-bit register known as the **source select register**. When this register contains all 1s (the number 255), the station will receive a minipacket addressed to it from any source. When the register contains all 0s, the station will not receive minipackets from any source. Otherwise, the station will receive minipackets only from the source whose address is specified by the number in the register.

5.1.1 The Cambridge Ring hardware

Data is transferred serially around the ring over two links which, between them, carry the encoded data and clock signals. At intervals around the ring are **repeaters** which provide a means of accessing the ring and regenerating the data in it. The data rate between repeaters is 10 Mbps. The communications medium used is the standard twisted-pair cable widely used in telephone systems. Two twisted pairs, enclosed in a single sheath, are used to implement the two links. Included in the repeaters are transformers which remove any common mode interference or low-frequency noise. Screening of the twisted pairs is not found to be necessary for satisfactory operation.

The repeater design has been found to operate with up to 200 m of cable between repeaters, but 100 m is recommended as the upper limit for routine use. Many repeaters are, of course, very much closer together than this. A twin fibre-optic system has also been used between two repeaters in the ring. The attenuation and dispersion encountered on this link were so low that the current design could be expected to drive several kilometres of fibre cable.

The use of two channels enables a simple self-clocking system of encoding to be used. In each bit time a transition on both channels denotes a 1 and a transition on one or other of the channels only denotes a 0. Under normal conditions, therefore, there is at least one transition per bit time and so it is possible to recover a clock signal. This scheme is illustrated in Fig. 5.1. The waveform on each channel is fully balanced and unlike the well-known Manchester or biphase encoding schemes, there is no half-pulse ambiguity. Each repeater incorporates a phase-locked oscillator for the generation of a local clock. The twisted pairs used for signal transmission are also used to carry DC power at 50 volts for the repeaters, each repeater having in it a step-down DC transformer.

Because the operation of the ring depends on the repeaters working at all times, they are powered independently of the hosts which use them. This

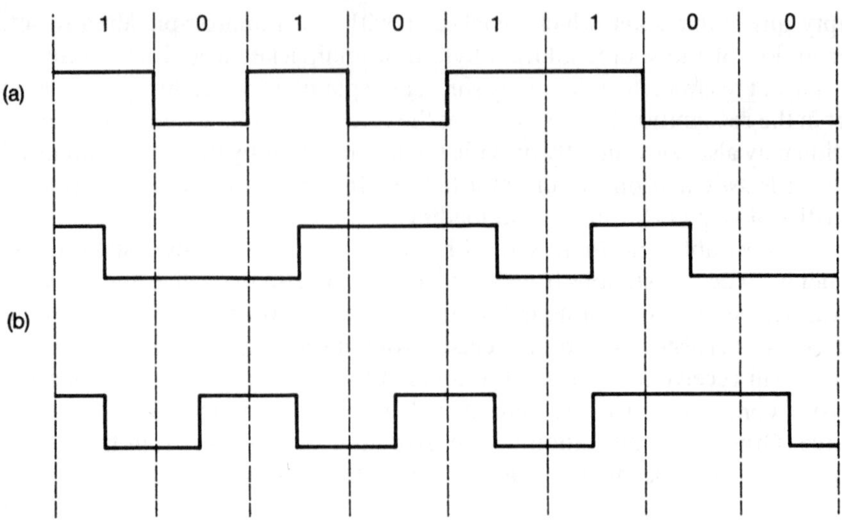

Fig. 5.1   The Cambridge Ring line encoding scheme: (a) NRZ encoding; (b) Cambridge Ring line encoding

power is supplied on the ring cables themselves by power supplies known as **power insertion boxes**, each of which can power up to six repeaters. The remaining components which make up a Cambridge Ring connection are normally powered from their associated host. Thus the repeaters, being independent of local sources of power, continue to work when their hosts are switched off and even after a single ring break.

A connection to a Cambridge Ring has three components. The repeater, as already mentioned, provides a connection into the ring. A device known as a **station** contains all the circuitry associated with transmitting and receiving packets. Finally, the **access box** provides an interface between the station and the host device. All repeaters are identical and the station units differ in only one detail, a coding plug which gives each station a unique 8-bit address. The structure of a Cambridge Ring connection is shown in Fig. 5.2.

Around the ring there is an appreciable delay, both in the wire itself (5 ns per metre) and in the repeaters which delay data by three bit times. This delay is occupied by a fixed number of slots or minipackets. The slots follow one another head-to-tail up to the capacity of the ring. The train of slots is terminated by a sequence of 0s referred to as the **gap**. These 0s, together with the first bit of the slots, are used for minipacket framing and counting. Since the delay in each repeater is only three bit times, the total number of minipackets circulating in the ring tends to be small. Most Cambridge Rings in operation at present have only one or two slots on them.

The minipacket format is shown in Fig. 5.3. The first bit is always a 1, and indicates the start of the minipacket. The second bit is the full/empty bit which indicates whether the minipacket is in use or not. The third bit is the monitor-

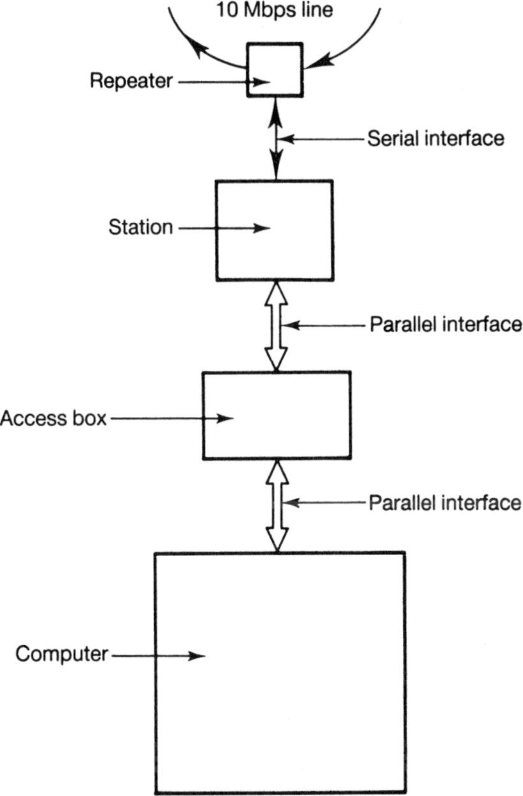

Fig. 5.2   Structure of a Cambridge Ring connection

passed bit. After that come the destination and source addresses, each of 8 bits, followed by 16 bits of data. These are followed by two response bits which are both set to 1 when the minipacket is launched. If the destination is absent or switched off they will be unchanged when the minipacket returns to its source. Otherwise they will be changed by the destination, according to the code shown in the figure, and indicate whether the minipacket was accepted, was rejected because the destination was not ready to receive another minipacket or was rejected because the station was deaf (unselected) to the particular source. The last bit in the minipacket is a parity bit which is used to detect errors in the transmission system.

The interface between a repeater and a station unit consists of four lines of which two are data lines. One of these passes the bit stream received from the ring to the station unit and the other is used by the station unit to pass data to the repeater for transmission onto the ring. The third line supplies the station with a clock which the repeater derives from the incoming data. The fourth line is a gating signal from the station which causes the repeater to inject the station's data onto the ring. This line is routed through a relay in the repeater

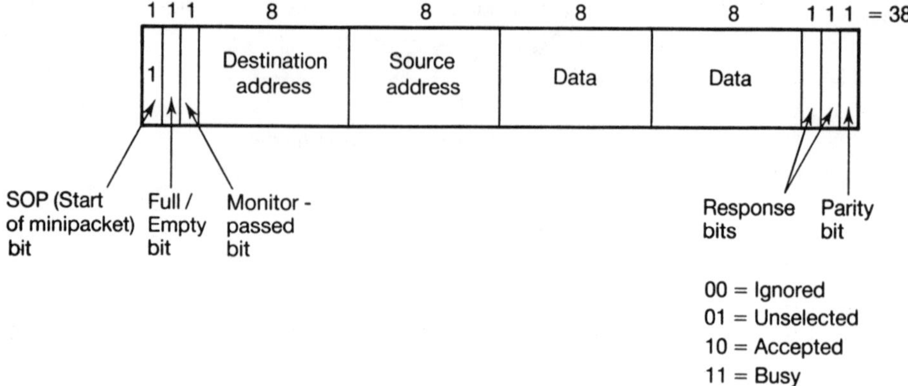

Fig. 5.3   Minipacket format of the Cambridge Ring

which is closed by the station unit's power supply. Therefore, when the station unit is off data cannot be accidentally injected onto the ring.

The station unit contains framing circuits that synchronise themselves to the passing slots using the leading 1s and the gap digits. It also contains the parity generating and checking circuits, and the circuits for dispatching a maintenance minipacket when one is necessary. The maintenance minipacket is easy to generate since, apart from the source byte and the full/empty bit, all bits are 0s.

The station unit also contains transmission and reception circuits. These are independent of each other and permit full-duplex access by the host via the access box. On the receiving side there are circuits which continuously monitor the data stream received from the repeater and which are capable of recognising minipackets addressed to the station. As long as the station is free, that is, not busy dealing with a previously received minipacket, the data flows into a receiving shift register. When a minipacket addressed to the station is recognised a note is made of the fact and, if it subsequently appears that the minipacket has come from a source to which the station is deaf, shifting ceases. When it is known whether or not the minipacket is to be accepted, the front part of it will have already passed the repeater. However, since the response bits come at the end of the minipacket, there is plenty of time for the minipacket to be marked as accepted or rejected. If the minipacket is accepted, it remains in the receive shift register until that register is cleared by a signal from the access box. If any further minipackets addressed to the station arrive before this has happened, they are marked busy.

There is a separate shift register for transmission. The destination address and data bytes are written into this in parallel from the access box and, on an appropriate signal from the access box, are ready to be inserted into an empty slot when one arrives. The source address and control bits are added automatically. The transmitting shift register is circular and retains a copy of the transmitted minipacket. Therefore, the minipacket can be retransmitted, if necessary, without reloading the shift register. During the design process, it was decided to take further advantage of the retention of a copy of the transmitted minipacket by providing circuits for checking, bit by bit, that the data and address bytes in the minipacket returning from the ring are identical to those transmitted.

When the minipacket has returned, some status information is available for reading by the access box. This contains the response information which was brought back from the destination and also an error-checking bit which indicates if the returned minipacket contained the same data and addresses as the one which was transmitted. This status information must be inspected before it can be decided whether to retransmit the minipacket that has just returned or whether to send a new one. It is, therefore, not possible for the access box to fill the slot immediately after the slot that has just been used, even if it is empty. When allowance is made for this and for the fact that only 40% of a minipacket carries user's data, it is found that the fastest that one station can transmit data to another is about 1.6 Mbps on a ring with a single slot. There is a further mechanism built into the hardware which comes into operation when two consecutive minipackets to the same destination have come back with the busy response. When this occurs the station delays the signal which says that a minipacket has returned. Thus, when a destination is slow at receiving minipackets the transmitter is forced to slow down by this mechanism. This reduces the load on the ring under such circumstances, as well as the time that the transmitting host spends performing transmissions.

The interface between the station unit and the access box consists of two 16-bit buses, the digits of which are denoted by TB_0 through TB_{15} and RB_0 through RB_{15}, respectively, and 17 control signals CS_1 through CS_{17}. There is also a disabling line which controls the relay in the repeater. This is used only during switching on and switching off. The functions of the various control signals are given below.

CS_1 Sets the 8-bit source select register from RB_0–RB_7.

CS_2 Gates the first data byte from the receive shift register to RB_0–RB_7.

CS_3 Gates the second data byte from the receive shift register to RB_8–RB_{15}.

CS_4 Gates the source address from the receive shift register to RB_0–RB_7.

CS_5 Gates the source select register to RB_0–RB_7.

CS_6 Gates a 1 to RB_6 if the station has rejected a minipacket from an unselected source at any time since the source select register was last set.

CS_7 Echoes the logical OR of CS_1–CS_6 and CS_{16} (handshake response to access box).

CS_8 Sets the first data byte in the transmit shift register from TB_0–TB_7.

CS_9 Sets the second data byte in the transmit shift register from TB_8–TB_{15}.

CS_{10} Sets the destination address in the transmit shift register from TB_0–TB_7.

CS_{11} Gates the response bits for the last minipacket returned to TB_0–TB_4. These bits are not valid until CS_{14} has gone high.

CS_{12} Echoes the logical OR of CS_8–CS_{11} and CS_{13} (handshake to access box).

CS_{13} Causes the minipacket in the transmit shift register to be transmitted (transmit command).

CS_{14} Falls at the end of CS_{13} and rises again when the transmitted minipacket has returned (minipacket returned signal).

CS_{15} Falls at the end of CS_{16} and rises again when a minipacket has arrived in the receive shift register (minipacket received signal).

CS_{16} Discard information in the receive shift register and prepare the station unit to receive (receive command).

CS_{17} Signals appearing on this line indicate that the ring is up and working.

5.1.2 Synchronisation of the ring

The ring has to be synchronised during power up both at the bit level and at the slot level and synchronisation has to be maintained during operation and re-established when errors occur. It is the responsibility of the monitor station to perform these functions.

To establish bit-level synchronisation all the oscillators in the ring have to be phase-locked. When first switched on the monitor station uses a 10 MHz fixed-frequency oscillator to put out the bit stream. This is at the centre of the range of the next phase-locked loop downstream which locks to this frequency. This continues with all phase-locked loops round the ring until the one preceding the monitor station. Now the monitor station removes the 10 MHz fixed-frequency reference and itself locks to the incoming bit stream. This may require the operating frequency to change slightly so that there is a whole number of bits round the ring. Under error conditions, for example during a ring break, the oscillator immediately downstream from the break is designed to move to the centre of its range and thus the clocking regime is maintained, albeit now on a unidirectional bus.

The station units contain a simple algorithm, embedded in their framing circuitry, which synchronises them to the slot structure. The framing logic can be in one of two states, **InGap** or **NotInGap**. When a station powers up it may come on in either of these states at random. While a station is InGap it skips over bits 0 arriving at the input. When a 1 arrives it takes this to be the start of the slot train and becomes NotInGap. In this state it counts 38 bits from the 1 it received and looks at the next bit. If this is a 1 it remains in the NotInGap state and waits another 38 bits. If it is a 0 the station goes to the InGap state. Eventually, this process will get the station into synchronisation with the ring.

The station logic does not use the number of slots in the ring as part of its synchronisation process. The number of slots is used solely for determining when a transmitted minipacket has returned.

The monitor station initialises the slot structure when it powers up or when a serious error occurs. Its mode of operation when it does this is known as **start mode**. When in start mode it writes a train of slots onto the ring which are marked full but otherwise contain 0s. It then starts writing the gap digits. While it is doing this it looks at the incoming data which has been right around the ring and when it sees a 1 it takes this to be the start of the slot train and starts writing the slot train again. Because stations will not synchronise immediately to these slot trains they will probably become mutilated as they pass round the ring and stations try to correct parity bits which are not really parity bits. Stations may even try to transmit in the slots. Therefore, the monitor keeps on putting out slot trains until the returning trains show no signs of error. One can argue that the first station downstream will synchronise and thereafter stop writing erroneous bits followed by the second station and so on. Once the incoming bit stream is correct the monitor sends out a train of empty slots and enters another mode known as **run mode**. In this mode it simply monitors the ring for errors and adjusts the monitor-passed bit in minipackets. If a serious error occurs it will re-enter start mode to initialise the ring.

5.1.3 Provision for maintenance

It was realised at an early stage in the design of the Cambridge Ring that some aid would be necessary to enable breaks in the ring to be readily located. A proposal for continuously monitoring the ring and reporting errors to a logging station was made by Hopper and Wheeler (1979). This proposal was so attractive that the ring was rebuilt to implement it.

In this system, the last bit of each minipacket is used as a parity bit. As the minipacket leaves each station, including the station at which it is launched, this bit is adjusted so that the minipacket will have even parity. When a minipacket enters a station, the parity is checked by separate circuits. If it is found to be correct no action is taken. If it is incorrect the station that has discovered the error proceeds to transmit a maintenance minipacket to a logging station, which has address 0. Thus, if one of the repeaters develops an intermittent or marginal fault, or if noise enters the ring from outside, the logging station will begin to receive reporting minipackets from the station immediately downstream of the trouble. The faulty minipacket continues on its way but, since the parity bit is reset as it leaves each station, the stations downstream of that at which the parity was found to be wrong will not produce further reporting minipackets.

The logging station is placed just ahead of the monitor station and reporting minipackets are launched with the monitor-passed bit already set so that they are removed by the monitor station without making a complete circuit of the ring. As an alternative to providing a separate logging station, facilities for recording information arriving in maintenance minipackets may be built into the monitor station.

The monitor station fills empty minipackets with random bits (except for the full/empty bit) and these minipackets are subjected to the procedure just described in exactly the same way as full ones. The functioning of the ring is thus continuously monitored whether or not it is carrying traffic. The staff responsible for the maintenance of the ring can thus receive immediate indication that trouble is occurring and are not dependent upon reports received from users. It is suggested that this should be a design requirement for any digital communication system from which a high degree of reliability is expected.

The leading digit in a minipacket is always a 1 so that a station can never in normal operation receive a long unbroken stream of 0s. If this situation does occur, as it would if the ring became broken, the design of the station is such that it will emit a sequence of maintenance minipackets as long as the condition persists. The stations downstream of the one after the break will see what appears to be a normal stream of minipackets but without a gap. Thus the maintenance system enables breaks in the ring, as well as intermittent faults, to be located.

5.2 Cambridge Ring protocols

The protocols in use on the Cambridge Ring in service at the University of Cambridge Computer Laboratory will now be described. The majority of data transmitted on the ring is sent using the **basic block protocol** (Walker, 1978). This provides a mechanism for transferring up to 2048 bytes of data from one host to another and corresponds to a packet on an Ethernet or token ring. Two higher-level protocols have been implemented on top of the basic block protocol, these being the **single-shot protocol** (Ody, 1979) and the **byte stream protocol** (Johnson, 1980). From these protocols has grown a set of standard protocols now used on most Cambridge Ring installations and known as **CR82** (Larmouth, 1982).

5.2.1 The basic block protocol

The transmission of data across the Cambridge Ring is almost exclusively performed in terms of the basic block protocol (BBP). A basic block is a sequence of minipackets and begins with a **header** minipacket. Following this is a **route** minipacket and this is followed by between 1 and 1024 **data** minipackets. Finally, there is a **checksum** minipacket which is used for error-checking.

The header minipacket contains a 4-bit pattern to identify it as a header, a 2-bit type field and a 10-bit size field which indicates how many data minipackets there are in the block. The pattern field is only a weak identification of the minipacket as a header, since data minipackets are quite

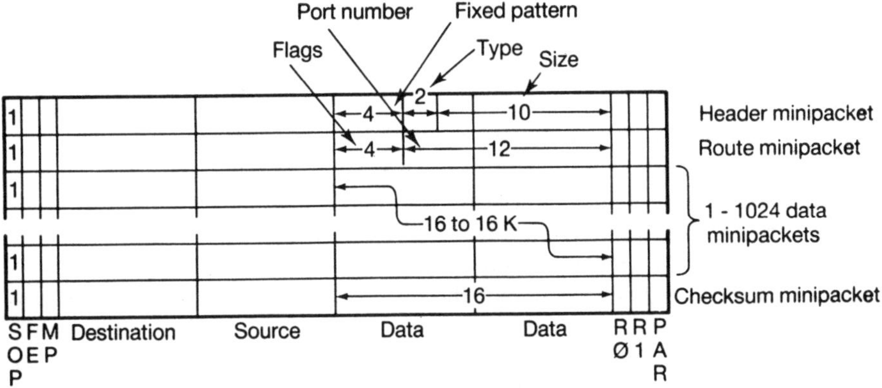

Fig. 5.4   Format of a basic block

likely to contain this pattern also. The route minipacket contains a 12-bit port number which is used to direct the block to the appropriate place within the destination. The remaining 4 flag bits are used for assorted purposes in intelligent access boxes and bridge computers. The format of basic block is shown in Fig. 5.4.

The type field in the header identifies the block as being one of four types. The most common type consists of a block with data and an end-around-carry checksum packet. A second type has a checksum of 0 and a third type consists of just the header minipacket with 10 bits of data in what would normally be the length field. Such 'blocks' have been used to carry digitised voice samples around the ring. The fourth type is a slightly different form of the first mentioned type, in which the second minipacket contains the block length in bytes and the third minipacket is the route.

Current implementations of the basic block protocol limit the number of blocks being transmitted or received at any one device to one, although the protocol itself does not impose any limit. One method of implementing the reception of basic blocks is simply to receive all their minipackets and discard the data if it is not wanted or if it is too big for the available buffer. The hardware of the station unit contains a facility which may be used to advantage in this situation, however. This is the **source select register** which was mentioned in Section 5.1 and its use in the basic block protocol will now be described.

A station which is not currently receiving a basic block will set its select register to 255 to receive minipackets from anyone. When it receives a header packet from someone it will then set its select register to accept minipackets only from that source. It will then receive the rest of the minipackets in the block and then set the select register back to 255. If it decides at any time that it does not wish to receive the block then it sets its select register to 0 and the transmitter will see its minipackets being unselected (rejected) and hopefully stop transmitting. The destination will wait a while and then set its select register back to 255. It will probably decide that it does not want the block quite early on, either because it did not like the source or the length was too great or because the port number was unsuitable.

When transmitting a basic block the transmitter will repeatedly transmit the header until it is accepted and will then transmit the rest of the block. If at any time after the header a minipacket comes back unselected, the transmitter will stop and conclude that the source did not want the block for some reason. This method of working has the advantage that some higher-level information can be conveyed to the source in the form of the unselected response and also that the number of unwanted minipackets which are transmitted is much reduced. Another advantage is that the processing load on the destination is reduced, since it knows implicitly where minipackets are coming from during the block and does not need to worry about minipackets from other sources. A disadvantage is that multiplexed reception from multiple sources is not easy. This has only proved to be a problem in a small number of cases.

At Cambridge, the majority of hosts implement the basic block protocol using the select register mechanism. One or two do not and in either case blocks may get lost. For example, a received block in which the checksum is incorrect will be discarded. The basic block protocol is therefore only viewed by higher-level protocols as a means of getting blocks to their destination with high probability.

5.2.2 The single-shot protocol

The single-shot protocol (SSP) is based on the basic block protocol. It is a request/reply protocol in which the requesting host sends a single basic block containing the request and receives a single basic block in reply. The blocks are identified as belonging to this protocol by reserving the first three data minipackets to contain identification and parameters as shown in Fig. 5.5.

The receipt of a reply block is taken as evidence that the request was received and if no reply is received within a certain time the protocol specifies

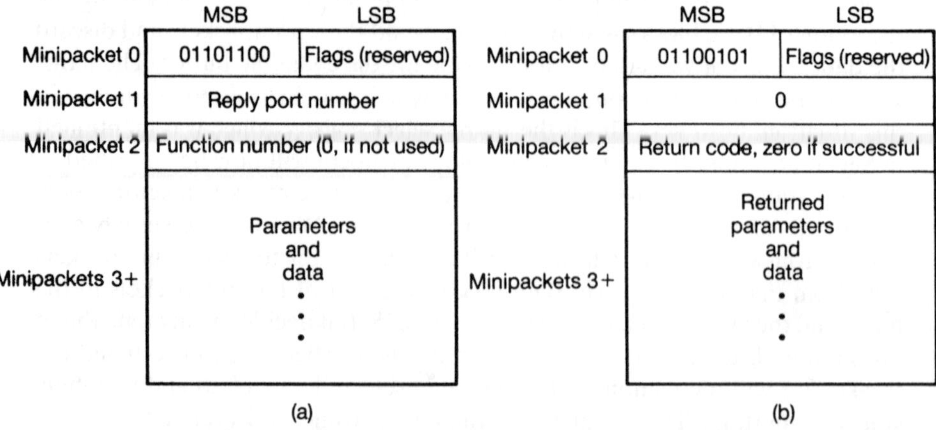

Fig. 5.5   A basic block carrying SSP data: (a) SSPREQ block; (b) SSPRPLY block

that the request be made again. It is possible that the request was received and the reply lost in such cases and so it is important that the request should be for an idempotent (i.e. repeatable) operation.

A typical example would be a request for the time of day. The requester sends a block asking for the time and receives a block containing the time in reply. Another example is a request to write page 52 of file FRED on a remote computer. The request would specify the file, the page and the data, the reply would simply say that the operation had succeeded. An unacceptable (i.e. non-idempotent) operation would be to append a page to the end of a file. If the request succeeded but the reply was lost then another request would be made and two append operations performed.

5.2.3 The byte stream protocol

The basic block protocol provides unidirectional transmission of usefully sized units of data with acknowledgement and flow control at the minipacket level. In order to provide a connection-based protocol with flow control at the block level, the byte stream protocol (BSP) was defined. This protocol provides bidirectional flow of bytes contained within basic blocks between two hosts. The transmission and reception of byte streams is symmetrical and a transmitted block can contain information which is relevant to both data directions. Flow control is performed by providing protocol commands which direct a remote host not to send more data. Synchronisation is provided by associating a sequence number with each command, so that commands which arrive with an out of order sequence number are ignored. The protocol is normally operated with a fixed window size of 1 but larger windows are possible. The byte stream protocol corrects errors detected by the basic block protocol. Correction takes the form of the recipient not transmitting an acknowledgement, thus causing the source host to retransmit the block.

BSP commands

Basic blocks transmitted in the byte stream protocol can be divided into two groups. Either they contain commands relating to the transmission and reception of data or they contain commands which relate to the state of the connection as a whole. The two possible formats of BSP blocks and the command layout are shown in Fig. 5.6.

A **data block** starts with a command referring to the reception of data and is followed by a command relating to the transmission of data. Both of these commands are defined within the context of the source host, that is, the reception command relates to reception of data at the source host and so on. The rest of the block data field, if present, contains the information to be transported. A **connection control block** contains only one command. This may be followed by command-dependent data, if necessary.

A command generally consists of three fields – a 4-bit command identifier, a 4-bit sequence number calculated by addition modulo 16 and finally a byte of command-dependent information. When referring to BSP commands it is

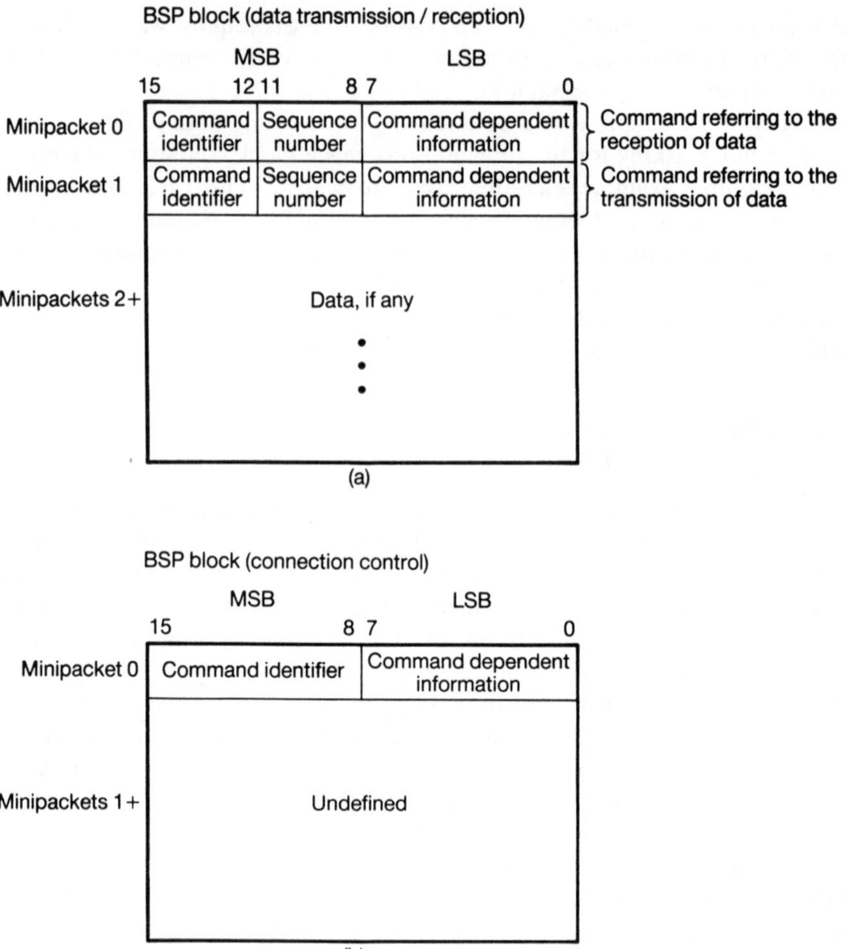

Fig. 5.6   The two types of BSP blocks: (a) data transmission/reception; (b) connection control

customary to write the sequence number relating to a command as a subscript of that command, e.g. $DATA_n$. The only commands which do not follow this format are the connection control commands. In these the identifier is extended to 8 bits and there is no sequence number. A list of the BSP commands and their associated identifiers are given in Table 5.1.

Commands which refer to the transmission and reception of data can be divided into two categories, essential and non-essential elements. An essential element is a command which conveys information about the state of a data buffer. For example, the DATA command says 'my transmit buffer is now full and here it comes'. The RDY command says 'I now have a free input buffer, so you can transmit to me'. The role of a non-essential element is to defer passing that information since the buffer condition is not yet valid. In addition to non-

Table 5.1   BSP commands and their identifiers

Command	Code	Meaning
OPEN	01101010	Request to open a byte stream
OPENACK	01100101	Response to a byte stream open request
NULL	00000000	Null command
RDY	$0011xxxx$	Blocks with sequence number less than $xxxx$ have been received and a new data buffer is ready for reception of further data
NOTRDY	$0101xxxx$	Blocks with sequence number less than $xxxx$ have been received but there is no buffer free for the reception of further data
DATA	$1010xxxx$	The current block contains data with the associated sequence number $xxxx$
NODATA	$1100xxxx$	The transmitter has no more data to send
RESET	01100011	Reset the state of both the transmit and receive halves of the byte stream
CLOSE	01100110	Close the byte stream

essential elements providing information on buffer status, they also exercise the block-level flow control. For example, NODATA gives the information that the source transmit buffer is not ready to be sent. NOTRDY conveys the information that a receive buffer is not ready and in so doing prevents the remote host from transmitting.

A finite state machine with three states describes the operation of the byte stream protocol. A single-state machine describes a source-sink relationship between two hosts. The transmission and reception of data at a host are symmetrical and so there will be two copies of the state machine during the lifetime of a connection. The state machine is shown in Fig. 5.7. The three states in the machine are:

E   An essential element has been transmitted and an acknowledgement is awaited. If the response is not received before the expiry of a timeout, the essential element is repeated.

N   A non-essential element has been transmitted. No response is expected.

I   A non-essential element has been received. It is not necessary to transmit anything, although the previous essential element may be repeated.

A transition from one state to another is made on the execution of an event. There are five possible events:

Erep   Repeat reception of an essential element.

Eexp   An essential element which bears the expected sequence number is received.

Event \ State	Erep $Data_{n-1}$ / RDY_n	Eexp. $Data_n$ / RDY_{n+1}	Nexp $NODATA_n$ / $NOTRDY_{n+1}$	Timeout	Buffer ready
E	Retransmit RDY_n / $DATA_n$ E	Empty / Fill buffer $n + := 1$ Buffer ready? Yes No RDY_n / $NOTRDY_n$ / $DATA_n$ $NODATA_n$ E N	— I	Retransmit RDY_n / $DATA_n$ E	— E
N	Retransmit $NOTRDY_n$ / $NODATA_n$ N	Protocol error	Protocol error	— N	Transmit RDY_n / $DATA_n$ E
I	Protocol error	Empty / Fill buffer $n + := 1$ Buffer ready? Yes No RDY_n / $NOTRDY_n$ / $DATA_n$ $NODATA_n$ E N	— I	— I	— I

Fig. 5.7 The BSP state machine

Nexp A non-essential element which bears the expected sequence number is received.

Timeout Expiry of a timeout counter.

Buffer ready A buffer becomes ready for transmission or reception.

The DATA command is used to transport a block of data from the source host to the destination host. The sequence number contained in the command field identifies the position of the data with respect to the whole. $DATA_n$ is an essential element and is only sent when there is data to be transmitted. The non-essential element which is related to the DATA command is NODATA. This command tells the remote host that although it may have a buffer ready to accept data, the local host does not have any to give yet. The response to transmission of a DATA command is to transmit either a RDY or a NOTRDY, depending upon whether further buffer space is available.

The RDY command informs the correspondent host that the originator has a data buffer free and is willing to accept data. RDY is therefore an essential element. The non-essential element associated with RDY is NOTRDY which informs the remote host that there are no buffers available. RDY_n and $NOTRDY_n$ act as acknowledgements within the protocol, telling the source of the data that blocks with sequence numbers less than n have been successfully received. The response to the transmission of a RDY is to transmit either a DATA or a NODATA, depending upon whether a data buffer is available.

There is also a NULL command and this is used where the protocol does not dictate the transmission of any particular command.

There are two commands which are defined to relate to the connection as a whole. These commands are RESET and CLOSE. RESET can either be generated within the protocol, due to a serious error condition, or may be forced by higher-level software. Whenever a reset condition arises, the RESET command is transmitted and the local state of the connection is set to a well-defined state. All outstanding data transactions are discarded. On receipt of a RESET command, a host should also return to a safe state and then transmit a RESET block back to the original host as an acknowledgement. Passing a RESET in both directions ensures the symmetry which means that a pair of corresponding hosts which simultaneously enter error states will not hang up. In addition to notifying the remote host of the reset state, the local user of the byte stream must also be notified.

Transmission of the CLOSE command requests termination of the connection with the remote host. It is acknowledged by a similar CLOSE block. This command is generally generated upon request from the user, but may also be transmitted as the result of an irrecoverable error.

At the beginning of a connection and after a connection reset, both hosts should be in a standard state in which both transmitters are in state I with a sequence number of 15 and receivers are in state N with a sequence number of 0. Thus, as soon as the first buffer becomes available at the receiver, a RDY_0 is transmitted and state E entered. When the transmitter receives this command, it increments its sequence number and transmits either a $DATA_0$ or a $NODATA_0$.

It may be the case that during a connection one of the host devices dies. This might not be acceptable to some devices and so the option of implementing an idle handshake has been introduced. When a host enters the I-state, having just received a non-essential element, it starts a timeout counter. If this counter expires, the host retransmits the previous essential element and then re-enters the E-state. If the remote host is still not ready, a response of a non-essential element should then be received, returning the local host to state I. In the case of the previous essential element being a DATA command, the local host is permitted to send only the command and not the complete data field, since reception of the packet has already been acknowledged.

Initial connection

The setting up of a BSP connection takes the form of a single basic block passed in each direction and is very similar to a SSP transaction. The blocks are referred to as OPEN and OPENACK blocks. The host wishing to initiate a byte stream transmits an OPEN block to a **ring service address**. This is a triplet which is designed to identify the intended correspondent at the remote host, and consists of an 8-bit station address, a 12-bit port number and a 16-bit function code.

The station number is the ring address of the station to which the intended correspondent is attached. The port number is a logical address within that host, to which incoming open requests are to be routed. It is contained in the route minipacket of the OPEN block. The function code allows further qualification of the open request.

The OPEN block contains information about where the destination should reply to and what buffer size the transmitter wishes to use for transmission and reception. If the destination wishes to have the byte stream opened it sends an OPENACK block back to the source containing the port, to which the source should send further data and information on the buffer sizes it wishes to use.

5.2.4 A sample BSP implementation

A sample implementation of the BSP protocol will now be outlined. The implementation chosen is that used on Z80 microcomputer systems attached to the ring installed in the University of Cambridge Computer Laboratory. The hardware of these systems, the Types 1 and 3, is described in Chapter 6, Section 2.2.

The state of the protocol is internally represented by three control blocks in memory, a channel control block (BSPCB), a transmit buffer control block and a receive buffer control block. During the lifetime of a connection there should be corresponding copies of each control block in both hosts.

An appropriate way of describing a protocol implementation is to discuss the interface between the protocol software and the programs which use it. The user program communicates across the network by using the protocol through a number of procedures. These procedures semantically represent actions which occur in the lifetime of a connection. The most important procedures in terms of illustrating the implementation are:

1. **BSPOPEN**   This is called to set up a byte stream connection to a remote host. The user supplies the textual name of the intended partner in the connection. The three control blocks are set up and the ring service address corresponding to the supplied name is looked up in a name-server. The address received is copied into the BSPCB and an OPEN block is sent to it. When the OPENACK block returns the procedure returns with a return code indicating whether or not the connection opened successfully.

2. **RCVOPEN**   This is called in a host when an OPEN block arrives and it is required to open a byte stream. The three control blocks necessary for the connection are created and an OPENACK block is sent back to the host which sent the OPEN. That this procedure can be called at all implies that in every host there must be a continuously running program which checks on blocks arriving from the ring and interprets them in order to take the appropriate action. In the Z80 implementation this is achieved using co-routines and in some systems a separate task performs this function.

3. **BSPWRCH**   This procedure is called to send a byte of data down the byte stream. Normally the byte is just placed in the transmit buffer but if the buffer becomes full then a buffer full event is generated. The protocol then attempts to transmit the necessary DATA command. This may involve waiting for the remote receive buffer to become ready.

4. **BSPRDCH**   This procedure is called to read a byte from a byte stream. If the last byte of a buffer is read, then a buffer empty event is generated. This may cause a RDY command to be sent to notify the other host that more data may be sent.

5. **FORCETX**   A buffer full event is forced on a transmit buffer. This will cause a DATA command to be sent.

6. **BSPRESET**   A RESET block is sent to the remote host and the byte stream control block is set to the stable state. The channel transmit and receive control blocks are cleared of references to existing transactions.

7. **BSPCLOSE**   A CLOSE block is sent to the remote host. No other references should be made to a byte stream channel which has been the subject of a BSPCLOSE.

8. **TIMER**   The TIMER procedure decrements timeout counters in all active byte stream control blocks. If a timeout counter reaches 0, the relevant protocol event is generated. If a timeout counter is already at 0 when TIMER is called, the channel is deemed to be in an error state and an internal CLOSE command is generated. The TIMER procedure should be called by the host device roughly every 100 ms.

The operation of a single BSP channel involves the execution of a considerable amount of work. All of the protocol levels, from the basic block and up, are implemented in software on the host. Even if the host device was a high-performance processor, the time spent maintaining a network connection reduces the time which can be spent on user tasks. The amount of work to be performed is directly proportional to the number of byte stream channels open. In a network-server, such as a file-server, this quantity may be large and so the service experienced by each user will deteriorate as the number of channels increases. One solution to this problem is to increase the power of the host's access box so that it can deal with the lower-level protocols and leave the host to get on with the real work. This approach is described in Chapter 6, Sections 3 and 4.

5.3 Integrating the Cambridge Ring

When the development of the Cambridge Ring had been completed, and it had proved itself to be a useful and reliable network, attention was turned to improving it. The major interest was in integrating as much of the hardware as possible onto a chip. This would reduce the cost of connection considerably and enhance reliability since fewer active components would be used.

The cost of connecting a device to a local network can be attributed to several components which make up the connection. The first is the cost of the transmission medium and its associated connectors. A large part of the expense of any network is the cost of laying the cable. In addition to this is the cost of implementing the network architecture in either hardware or software. Most networks have a number of similar features which only vary in detail. These include framing, addressing, error-checking and maintenance. In general, these features are implemented in hardware for reasons of speed. Occasionally, to reduce cost, they may be performed in software, but such systems tend to be rather simple and shifting problems to software does not always mean a lower total cost.

Once a system for delivering data between nodes has been devised the cost of interfacing machines can be considered. Here the problem is more general as it may be required that both very simple and also sophisticated devices are easily connected. For a simple device it is sufficient to ensure that the network buffers at least the smallest unit which the hardware delivers at full speed. In this way there is no minimum speed constraint on the attached devices. For more sophisticated devices, Direct Memory Access and other high-speed access methods become important and the interface design should not preclude such techniques.

Another major cost is that of writing software to drive the network. Each different host and different operating system may require a new set of network software. A recent trend has been towards making the access box intelligent by incorporating a processor of some kind in it. This processor is then responsible for many of the operations which would otherwise have to be implemented on the host. By standardising the software interface which the access box provides to the host, it should be possible to reduce the amount of software which must be written specifically for the host. Such topics will be discussed in Chapter 6.

5.3.1 What can be integrated?

When considering an LSI chip design, it is important to integrate as much of the system as possible so that the complexities of the design are hidden from the user, who has a simple and well-specified interface. Each layer of the architecture is considered in turn.

A common and cost effective transmission medium is twisted-pair wire. It is important to consider the design of line drivers and receivers for this medium. On the driving side, sufficient signal must be injected into the wire to ensure that at the receiving end the data is decoded correctly with minimum distortion. With baseband signals and twisted-pair wire, transmission over distances of around 100 m and also encoding of the data to enable the recovery of a clock signal is desirable.

At the receiving end, a differential amplifier to counter the effects of line attenuation and induced noise should be included. Incorporating hysteresis in the inputs is also important so that a broken cable does not introduce random data.

In addition to the line driver and receiver, a chip design should also consider the clocking system. In some schemes the clock is passed round on separate wires and can be regenerated easily. However, if the clock and data paths are shared, some form of clock extraction mechanism is required. If jitter has been introduced, some averaging may have to be performed. This can be done either digitally using a high-speed counter or gate delay chain or in a more conventional way, using analogue phase-locked loop techniques. In summary, it is important that any chip design considers the line-driving, receiving and clocking systems, as often these are the most complicated or sensitive parts of the system and are typical of the kind of complexity that should be hidden from the user.

At the network design level it is necessary that the chip performs the basic network functions of address recognition, framing, error-checking and maintenance. Such functions normally have to be done within a very short time and are thus implemented in hard logic.

The buffers which store data to be transmitted or received must be considered. One of the advantages of the Cambridge Ring is that the data buffering requirements for minipackets are very modest: minipacket buffers could be implemented on a chip in addition to the control logic. However, if a wide bus interface is required this scheme may not be appropriate since the number of pins available on a chip will probably be too small. A byte-wide interface would probably be possible but nothing wider than this.

On the Cambridge Ring no error-checking facilities are provided for the user, who normally implements an external checksum over a number of minipackets which make up a message. This error check could be implemented in hardware within the network chip. However, performing the error check close to the network may be unsatisfactory since there will still be an unchecked path between the hardware error checker and the memory of the host device, which may be as error prone as the ring itself. Error-checking is best done when the data is actually in the host's memory since that it where it will actually be used.

At the next level the interface has to be specified to the user in a way that is both convenient and which allows high-speed data transfer. However, there is an overall constraint on the number of pins on the package. An interface which is both easy to use and which allows high-speed access logics to be built, is one in which there is a general purpose data bus and separate control signals for commands to the network logic. The Cambridge Ring interface was designed in this way. Such an interface would be very difficult to implement on a chip because of the limited number of pins available. The best that can be hoped for on a chip is a single data bus of 8 or at most 16 bits and some control lines onto which encoded commands for the internals of the chip are placed. The Cambridge Ring scheme of one line per function would require too many of the chip's pins.

Such a chip would then have an interface very similar to the wide range of microprocessor peripheral chips which are available. This would be a distinct advantage in those cases where the chip is to be interfaced to a micro but the interface would be a bottleneck for faster systems, unless extra logic were used to speed up the interface operation. An alternative scheme is to have a simple, fast interface on the chip which is not the true interface, but which is designed to allow the construction of arbitrary host interfaces with a small amount of extra logic.

5.3.2 The design of the Integrated Cambridge Ring

The design constraints for the Integrated Cambridge Ring (ICR) were to encapsulate as much of the design as possible on a chip, without restricting the options open to the network designer. It was not an original design goal to make the ICR system directly compatible with the original MSI system at the wire level, although it was thought this would be desirable at the access box level.

The choice of technology was constrained by a number of factors. It was thought that the package size should not exceed 40 pins since larger sizes become prohibitively expensive. The target design speed of the system was 10 MHz which suggested a typical gate delay of less than 10 ns. At the time, available CMOS technology was not capable of providing this performance, particularly with 5-volt power rails. This directed attention towards a bipolar process. The technology would also have to provide facilities for analogue circuits to enable the line drivers and receivers to be integrated. An estimate of the gate count indicated that the whole system could be integrated on several thousand gates and that a system with external minipacket buffers would require under 1000 gates. It was also a requirement that the design be completed rapidly, perhaps at the expense of silicon area. For these reasons the technology chosen was the Ferranti Uncommitted Logic Array (ULA). These arrays are uncommitted at the transistor level and thus can be used to construct analogue structures as well as digital functions. Various sizes were available at the time, the largest providing about 500 gates for the designer.

Thus, a two-chip implementation was planned with the logic being partitioned roughly equally between the two. The minipacket buffers were to be external to the chips and implemented using standard MSI parts. One of the major problems was in partitioning the logic in such a way that both chips contained the right amount and that the number of pins needed to communicate between them was minimised. Eventually, the logic was successfully partitioned into two sections. The first, the **repeater chip**, performed the transmit and receive functions and the second, the **station chip**, decoded minipacket frames and transmitted and received user data from the external buffers. Because the gate utilisation on the two chips was still uneven, some of the station logic was implemented on the repeater chip. With this partitioning most of the criteria of pin count, gate count and cost were met (Hopper, 1981).

The repeater chip had line drivers and receivers built in and was capable of driving twisted-pair cables directly. It also incorporated a phase-locked oscillator to recover the clock from the incoming data. A number of user options were also introduced into the new design which allowed the construction of a variety of slotted ring networks.

Variable data field

The number of data bytes per minipacket was made variable in the range 1–8. Three pins on the repeater chip allowed the required size to be specified. The performance of a ring changes with minipacket size in two ways. As the number of data bytes increases the ring becomes more efficient in use of data and so the effective system bandwidth improves. Increasing the number of data bytes also means that a single user can transmit more data each time he acquires a slot. However, as the slot size increases, so the number of slots for a given ring size will decrease and thus the degree of sharing of bandwidth will tend to decrease. This means sharing will be at a coarser level and the upper bound of the access time will increase. Another effect of changing the number of data bytes is on the design of the interface. As the Integrated Cambridge Ring interface was implemented externally to the chips, an interface to suit the slot size in use could be designed.

User control bits

The addition of two user control bits to the minipacket format was the main change which makes the Integrated Cambridge Ring incompatible with the original Cambridge Ring. The two extra control bits are available to the user who can load them and read them as required. The hardware treats these bits as an extension of the data field and does not change them in any way. Their primary use is to mark minipackets as belonging to some category, by higher-level protocols for instance. Another way of using the control bits is to allow hardware to interpret them in a specific way. For example, one could envisage a system where voice minipackets are marked with a special pattern of control bits.

Broadcast addressing

A broadcast address was implemented to permit a single minipacket to be recognised by every destination. It is characteristic of a ring that all minipackets pass all destinations. Thus it is easy to reserve one address (255) which is detected by each station. Minipackets are then received in the normal way. There is problem here with the response bits as it is difficult to inform the source of each station's response. To make this option more useful the responses were changed so that for broadcast minipackets only one bit is used. It is set by any station which accepts the minipacket. Thus, the response information available at the source indicates whether at least one station has received the minipacket.

Improved logic design

One of the most important limitations of the transmission speed on the Cambridge Ring is that the transmit command cannot be issued until the previous minipacket has returned. Since this command is asynchronous to the network clock, by the time it has settled the next full/empty bit has passed. To improve this, a **transmit-on-accepted** mode was introduced in which two extra signals are provided. These are the transmit-on-accepted command and the buffer empty status line. The transmit-on-accepted command can only be issued while a previous minipacket is making its way round the ring. Its effect is to launch the next minipacket if the previous one was accepted. Because the transmit-on-accepted command can be early, synchronisation can also take place early. The buffer empty response indicates when a minipacket has been shifted out and a new one can be loaded.

Higher transmission rates

Another mode of operation was provided in the ICR for use where either very high bandwidths are required or where the service times of the ring must have a very precise specification. This is called **channel** mode and allows a station to replenish data in a slot. Thus, once a station has acquired a slot, there is no compulsion for this slot to be released. The service time is deterministic and part of the ring bandwidth has been allocated to that station for as long as it desires. To use this mode the interface has initially to issue a normal transmit command which will use the next available slot. When the buffer empty response indicates that the minipacket has been moved out of the transmit shift register, a new minipacket is loaded and the **transmit-in-same-slot** command issued. The returning slot is not marked empty, the new data is inserted and the next transmit command can be issued.

In channel mode there is a difficulty in handling responses. Because new data is inserted into a slot before the responses are read there is a possibility that minipackets will be received out of order. This happens whenever a minipacket is not accepted at a destination. Thus, in this mode it is important that the destination can receive from the ring at full speed.

5.3.3 Summary

Despite successful implementation of the ICR chips they did not prove popular in practice. The prototype chips functioned correctly at approximately half speed (5 to 6 MHz) and this may have discouraged their use. It was not widely appreciated at the time that the point-to-point bandwidth of an ICR system was nearly the same as that of a Cambridge Ring despite the difference in clocking rates.

A more serious problem was that they were incompatible with the already existing Cambridge Ring because of the addition of the control bits. Thus, users who already had a ring and wanted to add more stations to it could not do so with the ICR despite the fact that the hardware cost would have been around one tenth of that of the non-integrated Cambridge Ring.

Recently Cambridge Rings have been constructed with the two control bits and a 40-bit minipacket and commercial systems often have a switch to allow them to function with or without the control bits. This 40-bit ring has been adopted as a standard within the UK and is referred to as **CR82** (Sharpe and Cash, 1982).

5.4 References

Hopper, A., 1981. 'Cambridge Ring LSI system specification 1.2'. Project Note, Computer Laboratory, University of Cambridge, October.

Hopper, A. and Wheeler, D.J., 1979. 'Maintenance of ring communication systems'. *IEEE Trans. Comm.*, COM-27 (4), 760–61.

Johnson, M.A., 1980. 'Ring byte stream protocol specification'. Project Note, Computer Laboratory, University of Cambridge, April.

Larmouth, J., 1982. 'Cambridge Ring 82 – protocol specifications'. UK Science and Engineering Research Council, Joint Network Team, November.

Ody, N.J., 1979. 'A single-shot protocol'. Project Note, Computer Laboratory, University of Cambridge, April.

Sharpe, W.P. and Cash, A.R., 1982. 'Cambridge Ring 82 – interface specifications'. UK Science and Engineering Research Council, Joint Network Team, September.

Walker, R.D.H., 1978. 'Basic ring transport protocol'. Project Note, Computer Laboratory, University of Cambridge, November.

Wilkes, M.V. and Wheeler, D.J., 1979. 'The Cambridge digital communication ring'. Local Area Communications Network Symposium, Mitre Corp. and Nat. Bur. of Stand., Boston, May, p. 47.

Chapter 6 Interfacing to local networks

This chapter discusses interfacing techniques for local networks. A general introduction to the subject is given and then a number of different interfaces which have been designed for the Cambridge Ring are described. The small packet size of the Cambridge Ring presents some special problems when designing high-speed interfaces but many of the aspects discussed here are applicable to most types of local network.

6.1 Introduction to interfacing

The function of a network interface is to provide a physical and logical connection between a host device, which is normally a computer, and a network. The physical connection is at the electrical level, where the buses of the host device meet the buses of the network node. Interfacing at this level may involve adapting the widths of the buses so that they coincide and providing a connection between two different logic families which use different voltage levels to represent logical values.

The logical connection provides a bidirectional flow of data between the host and the network. The complexity of the interface can vary from a simple device, which maps the network control lines onto the memory space of the host, to a sophisticated device which handles all interactions with the network autonomously. The designer of an interface must therefore make several decisions relating to the complexity of the interface and how it affects cost, the amount of work that is necessary for host–network interaction and the development time of the interface.

Since a network interface might well be a sophisticated device in its own right, with its own processor and support chips, it is referred to as an **access box**. The term **interface** is reserved for the electrical and operational boundaries between functional units. Hence, a complete network connection can be viewed as having three components with two interfaces interconnecting them. The components are the host device, the access box and the network hardware while the interfaces are the host/access box interface and the access box/network interface. This arrangement is shown in Fig. 6.1. An important function of the access box is that it allows all instances of the network hardware to be identical. The access box can be viewed as a means of customising the network hardware to a particular type of host computer.

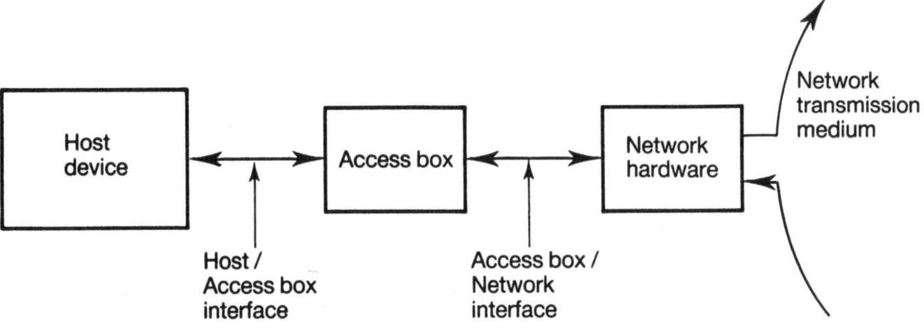

Fig. 6.1 Components of a network connection

There are a number of ways of attaching the access box to the host. Probably the most common is to attach it to one of the buses within the host. Some hosts may have only a single bus with which they communicate with the memory and peripherals, others may have separate buses for memory and input/output operations. The access box will be connected to one of these buses and assigned a range of bus addresses with which the processor can read and write data into registers in the access box. The interrupt lines of the processor may also be made available to the access box in this way so that the access box is able to interrupt the processor. With this style of interface a number of modes of operation are possible. The first involves the processor polling the access box registers to find out when packets are transmitted and received. Another method involves the access box interrupting the processor when a packet is received or transmitted. Sometimes a combination of these two modes is appropriate. In either case the computer must copy the packets to and from memory under program control. If the access box is more sophisticated it may perform this copying itself using Direct Memory Access (DMA) and only notify the processor when the copying is complete.

A simpler way of interfacing, which is suitable for slow LANs and does not involve the complication of interfacing to the host's bus, is to use an existing standard interface on the host, such as an RS-232 serial line. The data rates available on such lines are limited but there are very few computers made which do not have one and this is a great advantage of this method. Provided the access box can drive an RS-232 line, then it will allow interfacing to a great many computers without modification.

The access box/network interface will normally consist of either one or two data buses and a set of control lines. If the network can operate in full-duplex mode at the interface level, then there will be two data buses, one for transmission and one for reception. If the network can only operate in half-duplex mode at this level, then there will only be a single transmit/receive data bus. The control lines will be used to read and write data, give commands and read status information from the network.

At its most simple, the access box will take the host/access box interface and map it directly onto the access box/network interface. In this case the access box performs no function other than mapping the two interfaces. As a result the host computer must have a complete knowledge of the network and how it operates. For example, it would have to know the size of the basic transmission unit of the network and what other information is necessary for the initiation of a transmission. Once a transmission has been started, the host would have to wait for any feedback that is available from the network and then interpret it. This might include response information from the remote network hardware or an indication as to whether any problem occurred during the transmission. In the case of a system based on short packets, such as the Cambridge Ring, this level of access box can impose an enormous work load on the host device because many interactions with the network hardware are necessary to send a reasonable amount of data.

At the opposite end of the spectrum is the access box which hides unimportant details of the network from the host. Such details as packet size and retransmission strategies may be usefully hidden. For such an access box, the logical access box/host interface would be defined in terms of a high-level protocol and data would be exchanged between the host and the access box as complete messages. The host has no knowledge of the mechanisms involved with the transmission or reception of that data. The only details of the network that the host may need to retain will relate to network addresses, since it is necessary for it to be able to identify a remote host device. However, a very high-level interface might allow the host to refer to remote hosts solely by name. When it becomes necessary for such a name to be resolved into a network address, the access box would call a **name-server** on the network. The function of a name-server is to translate textual names into network addresses.

The user processes in a host device do not need any knowledge of the details of the network to which it is attached. In fact, in some distributed computer systems, the user software may not even know that the connection exists. So the details of the network and how interactions take place must be provided somewhere between the user software and the network node. The choice of location for this knowledge is therefore restricted to either low-level system software in the host device or to the access box.

The characteristics of the network and the network node hardware to which a host device is to be connected, affects the design of the access box. In particular, the size of the basic transmission unit, the speed at which data must be sent to the network and the amount of data buffering in the network node are of great importance. With a network like the Cambridge Ring, where data is transmitted in very small units and a complete minipacket is buffered in the station, there is not a great requirement for the access box to provide additional buffering. However, if the network hardware of a token ring, which allows the transmission of large packets, does not provide buffering for an entire packet, then either the access box must include some packet storage or there must be direct access to buffers in the memory of the host device. Since the transmission speed of local area networks is typically very high, this imposes the requirement that the access box can acquire the host's bus at short notice and keep it for the duration of a packet.

6.2 Ring interfaces at Cambridge

A number of interfaces have been developed at Cambridge for attaching a variety of devices to the Cambridge Ring. These range from microprocessor systems which provide access to devices such as line printers, to interfaces which provide a complete communications service, including session-level protocols, for an attached host computer. Some of these interfaces will now be described in roughly chronological order.

6.2.1 Early ring interfaces

Three of the first computers to be interfaced at Cambridge were a Data General NOVA, a DEC PDP11 and the Cambridge CAP computer. The NOVA and PDP11 had the ring interface mapped into their memory space and were able to work in either polled or interrupt-driven mode. The NOVA was mainly used for testing new stations before putting them into service and its interface was not fully supported by software. The PDP11 ring software was a more complete implementation and considerable effort went into making it transfer data as fast as possible. It was this effort which highlighted one of the difficulties of interfacing to the ring. The PDP11 interface was interrupt-driven and the amount of processing required for each minipacket of a basic block was so great that almost all of the CPU cycles were used when a ring transfer was taking place. A useful description of interfacing techniques for the Cambridge Ring may be found in Gibbons (1980).

It would have been possible to make the PDP11 interface run faster by dubious programming methods, for instance exploiting the extended instruction set of the PDP11/45 on which the first interface was designed. This would have made the system non-portable to other members of the PDP11 family and it was decided to keep to a straightforward implementation and be forewarned of the difficulties when designing subsequent interfaces.

The CAP computer is an experimental machine built at Cambridge for research into protection architectures (Wilkes and Needham, 1979). It is a microcoded machine and the ring interface for it is mapped into the microprogram memory space. Instructions have been implemented in the microcode which control the transmission and reception of basic blocks as well as for transmitting and receiving single minipackets. Building the interface at this level has proved very successful and the CAP computer is capable of transmitting and receiving as fast as the ring will permit. Unfortunately, not all computers allow access at such a low level and other methods of achieving high transmission speeds must be found for them.

6.2.2 The ring interface of the Type 1 computer

A Type 1 is a small Z80-based microcomputer which was developed at Cambridge specifically for attachment to the ring. It was envisaged that it would be used to interface devices such as printers and plotters to the ring and also allow the connection of several terminals to a single ring station (a Terminal Concentrator).

A number of microprocessors were considered as the basis of this system and the Z80 was finally chosen because it offered some 16-bit operations and support for dynamic RAM memory. The Type 1 was, in fact, constructed using static memory but it was the intention to build larger systems with dynamic RAMs at a later date.

The Type 1 consists of a 1 Kbyte EPROM, 4 Kbytes of static RAM, a handful of simple chips for the ring interface and general support logic. The system is sufficiently small to occupy half of a board about 120 mm by 160 mm. Static RAM, as opposed to dynamic RAM, was used for reasons of simplicity and because of the small quantity required.

It was decided that the EPROM would contain only sufficient code to allow loading the RAM via the ring and debugging of the Z80. Thus, all Type 1s would have the same EPROM and application-specific code would be loaded into RAM via the ring. This has many advantages, the most important of which is that Type 1s may be swapped around at will since they are all identical.

Several ways of interfacing to the ring were considered. The simplest involved memory mapping the ring station's interface, the most complex required a DMA system to transfer basic blocks directly between the Type 1's memory and the station unit. An interrupt-based system was also considered, with one interrupt being generated for each ring packet received or transmitted. With ring packets potentially arriving every 20 μs or so, interrupts were discounted since the interrupt entry and exit sequences alone were likely to take that amount of time to execute. The DMA scheme is too complex (and expensive) for the simple applications envisaged for the Type 1, which were to provide small, simple but efficient interfaces for peripherals to the ring. Since the data rate to peripherals is generally quite low, it is not appropriate to provide such a complex interface when the CPU is expected to be idle most of the time.

A very simple interface is therefore used and the processor made to do as much of the work as possible (checksum calculation, transferring data to memory, etc.). The various registers of the ring station are mapped into the Z80's memory space. Status lines are also mapped into the memory. These are polled by software to find out when packets have been transmitted or received. A diagram of the Type 1 and its ring interface is shown in Fig. 6.2.

The memory map of the ring interface of the Type 1 is given in Table 6.1. The ring is mapped into memory addresses beginning at X'FE00'. The 16-bit data buses of the ring station are 'folded' together to give a single 8-bit bus which is compatible with the Z80 data bus.

It will be noted that the received ring packet data register appears twice in the map. Reading address X'FE01' will automatically cause the receive logic of the station to be reset. It is therefore typical to access received minipackets by reading a word from X'FE00/1', not only obtaining the data of the minipacket but automatically acknowledging receipt of the minipacket as well. The data

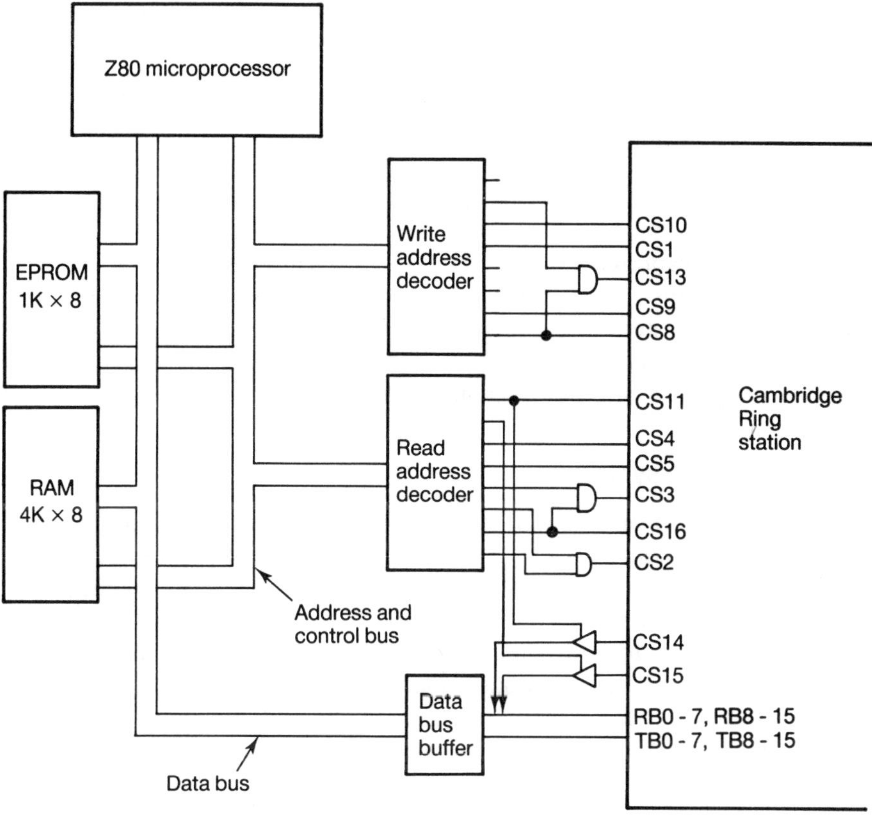

Fig. 6.2 The Type 1 and its ring interface

Table 6.1 Type 1 memory map

Address	Read register	Write register
FE00	Received data (low byte)	Transmit data (low byte)
FE01	Received data (high byte) (and reset receiver)	Transmit data (high byte) (and start transmission)
FE02	Received data (low byte)	
FE03	Received data (high byte)	
FE04	Source address	Destination address
FE05	Select register	Select register
FE06	Receiver status	Start transmission
FE07	Transmitter status	

can be read without acknowledgement from X'FE02/3' but eventually a read cycle will be performed on X'FE01' to acknowledge receipt of the minipacket.

There is no point in loading data into the transmit data register without actually issuing the transmit command, so output locations X'FE02/3', unlike the corresponding input locations, are not used. However, it is convenient to be able to retransmit the previous packet. This is done by writing to address X'FE06'. Data written into this location is discarded. Causing the address to be decoded initiates the transmission of data.

The other locations are self-explanatory. The status registers are, in fact, a merge of status bits explicitly available from the station as individual signals and the status registers of the ring station available via the main buses. The most important status bits are arranged so that they can easily be shifted into the Z80 carry bit for fast and efficient testing.

6.2.3 The Type 3 system

The first proposed application of a Type 1 interface was as a Terminal Concentrator. Although a Type 1 was built for this purpose, it was never used. This was because the complexity and size of the software to implement such a system had been underestimated. The concentrator was intended to support 8 terminals at rates up to 9600 baud. On each of these terminals it was proposed to allow up to 10 virtual connections to machines on the ring. Such a level of use has never been seen but it is not uncommon for all 8 lines to be in use, each with two or three virtual connections. The memory requirements of the terminal concentrator are much greater than the 4 Kbytes of the Type 1. For this reason, the Type 1 was redesigned to become the Type 3 (the design of the Type 2, a completely different system, came between the two). The Type 3 was simply a Type 1 with more memory. Dynamic RAM was used to provide 32 Kbytes of RAM but the rest of the system remained the same. The ring interface was identical and Type 3s could be substituted for Type 1s at will. The Type 3 was, in fact, slightly cheaper to build than the Type 1!

The jobs to which the Type 1 and Type 3 systems have been applied are many and varied. Each ring has a name-server which translates the textual names of ring services to addresses. This was first implemented with a Type 1 and, as the size of the name table grew, with a Type 3. An error logger, which receives and prints out maintenance minipackets, was built with a Type 1. A controller for a 'pointing machine' which aids in the construction of wire-wrapped prototype boards is controlled by a Type 1. In this case a larger computer on the ring processes a file which contains a list of connections to be made on the board. It then sends simple commands to the Type 1 which controls the stepping motors that position the wire-wrap gun on the machine.

The Type 3 systems, and their latter day relatives the Type 3A which have 64 K of memory, are extensively used as **servers** which provide a service to other machines on the ring. In this case they do not have peripherals attached but are used purely as small, cheap computer systems in their own right. This topic will be discussed further in the next chapter.

While the Type 1 systems were programmed in assembly language, thought had been given to the provision of a high-level language for use on the Z80 systems, principally the Type 3s. The language which was chosen was a local dialect of ALGOL68 called ALGOL68C. This is cross-compiled on a larger machine and then downloaded into the Z80 systems. It has enabled larger and more complex programs to be implemented more easily than would have been possible using assembly language.

6.3 The Type 2 interface

Whereas the Type 1 system was designed as a low-cost, general purpose computer, the Type 2 is an intelligent access box designed specifically to interface a variety of 16-bit computers to the ring. As part of an experiment in distributed computing, the Computer Laboratory at Cambridge had purchased a number of General Automation LSI4 processors and it was desired to connect these to the ring. A requirement of the interface was that it should be fast and it should not consume many of the LSI4's cycles. An additional requirement was that it should be possible for the access box to exert complete control over the LSI4. That is, it should be able to load, start, stop and debug it by means of commands given over the ring.

Interfacing the PDP11 to the ring had shown that dealing with individual minipackets was a good way of using up CPU cycles and therefore the Type 2 was designed to present an interface to its host at the basic block level. Thus the host would be interrupted when a basic block was transmitted or received. This implied that a DMA type of interface would be required so that the Type 2 could use the host's memory as buffers for basic blocks.

6.3.1 The Type 2 hardware

Having decided what the Type 2 should do, it was then necessary to decide how to implement it. The high rate at which minipackets come and go meant that a fast processor would be required if a totally hardware-based solution was to be avoided. Because the processor's only responsibilities were in dealing with the ring and with requests from the host, it would be quite acceptable for it to poll these things rather than use a slower, interrupt mechanism. A number of processors were considered as the basis for the Type 2. Potentially the fastest system would be achieved with a bit-slice microprocessor, such as the AMD 2900 series. However, this had the disadvantage that a large amount of development work would be necessary to set up such a system. An alternative was to use a conventional microprocessor such as the Z80. Here the disadvantage was one of speed because the Z80 and similar micros could not execute instructions fast enough to keep up with the ring. By providing a large amount of hardware support, such as the automatic calculation of block checksums, this deficiency could be avoided but this put the cost and complexity above that which was permissible.

The solution which was chosen was a compromise. A processor known as the 8X300 provided roughly the performance that was needed. It is an 8-bit, bipolar microprocessor which has been optimised for control applications. It can execute an instruction in 250 ns and has a useful variety of bit manipulation instructions. Its instructions for controlling the program flow are less than adequate and its overall architecture is unconventional by comparison with other microprocessors. Nonetheless, it seemed the best choice and so a system was built around it.

The architecture of the Type 2 is illustrated in Fig. 6.3. The system consists of four boards. The board containing the 8X300 also contains the ring interface which is simply mapped into the address space of the micro. Two more boards implement two identical DMA channels and each contains an I/O port. These three boards are designed to be machine-independent and the fourth board is specific to the particular host. This board is contained within the LSI4 and maps the general DMA interface presented by the channel boards into a form suitable for the LSI4 bus.

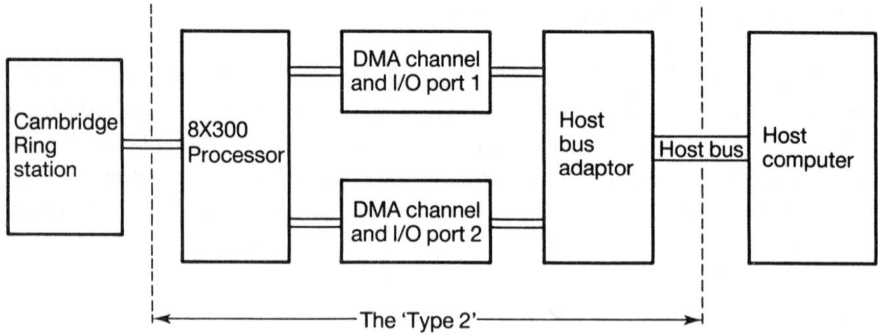

Fig. 6.3   The architecture of the Type 2

The DMA channels contain auto-incrementing address registers and are suited to the transfer of vectors of contiguous memory to and from the ring. Because of the need to accumulate checksums, all data passes through the 8X300 on its way to and from the ring. The I/O ports provide a facility for exchanging single 16-bit words between the host and the Type 2 and on the host side an interrupt is generated to indicate that a word has been placed into a port by the Type 2. The Type 2 polls the ports to discover when data has been written to or read from them by the LSI4.

6.3.2 The Type 2 software

The 8X300 can only address up to 4096 instructions which limits the size of its programs. The program which was written for it in the Type 2 deals with the transmission and reception of basic blocks and with loading and debugging the LSI4. When transmitting basic blocks the Type 2 is required to generate the header and route minipackets, to copy the data minipackets from the LSI4's memory and to calculate an appropriate checksum minipacket. On reception, the header, route and checksum are removed by the Type 2 and the checksum is validated.

The way in which transmission and reception of basic blocks occurs is as follows. When the host wants to transmit a block it sends a command to the Type 2 which looks like the following:

> Transmit as the data of a basic block N words from the buffer B to station S, port P.

Reception is slightly more complicated. The LSI4 must state in advance where it wishes to receive from by issuing one or more reception requests of the form:

> If a valid basic block of up to N words arrives addressed to port P from station S then put it in the buffer B.

In this case the station S may be a wildcard and any block arriving for port P will be received. The Type 2 keeps a list of outstanding requests and scans it each time a block arrives.

The method by which these commands are sent to the Type 2 from the LSI4 and the means by which the Type 2 indicates their execution, is based on the use of the I/O ports. It would have been possible to define a protocol for passing all the parameters of a command through the port but this would have been complex and prone to errors. The method chosen is for the LSI4 to assemble the parameters into a **codeword** in its memory and then to pass the address of the codeword via an I/O port. It assumes that the Type 2 will pick up the address almost immediately and so no acknowledgement is required for this operation. The Type 2 will take the address from the port and read the codeword via one of the DMA channels. The Type 2 will therefore accumulate a number of transmission and reception requests. It is unlikely to process the reception requests in the order in which they were given but, since each codeword has a unique address within the LSI4, it is simple to indicate that a request has been satisfied by passing back the address of the appropriate codeword through an I/O port. The LSI4 is interrupted at this point and can then read the received data from the buffer.

A third command which may be given to the Type 2 is to cancel a given request. This may be necessary when part of a higher-level protocol times out. A byte stream may have to be closed because the remote host has crashed and it is then necessary to cancel all requests for reception from that host.

The above description has ignored the facility whereby the Type 2 is used to load and debug the LSI4. In this case requests in the form of basic blocks are being sent to the Type 2 itself and not to the LSI4. The Type 2 must, therefore, be able to distinguish blocks for itself from those for the host. This is done by using one of the spare bits in the flag field of the route minipacket. If this bit is set it indicates a block for the Type 2 rather than for its host. There is a further problem which is one of security. Any machine on the ring could generate such basic blocks for the Type 2 and thereby take control of the host computer. The only part of a basic block which is, for practical purposes, unforgeable is the source address. It is therefore arranged that the Type 2 has a coding plug indicating which station address is allowed to issue valid debug commands. Debug commands from this source are accepted by the Type 2 and this source may safely nominate additional sources to issue debug commands. The station which has this privilege is called the Ancilla and it is also responsible for loading the LSI4s when they start up.

6.3.3 Discussion

The Type 2 has largely met its design aims as a basic block level interface. The 8X300 has proved to be the limiting factor in most areas where improvement was desired. Because it is an 8-bit processor and the ring deals in 16-bit quantities, some pieces of code are longer than would be liked. Calculating the checksum, in particular, is a bottleneck on throughput. The 8X300 can have only 256 bytes of RAM and this limits the number of reception requests which may be outstanding at any one time.

These deficiencies apart, the Type 2 was a success. It removed much of the burden of dealing with minipackets from the host and provided an elegant way of remotely loading and debugging it. More importantly perhaps, it highlighted the areas to which special attention should be paid in the design of future interfaces. A thorough description of the Type 2 may be found in Garnett (1983).

6.4 The MACE

Some years after the implementation of the Type 2, the Computer Laboratory at Cambridge commissioned the design of some microprocessor systems built around the Motorola M68000 processor. These systems were similar to the LSI4s in that they were intended for connection to the ring via an intelligent access box. In this case the access box was known as the MACE and it was quite unlike the Type 2, although its aims were broadly similar.

While the Type 2 supported the basic block protocol, it was intended that the MACE should support the single-shot and byte stream protocols in addition to the basic block protocol. It was also expected that several different programs might be developed for the MACE for use in different applications. The prospect of programming the MACE in a high-level language was also contemplated and it was with these points in mind that the design was started.

6.4.1 The MACE hardware

The processor around which the MACE is built is a Motorola 6809. This is a MOS processor and has an 8-bit architecture with a good selection of 16-bit operations. It can execute a simple instruction in 1 μs and there is a wide variety of addressing modes which suit it to the running of high-level languages. The MACE also contains 4 Kbytes of EPROM for the 6809 and a variety of peripheral devices, including the ring, mapped into its address space. The remainder of the address space, nearly 60 Kbytes, is occupied by RAM.

The MACE occupies a single board and has a four-channel DMA system with which to make transfers to the host 68000. The 68000 has upwards of 512 Kbytes of memory and the MACE can copy data using DMA into any portion of this. Communication between the two is a little more complex than on the Type 2 since there are no I/O ports and all data transfer must be done by DMA. Each processor can interrupt the other to indicate that some action is required of it and data is placed at pre-agreed places in the host's memory to be passed between the processors. Like the Type 2, the MACE incorporates facilities for loading and debugging the host computer.

Unlike the Type 2, the MACE has a clock of its own and so can deal with ring timeouts by itself. The 6809 is interrupt-driven, interrupts coming from the ring station, the DMA controller, the host and the clock. A disadvantage of the MACE is that these interrupts are not individually vectored and so a search must be made for the interrupting device whenever an interrupt occurs. Later versions of MACE software use a polling mechanism for detecting events, rather than one using interrupts, and are faster as a consequence.

6.4.2 The MACE software

Various software systems have been written to run on the MACE. The first piece of code written was a small program to go in the EPROM and allow loading of the MACE memory with other programs. This program also provided a small set of debugging operations for the MACE processor.

The first real piece of software for the MACE was called Spectrum and this provided facilities similar to those offered by the Type 2 – the transmission and reception of basic blocks. The MACE was also able to provide facilities, such as timeout management, which the Type 2 did not.

The next major program written for the MACE, called SuperMACE, presents the host with a much higher-level interface. In particular, it hides from the host many details of the network and presents an interface based on the BSP and SSP protocols. Direct access at the minipacket level is denied to the host as is access at the basic block level. A similar step is taken with respect to ring addresses and ports. The host never needs to specify addresses to the MACE. Instead it supplies a textual **service name** which the MACE then maps to an address by consulting the name-server. SuperMACE is also intelligent enough to cache the results of these lookups to save itself work in the future.

6.4.3 Discussion

SuperMACE was the last major program to be written for the MACE. Though certain applications have been identified as being worthy of special MACE code, they have yet to be implemented. Performance comparisons of the MACE and Type 2 show that the Type 2 is slightly faster when it comes to transmitting and receiving minipackets but the extra functionality provided by the MACE and the comparative ease with which new systems can be written for it compensate for this.

The large amount of RAM available to the MACE and the powerful instruction set of the 6809 make it easy to program by comparison with the Type 2. In common with the Type 2, the major reason for its slowness in dealing with minipackets is the need to calculate checksums for basic blocks 'on the fly'. The MACE is described in detail in Garnett (1983).

6.5 Enhanced ring interfaces

Experience with the Type 2 and MACE has identified some areas where assistance could be given to speed up operations on minipackets. In both systems, data passing between the host's memory and the ring is routed through the processor for the purpose of accumulating the checksum. This ties up the processor and takes time – 15 instructions for the 8X300, 4 for the 6809. By providing hardware to accumulate the checksum, the data could flow directly from the DMA logic to the ring and vice versa.

A second area where hardware assistance could be used is in the provision of a **forward transmit buffer** (FTB). When a word is fetched by DMA and transmitted on the ring it is not known whether or not to start another DMA cycle until the transmission is complete. If the minipacket returns with a busy response then it must be retransmitted. If it comes back accepted another DMA cycle can be initiated. By having a forward transmit buffer into which the result of a DMA read is placed, a DMA cycle can always be initiated as soon as the FTB is copied to the ring. In this way the DMA cycle and minipacket transmissions are overlapped.

This system can be further enhanced by providing logic which automatically copies the FTB to the station when a minipacket is accepted. This logic might also retransmit minipackets automatically when they are marked busy and interrupt the processor when a minipacket returns unselected or ignored. In this way the processor would need to initiate just the first DMA cycle and the logic would then transmit minipackets automatically until the DMA controller signalled the end of the transfer.

Enhancements such as these were not placed on the MACE because there was not room on the board for them. A more advanced access box known as the Gizmo incorporates these features and others but is, as yet, unimplemented.

6.6 References

Garnett, N.H., 1983. 'Intelligent network interfaces'. PhD Thesis, Computer Laboratory, University of Cambridge, September.

Gibbons, J.J., 1980. 'The design of interfaces for the Cambridge Ring'. PhD Thesis, Computer Laboratory, University of Cambridge, September.

Wilkes, M.V. and Needham, R.M., 1979. *The Cambridge CAP Computer and its Operating System*. Amsterdam: North-Holland.

Chapter 7 A local network case study

This chapter describes a local network application in some detail. This is a distributed computing system developed at Cambridge and based around a Cambridge Ring. The system uses the protocols and interfaces described in earlier chapters.

The first half of the chapter introduces the reader to distributed computing and then describes the Cambridge system. The latter half then describes some measurements which have been performed on the ring in question and suggests some ways in which the ring might be improved in the light of experience gained from this system.

7.1 Distributed computer systems

Distributed computer systems have developed as a competitor to the traditional centralised approach to computer systems. As methods for interconnecting processors and other devices developed, experiments were performed to investigate how the service experienced by users of a system varied as the functions performed by that system were spread onto multiple processors. Originally, the requirement of highly efficient inter-processor communication dictated that cooperating processors had to be tightly coupled at the bus level. As local area networks developed, this opened the way for such computer systems to be more geographically distributed. This changed the emphasis from systems in which multiple processors cooperated on the execution of a single task to systems in which each machine has a particular service to provide. This is the current model of a distributed computer system, a series of machines which are linked together by an efficient communications system and in which each machine has a distinct role.

During a session a user will only use a subset of the facilities available and so will not disturb users of the other machines. This is as opposed to the centralised computing scheme where whenever any user does any kind of task it must, by definition, disturb the work of other users. The degree to which this disturbance takes place is dependent upon the nature of the individual tasks being executed and the implementation of the operating system. Hence, the user of a distributed computer system should see an increase in performance over that of a centralised computer system.

The benefits of distributing computer system functions also relate to system reliability. Given that component and other system failures do occur in computer systems, it is preferable to have the capacity of a system reduced rather than wiped out by such a fault. Furthermore, if functions in a distributed computer system are duplicated, it may be simple to reconfigure the system and proceed as if no failure had taken place.

The desire to distribute computer system functions between different machines has given rise to the concept of a **server**, which is an entity providing a single service in such a distributed computer system. Any other device on the system can use the server and are termed **clients** of the server. Similarly, one server may use another server in the course of its work. Not all users of a system will be clients of every server during a session, this depends upon the work to be carried out, but some servers will be used by every user.

Some but not all functions of a distributed computer system are seen by the user. The first, and perhaps most important, visible characteristic of a computer system is its ability to work for the user. Typically this entails editing files, compiling programs, executing the object code produced and generating results for the user. So a distributed computer system must provide processing power. Since more than one user will want to use the system simultaneously, many processors will have to be provided, although not necessarily of the same kind.

A key question in the provision of distributed computing power is where that power should be located. One school of thought supports the idea of locating all the processors in one area of the network, with the only access to them being via the network. Each user would then be provided with his own terminal which is also connected to the network. When a user wants to use the computer system, a virtual circuit is set up between the terminal and a free remote processor. The grouping of the processors into one area of the system need not be a physical constraint, it merely promotes the idea of a logical group of processors, any one of which can be used by any user. The second philosophy on the provision of processing power in a distributed computer system is to provide each user with his own personal workstation. This view has been supported by the reduction in the cost of processing power which has made the cost of a terminal and the cost of a personal computer roughly equivalent. The majority of the processing needs of the user are performed locally, without any network interaction. There may even be some provision of non-volatile storage at the workstation, such as hard or floppy disk drives. The user's need for other resources, such as high-volume data storage, high-power processing and I/O services would still be met by the other functions of the distributed system.

Of similar importance to the user is some method of storing programs, data and results. Traditionally this was done on the disks which were attached to the central processor. However, since a user may not use the same processor in the distributed system every time, there must be a centralised filing service for the whole system. The filing service is an important component of a distributed system, since it is likely that most or all users will require its services. Also, through its nature as a long-term storage device, the consequences of its failing are severe and reliability is an important consideration in its design.

The next service of a computer system that a user may wish to use is a printing service. In a distributed computing system printing will be performed by a printer-server which will be connected to the network via a local processor. The printer-server will handle the interaction with the remote host, control the printer functions and may perform some local processing of the text to be printed. In addition, it may play some part in the scheduling of files to be printed such as providing an internal queueing system for files or interacting with the filing system where they are queued.

In addition to the printer-server, a distributed system may provide other input and output facilities. These are likely to include both magnetic and paper tape writing and reading facilities and a plotter-server.

There are several components of a distributed computer system, some of which are also present in the centralised system, whose presence is not so obvious to the user. These are generally components which contribute to the control and operation of the system. An important service to any network is the name-server, or, as it would more appropriately be called, the address-server. In order to maintain the flexibility of service provided by a distributed computer system all services are referred to by a textual name. When a particular device is required, the actual location of that device must be obtained by interrogating the name-server. It is here that a mapping between the name of the required service and its network address takes place. Since the names of services, rather than their addresses, are the well-known quantity, the location of any service can be changed in order to improve performance or recover from a system component failure.

The presence of a service controlling the allocation of resources within the distributed computer system also may not be apparent to the user. The main application for such a device is in a system where processing power is provided remotely from the user terminals. Each time that a user wishes to initiate a session, a search of the processors must be made to determine whether a suitable one is free. If there is spare capacity, a virtual connection can then be established.

A further system function that may be invisible to a user is an authentication service. It is likely that when a session is initiated the user will have to quote a password. At this stage the authentication service will decide whether or not the password is valid, and grant access to the system appropriately. This service might not only be used at the beginning of a session, it may be that the authentication obtained at session initiation is retained for the duration of the session. Whenever a resource is required, that authentication, in some representation, will be presented as proof of identity and therefore of validity of the request. An example of this might be for file access. Each time a user wishes to access a file, a check can be made as to whether he has the right to inspect its contents.

Having described some of the characteristics of a distributed computer system, some of the features of a real system – the Cambridge Model Distributed System – are now described. Full details of the implementation of this system will not be given, since they are outside the scope of this book. Interested readers are directed to Needham and Herbert (1982).

7.2 The Cambridge Model Distributed System

The Cambridge Model Distributed System (CMDS) is the result of a large-scale research project which focused on the design issues of providing a coherent computer system by distributing functions across a local area network. The local area network used as the communications subsystem for the Cambridge Distributed System was the Cambridge Ring. Hence, each processor which provides a service in the system is interfaced to a ring station.

The design philosophy adopted by the designers of the CMDS was to provide a collection of processors which are remotely situated from the users' terminals. When required, a processor is allocated to a user for the duration of his work. When the user's session is completed, the processor is freed and thus made available to other users. The CMDS is organised around the server philosophy. Each distinct function is provided by a separate computer system dedicated to a particular task. This approach is only possible because of the low cost of the hardware. Separating system functions in this way means that the services are truly independent and so problems with interference caused by sharing a machine between services are eliminated. The interface between independent services is defined wholly in terms of the communications protocols which control the transfer of data across the network.

The operation of the CMDS and the individual services of which it is made up, will now be described. The description will follow the order in which services and servers are met during a user session.

A user who wishes to do some work as a client of the CMDS enters the system via a terminal. The terminal may have some processing capability of its own, although this is not necessary. Groups of up to eight terminals are attached to the Cambridge Ring by a **terminal concentrator**. The terminal concentrator is a Z80 microcomputer system which has the terminals and the ring as its only peripheral devices. The terminal concentrator software executes a byte stream with the remote device to which each terminal is logically connected. A user at a terminal can have a number of connections open at any time, so the terminal concentrator must be able to handle a large number of byte streams simultaneously. The user interface to the software driving a terminal concentrator is an example of a **virtual terminal protocol**. Once a connection with a remote device is established, no details of the concentrator or ring are obvious to a user. The only details of the concentrator which a user does utilise are those with which he can manipulate the various virtual connections which have been initiated.

Before a connection can be established across the network, the address of the remote `host must be obtained. This is performed by the terminal concentrator approaching the name-server. The role of the name-server is to translate names, which are simple text strings, into the address of a ring station. If there were no changes in the positions on the ring at which services were located, then those addresses could be embedded into the software which uses them. However, since the distributed system will constantly be evolving and in order to enhance the reconfigurability of the system, each time a ring address is to be used, the name-server is interrogated. Hence, when a new service is introduced or when the ring address of a current service changes, the only place where a reference to that address must be updated is in the name table used as the master address list by the name-server. The address of the name-server must, of course, be known to all who would wish to use it. This is the only ring address which is bound into the network software.

At the beginning of a user session, the terminal concentrator will request from the name-server the address of the **session manager**. The session manager and the closely related **resource manager** provide an informative user interface and control the allocation of processors within the system. The user interacts with these services through the session manager which provides an interface that allows the user to select a processor by one of a number of attributes. These attributes might be the processor type, memory size or possession of a floppy disk drive. A machine can also be chosen by name. In addition to the processor, the software to be loaded and executed must also be chosen. In general, the software used is one of a number of variants of the Tripos operating system developed in Cambridge. The list of which machines are free and which are in use is maintained by the resource manager and it is this service which actually performs the allocation of a processor to a user. An advantage of organising the allocation of resources centrally is that it promotes the use of accounting for system components. At the time of allocation a limit is set by the resource manager on the length of time for which the processor can be used and if the user has not completed his session when that time expires, it will be forcibly terminated. The allocation of processors by the resource manager is strictly on a first-come, first-served basis and when all the processors are in use the resource manager can only turn down connection requests.

As previously described, the processors in the CMDS are logically organised together and are therefore referred to as the **processor bank**. In practice, they are also physically located together since this simplifies their power wiring and access to the network. The present range of machines in the processor bank includes General Automation LSI4 processors with 128 Kbytes of memory and Motorola 68000 computer systems with up to 2 Mbytes of memory. Once a processor has been allocated to a user, it is as if it were his own personal computer. This brings all the benefits of having total control over the machine, such as being able to choose which operating system to run and being able to fully control the loading and execution of programs. The approach of providing the processor power of the system away from the user's terminal is particularly suitable where the computing needs of the average user changes regularly. If a range of machines is available in the processor bank, then the user can request the type which most suits his requirements. However, unless the number of processors matches the number of terminals, it must be assumed that demand for use of the machines will be limited. Even if the number of processors is calculated to more than match the average use, there may be periods when the demand overtakes the supply.

Since processors are shared over a long time by more than one user and one user will not always have the same machine allocated to him, processors cannot conveniently have local permanent disk systems. A depository for files is therefore required and this service is provided by the **file-server**. Any machine can access the file-server but, because each user may access the file-server from several machines, access privileges are a function of the user rather than the machine which he is using.

The Cambridge file server is an example of what Birrell and Needham (1980) called a universal file-server, that is, the functions it performs lie somewhere between those of a virtual disk-server and a file repository. A virtual disk-server only provides a basic list of primitives which operate at the page level and with which a remote disk can be treated as an extension of a local disk. The primitives provided by a virtual disk-server are 'allocate page', 'free page', 'write page' and 'read page'. The server software necessary to provide such a service would not be at all complex. However, this passes the responsibility to provide a coherent filing system onto the client code and hence the complexity of this code will be increased. A virtual disk-server does, however, provide the basis for a file protection scheme. The response to a call of the allocate page primitive will be an identifier which represents the page 'created'. This identifier will be needed for all future references to that page and can therefore be treated as a capability for the page. A file repository is located at the other end of the spectrum of filing system services. It provides a complete file and directory management system and therefore possesses a high-level interface with its client devices. Accordingly, the software complexity is removed from the client at the server, thus making it easier to design the client systems which use the filing system.

A universal file-server takes the service provided by a virtual disk-server and onto it applies a naming system for objects stored on the disk. The intention is to provide the client with a conceptually simple interface without committing it to any particular conventions with respect to text names or directory structure. This also allows the client to implement a number of different directory structures and naming schemes.

In the Cambridge file-server there are two classes of objects – files and indices. A file is simply an uninterpreted vector of bytes. Indices are structures which contain identifiers for files and other indices. The index structure has a base called a root index. A piece of client software can therefore impose a directory structure onto the index scheme in order to provide the type and level of service required. An example piece of client code is the file-server task which is implemented in the Tripos operating system. This task is the user interface to the file-server and a complex directory structure is provided for the user. The Cambridge file-server is currently implemented by two General Automation LSI4/30 processors with a total of 400 Mbytes of disk storage between them.

As well as user files, the file-servers also hold the operating system object code files which are to be loaded into a processor which has just been allocated. This loading process is performed by the **ancilla**. The ancilla is a small server, based on a Z80 microcomputer system, which performs the task of loading processors with the required operating system. In order to protect system integrity, the ancilla will only take the command to load a particular machine from the resource manager. On receiving such a request, ancilla confirms its validity by performing a reverse look-up of the source ring address in the name-server and then, if successful, approaches the file-server for the appropriate operating system object code files. It then loads the object code into the designated processor and initiates its operation. Since operation of the ancilla implies a knowledge of the low-level interface of the machines that it is loading, there must be a separate instance of the ancilla for each type of machine. Hence, in the Cambridge Distributed System there are two ancilli, one dedicated to the service of LSI4 processors and the other to the 68000 computer systems.

The result of the user interaction with the session manager is a byte stream connection being set up between the terminal concentrator and the processor which was allocated. The final initiation routine to be carried out is the authentication of the prospective user. The operating system performs this by referring to an authentication service. Having received a user identifier and a password from the user, the operating system performs a look-up operation at the authentication server. If the password is deemed to match the user identifier, a capability is returned to the processor. Once this has occurred the user session initiation is complete. The capability is then used in future interactions with other services in the distributed system. In particular, it is used to determine access privileges in the filing system.

Once a user session is fully underway on a processor bank machine, there are a number of available services provided by the distributed computer system. Probably the most commonly used service is the printing service. There are two printer-servers in the CMDS. One of them provides a standard line printer quality service and the other provides output on a high-resolution laser printer. The two printer-servers are implemented on independent processors, the line printer being attached to the ring via a Z80 processor and the laser printer interface being a M68000 system. There is also an archiving service provided by a magnetic tape server based on a NOVA minicomputer.

Specialist computing power is provided in the CMDS by connecting three different multi-user processors to the network. These are an IBM 3081 running the MVS operating system with a locally developed user interface system called Phoenix, a VAX-11/750 running under the UNIX operating system and the locally designed CAP computer running under CHAOS. These three machines provide a wide range of computing environments and language systems for the user. In addition, various hosts provide entry points to the SERC network (Janet) and other global networks, including Arpanet.

7.3 Performance of a Cambridge Ring

This section details a study made on the Cambridge Ring used as the basis for the Cambridge Model Distributed System just described. The traffic patterns and performance characteristics observed are typical for this sort of application, but other types of application may present a significantly different load. A comparison with another distributed system based around an Ethernet is made towards the end of the chapter.

7.3.1 The monitoring device

The measurement of traffic on a Cambridge Ring may be approached in several ways. If overall traffic patterns, such as the volume of data transmitted in a given time, are of interest then every minipacket which passes a given point on the ring must be inspected. The time between the arrival of consecutive minipackets is less than 4 μs and the operations which would have to be performed on a minipacket would take much longer than this using a conventional computer. A dedicated piece of hardware would perform the necessary manipulations much faster, but it could be quite complex.

It might also be desirable to observe traffic at the basic block level. Of interest are the number of blocks sent and their lengths and types when viewed as part of a higher-level protocol. A number of methods for monitoring at the block level have been suggested by Ody (1980). His 'promiscuous station' method uses a ring station capable of receiving minipackets from any chosen source without marking the response bits. This method allows monitoring of blocks between a given pair of stations and imposes no extra load on the network, which might upset the measurements.

An alternative method for monitoring blocks is to incorporate a facility in the software of each machine to send a logging minipacket to a logging device on the ring. Such minipackets would be sent at the start and end of a block and could provide information about the size of the block and its transmission time. This method will, of course, add traffic to the network, though hopefully an insignificant amount. A failing of both the above methods is that they do not allow inspection of the response bits of the constituent minipackets of a block and so are unable to correctly observe minipackets which are rejected and then retransmitted. Such information is of some importance in the design of ring interfaces.

The approach taken in designing the monitoring device was to use hardware to speed up certain operations. A small computer was used to control this hardware and perform calculations on the measurements obtained from it. The device is capable of counting minipackets with chosen contents at full ring speed. It can be configured to work as a promiscuous station while also allowing inspection of the response bits. It is attached to the ring at a repeater and is readily moved around to monitor at different points on the ring.

A diagram of the traffic monitor is shown in Fig. 7.1. The device contains a number of registers one of which, the packet register, is filled with a copy of each minipacket as it passes the repeater to which the monitor is connected. This register is therefore 38 bits long and synchronisation circuitry provides a pulse each time a new minipacket is loaded into it. Another register, the comparison register, is of the same length and may be written by the computer. The bits of this register are compared with corresponding bits in the packet register and the resulting bits fed to a third register, the mask register. The mask register is also written by the computer and its contents are ORed with the result of the previous comparison. It therefore selects the set of bits on which the comparison is made. The masked comparison bits are then ANDed together to give a signal which says whether or not the minipacket matched the pattern set up in the comparison and mask registers. If a match occurs then the packet register is copied into a fourth register, the capture register, where it may be read by the computer. A count register is incremented when a match occurs and it too is readable by the computer.

The device therefore provides facilities for counting and reading minipackets whose contents match a pattern set up by computer. While it is not

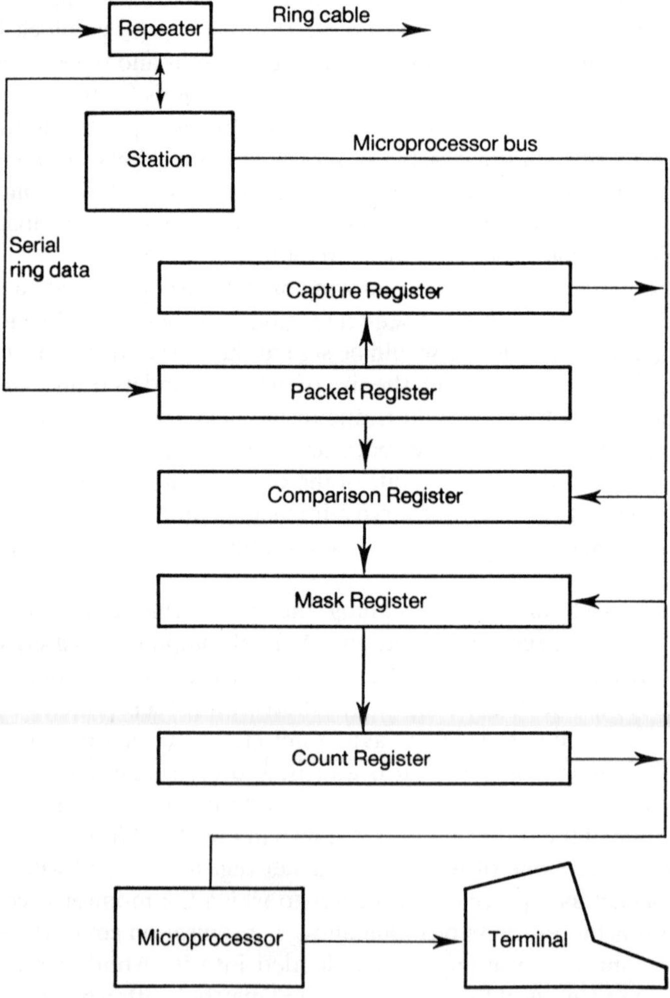

Fig. 7.1 Structure of the Cambridge Ring traffic monitor

possible to alter the pattern conditionally within a minipacket time, this can be done within a ring revolution time and this allows satisfactory monitoring of blocks.

A characteristic of the Cambridge Ring which makes traffic monitoring difficult is the use of response bits. These are marked at the destination station and thus the monitor must be placed after the destination if they are to be observed in their marked state. This means that if the monitor is correctly placed to observe minipackets sent from station A to station B, then it is not possible fully to observe minipackets from B to A without changing the monitor's connection to the ring. Two monitors can be used to solve this problem.

One of the first tests performed with the monitor was the measurement of ring utilisation, that is, the proportion of the available bandwidth in use over a given time interval. The fundamental measurement that the monitor must make for this experiment is to measure the number of full minipackets passing in a set time. The method used is described below to illustrate the use of the monitor.

7.3.2 Use of the traffic monitor

In order to count full minipackets the monitor is configured by the controlling computer as follows. The bit in the comparison register which corresponds to the Full/Empty bit is set to 1, indicating that a match should be given on full minipackets. The corresponding bit in the mask register is set to 0 and all others to 1, which means that a match will be given on any full minipacket, regardless of the state of any other bits in it. Having done this the counter is cleared by the computer and then allowed to start counting. The computer now waits for the desired time interval before stopping the counter. The counter may now be read and the average utilisation over that time interval can be calculated.

A slightly more complex use of the monitor is to look at basic blocks passing from one station to another. To do this the monitor must be positioned after the destination station in order to see the marked response bits. The registers of the monitor are initially set up to look for full, accepted packets with the appropriate source and destination and the basic block header pattern in the data field. This pattern is '100100' in the six highest bits of the data. If the ring carried completely random data then the chance of this pattern occurring in a data minipacket is 1 in 64. There is a possibility therefore, that one of these minipackets will be mistaken for a basic block header and the block checksum must be used to verify the validity of any block which is received. The data carried by the ring was not completely random and the chance of the header pattern occurring in data was rather less than 1 in 64 but still significant.

The computer detects the arrival of a minipacket which matches the pattern set up in the monitor by seeing the count register increment. It then reads the data field of the capture register to deduce the length of the block and reloads the data field of the mask register so that subsequent minipackets are captured regardless of the content of their data fields. The remaining minipackets of the block will now be captured by the monitor and placed in a buffer by the computer. When all have been captured the computer can validate the checksum and thus ensure that the first minipacket was really a block header.

A number of variations of this test are possible, such as measuring the time between successive minipackets and observing the number of rejected minipackets at various stages of the block transfer.

7.3.3 Observed traffic patterns

On the ring tested, the total bandwidth available to all stations, the system bandwidth, was 3.2 Mbps while the maximum bandwidth available to a single station, the point-to-point bandwidth, was 0.64 Mbps (20% of the system bandwidth). The ring was clocked at 9.8 MHz and contained 3 slots and a gap of 33 bits. There were 30 active stations and these connected the following computers to the ring:

  1 × IBM 370/165 mainframe

  2 × PDP11/45 minicomputers

  9 × LSI4 minicomputers (file-server and processor bank)

  2 × NOVA minicomputers

15 × Z80 microcomputers (small servers, terminal concentrators)

  1 × CAP experimental computer

The LSI4 machines and the Z80s make up the Cambridge Model Distributed System. The CAP computer has a virtual memory system which uses the file-server as secondary storage, while the remaining machines are connected mainly for convenience. For example, the IBM 370 is used for tape archiving. Terminal sessions and job submission on this machine are also possible from terminals on the ring.

Utilisation

The utilisation was observed to vary widely over short time periods. There were short-term peaks of activity, but over longer periods the average utilisation was moderately stable. At times of heavy use the utilisation was around 4% when measured over 30-minute intervals. Heavy use implies that most of the processor bank machines were in use, as was the CAP computer. At the time of the tests there were six active computers in the processor bank. All of these made frequent use of the file-server and this accounted for the majority of the traffic on the ring. At times of minimum ring use the utilisation was 0.1%, most of which can be attributed to the **logger**, a server which 'prods' each of the 255 ring addresses with a minipacket once per second. Over 24 hours the utilisation was typically 1.3%.

With short sampling times the utilisation can be much greater, although the majority of samples exhibit a very low utilisation: more than 80% of all 1 ms samples have a utilisation of well below 1%. A single station on the test ring could produce a utilisation of 20% if it transmitted at full speed and a basic block can consist of up to 1027 minipackets. It is reasonable, therefore, to expect to see utilisations of 20% lasting for up to 25 ms. This was indeed seen to occur but was never seen to exceed 20%, indicating the low probability of two stations transmitting at the same time. The only pair of stations which were capable of this transfer rate were CAP and the file-server, no other machines having ring interfaces of sufficient speed. An operation such as loading a processor bank machine with an operating system of 30 Kbytes lasts around 0.5 s, during which the utilisation is 10%.

This experiment demonstrates that ring traffic is bursty in nature and that a low level of background activity is interspersed with short periods of high activity. Overall, the utilisation remains low. At no time is the system bandwidth inadequate, though the point-to-point bandwidth is a limiting factor for those machines with inherently high transfer rates. The file-server could clearly benefit from higher bandwidth, but only if the stations with which it communicates could keep up.

Useful traffic

Useful traffic means the proportion of minipackets which are accepted by their destination. This may be influenced by the level of protocol above the minipacket level and also by the characteristics of the receiving computers and their ring interfaces. With the exception of the prodding minipackets sent by the logger, almost all minipackets in the test environment were part of basic block transfers.

Exact measurement of the overall numbers of minipackets with each of the four responses is not possible since one of the responses (ignored) cannot be counted properly. All minipackets are sent bearing this response initially and it is not possible, while monitoring a single point on the ring, to deduce whether an ignored response is implied or whether the minipacket has not yet passed its destination. A solution to this problem is to monitor empty packets which have a valid response in them. The monitor station (not the traffic monitor) may be configured to fill empty minipackets with 0s. By placing the traffic monitor just before the monitor station the relative numbers of three responses, including ignored, can be estimated. The busy response, encoded as 0s, cannot be measured in this part of the experiment. An assumption must be made that very few minipackets which have been marked empty at their source are re-used before they reach the monitoring point. This is reasonable at low utilisations and the figures given in Table 7.1 were obtained at a utilisation of 3.4% (over 30 minutes).

The measurements of Table 7.1 indicate that the basic block protocol is an efficient means of transporting data. The low proportion of unselected responses means that little bandwidth is wasted by excessive numbers of attempts to establish a block connection. The ignored responses can be largely attributed to the logger transmitting to non-existent addresses, while the slightly higher busy figure suggests that there is some degree of speed mismatch

Table 7.1   Useful traffic on a Cambridge Ring

Empty minipackets (not possible to count BUSY response)

Accepted	86200
Unselected	1030
Busy	?
Ignored	7200

Full minipackets (not possible to count IGNORED response)

Accepted	21800
Unselected	900
Busy	3600
Ignored + unmarked	65100

Combining these two gives an estimate for all responses

Accepted	86%
Unselected	2%
Busy	7%
Ignored	5%

amongst the various ring interfaces. The busy response is intended to promote efficient transmission in the event of such mismatches. A station getting a minipacket back with the busy response will retransmit it a short while later, by which time the receiver should be ready to receive it.

7.3.4 Block lengths

Measuring the lengths of blocks is performed as described previously. The header minipacket is accepted without regard for source or destination and the addresses found in that minipacket are used subsequently. When the block has been captured another block header is looked for, again regardless of source and destination. Clearly every block cannot be monitored in this way but over a long period of time (several hours) a representative picture of the distribution of lengths can be obtained. The results of this experiment are shown below in Figs. 7.2 and 7.3. The first histogram shows an overall picture while the second shows the low block length interval in more detail.

As expected there is a bimodal distribution of lengths, the majority of data being transmitted in maximal length blocks. However, the majority of blocks are quite short. Over 80% of blocks carry less than 16 words of data and 90% of the data is carried in the remaining blocks, most of which are 400 or 1024 words long. The blocks of length 400 are due to the processor bank machines having a 400-word buffer with which to perform transfers to and from the file-server.

Most of the small blocks are control blocks used in the higher-level byte stream protocol, many of these being associated with the terminal concentrators. These send large numbers of small data blocks, particularly when working in single-character mode and generate similar numbers of control

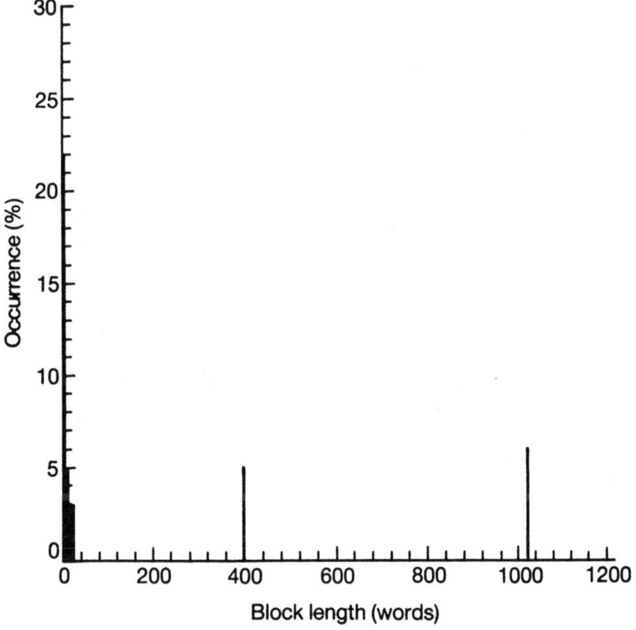

Fig. 7.2   Basic block lengths

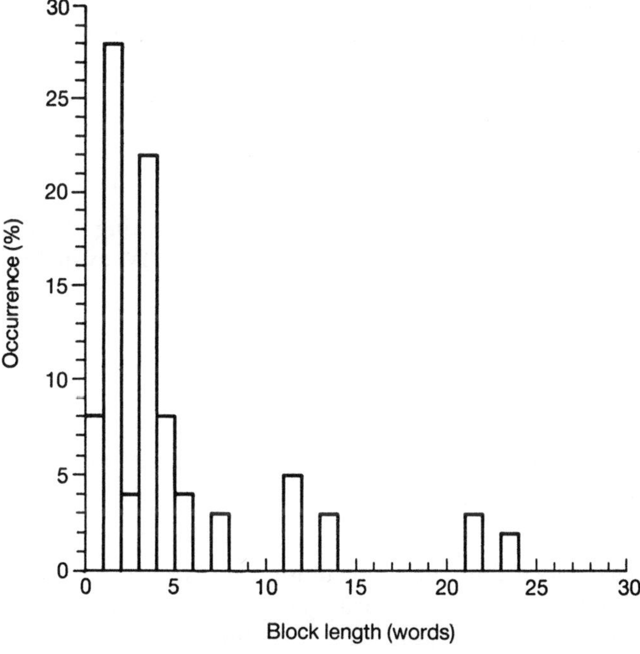

Fig. 7.3   Basic block lengths (low lengths only)

blocks. At times of heavy use it was observed that about 200 blocks per second were being sent.

7.3.5 Performance under heavy load

While the ring in the experiments described above was never heavily loaded, for example with a utilisation of 50% for a prolonged period, it is interesting to consider how the performance would change in such circumstances and what factors determine the bandwidth available. The system bandwidth (sysBW) is calculated as follows:

$$\text{sysBW} = \frac{\text{Number of data bits on ring}}{\text{Total number of bits on ring}} \times \text{clocking rate}$$

On the test ring there were 3 slots and a gap of 33 bits, the clocking rate being 9.8 MHz. Hence the system bandwidth was:

$$\frac{3 \times 16}{(3 \times 38) + 33} \times 9.8 = 3.2 \text{ Mbps}$$

Provided that the gap is small (less than 5 bits) the sysBW is roughly independent of the number of slots and in 10 MHz rings is just over 4 Mbps.

The point-to-point bandwidth (ppBW) is dependent on the number of slots for the following reason. Consider a ring with N slots; when a station transmits it must wait for the minipacket to return (N slot times + gap time) and then wait a further 2 slot times before transmitting again. This wait is a feature of the Cambridge Ring and could be reduced to one slot time by redesigning some of the circuitry. Thus the minimum time between transmissions is $N + 2$ slot times (plus the gap time). Assuming the gap to be small then we have:

$$\text{ppBW} = \frac{\text{sysBW}}{N + 2}$$

This assumes that no other stations are using the ring. If M stations are transmitting as fast as the ring will allow, then the ppBW available to each is as follows:

$$\text{ppBW} = \frac{\text{sysBW}}{M + N} \quad (\text{given } M > 1)$$

and the utilisation under such conditions is:

$$\text{Utilisation} = \frac{100 \times M}{M + N} \ (\%)$$

Note that this means that two stations may transmit with the maximum ppBW without interfering with each other. Computer simulation of situations in which many stations compete for bandwidth indicates that it is shared fairly and an experiment involving up to six stations was performed which verified this. A number of microcomputers were loaded with a program which caused them to transmit minipackets as fast as the ring would allow. The resulting utilisation when one to six of the microcomputers were transmitting was measured with the traffic monitor and found to agree with the predicted figures.

A graph of ppBW as a function of the number of slots is shown in Fig. 7.4. Several sets of points are plotted, representing different numbers of stations transmitting at full speed. A graph showing utilisation for similar parameters is shown in Fig. 7.5. From the first graph it can be seen that a single slot ring provides the highest ppBW and that the degradation in ppBW with increasing load is quite gradual in rings with several slots.

The ppBW can be increased by reducing the number of slots in a ring or by increasing the sysBW. Increasing the clocking rate increases the sysBW and the number of slots on a ring of fixed size. Thus the ppBW remains approximately constant. Increasing the sysBW can also be achieved by increasing the amount of data in a minipacket, though this is a design change and so not applicable to early Cambridge Rings. If we consider the present minipacket format enlarged to hold 8 data bytes then the sysBW would become 7.44 Mbps (assuming a small gap and 10-MHz clock). The number of slots on a ring of fixed size will be roughly halved and the ppBW will be more than four times that of a Cambridge Ring of the same size.

Reducing the number of slots amounts to reducing the delay in the ring. This is made up of delay in the ring cables and a 3-bit delay at each repeater. It is

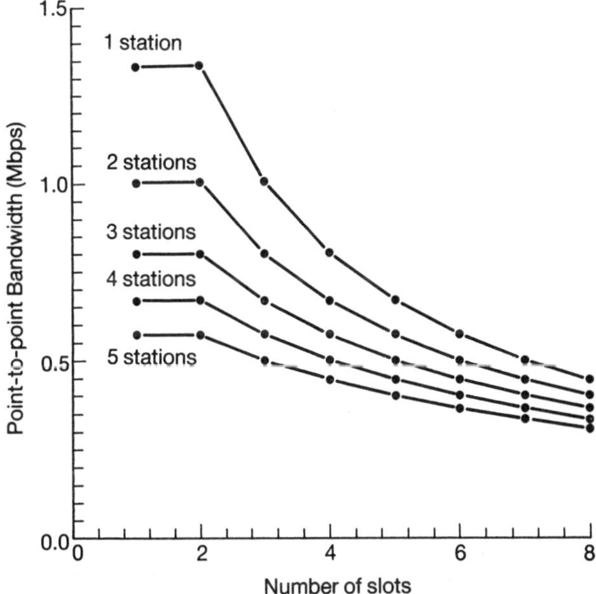

Fig. 7.4   Point-to-point bandwidth of the Cambridge Ring

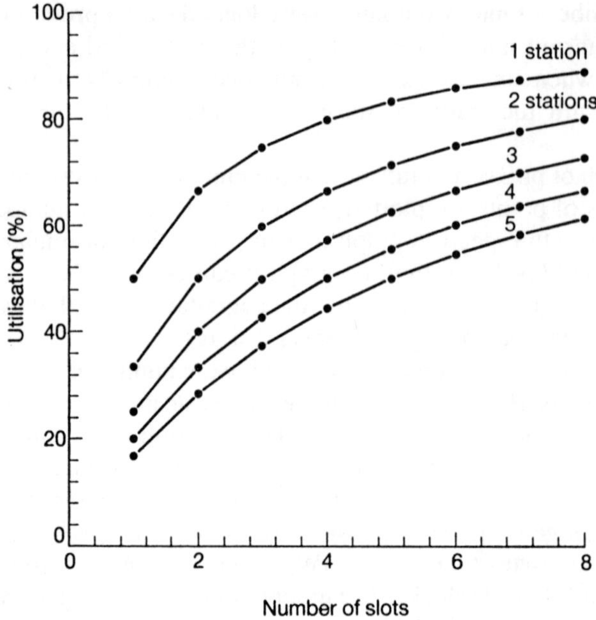

Fig. 7.5   Utilisation of the Cambridge Ring

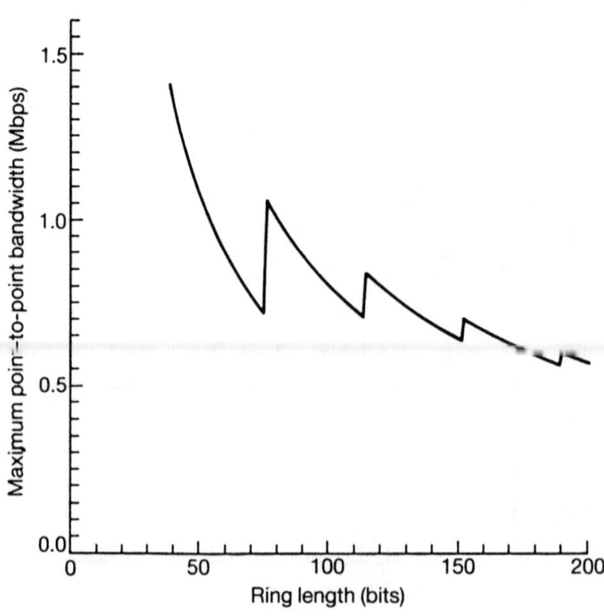

Fig. 7.6   Point-to-point bandwidth as a function of a ring length

possible to use a **repeater extender** which allows up to six stations to use a single repeater and will reduce the ring length by up to 9 bits. However, it is possible to cause a fall in bandwidth in this way, since a ring with a large gap has less ppBW and sysBW than a ring with one more slot and a small gap. This may be seen in Fig. 7.6.

A more drastic way of reducing the slot count of a large ring is to separate it into two smaller rings joined by a bridge device (normally a dedicated computer). In this way ppBW on the two rings will be increased, though traffic through the bridge may be slower and care must be taken in deciding which machines should remain on the same ring and which can tolerate slightly slower communication through the bridge. This course of action has been taken on the Cambridge system; the file-server, processor bank machines and CAP are sited on the same ring, while the terminal concentrators and printing servers are on the second (larger) ring.

A further worthwhile consequence of splitting rings in this way is that reliability is enhanced since the failure of one ring will not affect the operation of the other. Of course, it may be that machines on the working ring require resources on the failed ring, but the situation is nonetheless better than if everything were on a single broken ring. Bridge design and the splitting of rings are discussed in Leslie (1983).

7.3.6 Comparison with Ethernet

A series of experiments have been performed by Shoch and Hupp (1979) of Xerox PARC on an Ethernet in an environment similar to that described above. The Ethernet was a prototype version running at 3 MHz. Table 7.2 compares the two systems over some interesting parameters. One of the major differences between the two systems is in the location of disk files. Processors of the Ethernet have a disk drive directly connected to them, which is used for most short-term storage. There are also file-servers but these are mainly used for shared data and longer-term storage. Processors in the CMDS have no local disks and all files are kept remotely on the file-server. This is probably the reason for the much larger volume of traffic moved, on a per station basis, by the CMDS.

Another difference is in the maximum observed utilisation over short time periods. The Ethernet's maximum over one second was 37% compared to only

Table 7.2   Comparison between Ethernet and CMDS

	Ethernet	*CMDS*
Number of active stations	120	40
Daily throughput (Mbytes)	300	430
Average utilisation over 24 h (%)	0.86	1.3
Maximum utilisation over 1 h (%)	3.6	3.7
Maximum utilisation over 1 s (%)	37	20

20% on the ring. This reflects the fact that a single host on the Ethernet can induce close to 100% utilisation by sending consecutive long packets, whereas a single host on a (3-slot) ring can only produce 20%.

An Ethernet packet can contain up to about 540 bytes of data and so is comparable to the ring's basic block in size and also in function. The Ethernet experiment demonstrated a bimodal distribution of packet lengths, with the average size of short packets being somewhat larger than that of short ring blocks. The Ethernet median was 28 bytes and the ring median 4 bytes. This disparity disappears when one considers that all Ethernet packets contained protocol information for internetworking and thus contained 11 words over their true data content. The Ethernet's use of short packets is much the same as its ring counterpart, that is, they are largely protocol acknowledgements and terminal traffic. On the Ethernet 17% of packets were 'long' as opposed to 11% on the ring and 66% of data was carried in these long packets (94% on the ring).

Under normal operating conditions the Ethernet and ring are remarkably similar, both in terms of their usage and the traffic characteristics which are observed.

7.3.7 The growth of the CMDS

The CMDS configuration described earlier in this chapter has evolved and grown since the traffic study was made. The number of stations increased until the ring had 4 slots and a large gap. Further stations would have meant a 5-slot ring and transactions with the file-server had become unacceptably slow by this stage. This was due in part to the increased number of clients of the file-server, but was mainly because of the lower point-to-point bandwidth of the ring.

To remedy the latter failing, the ring was split into two and the new rings joined by a bridge computer. The faster ring of the two had 2 slots and connected the processor bank machines and file-server, along with a small number of essential servers. The remaining machines, including the terminal concentrators, were placed on the other ring which had 3 slots. Interactions between the file-server and processor bank machines could now proceed at high speed, while the less demanding terminal traffic passed through the bridge.

The bridge is a computer with two ring interfaces, one on each ring. Rather than passing minipackets from ring to ring, the bridge deals in basic blocks. If minipackets were passed the responses would be useless and different protocols would be required. The use of basic blocks as the unit of bridge traffic also means that the same station address can be used on both rings and more than 256 stations can be accommodated on the combined network. The method of bridge operation is as follows.

On the CMDS system, hosts and the services they offer are identified by textual names. The name-servers, whose addresses are known by all hosts, are used to translate the names into ring service addresses. When a name-server is asked to translate a name to an address which is on another ring, it supplies not the true address, but the address of the bridge which is used to reach the address. It also supplies a unique port number and notifies the bridge that it should retransmit any incoming basic blocks which have that port number to the true address. The host which originally asked for the name to be translated sends basic blocks bearing the appropriate port number to the bridge, which then retransmits them to their proper destination.

The bridge is a potential bottleneck since the current design can only be receiving one basic block at a time. This can cause problems when a machine sends many long blocks through the bridge. There is a chance that other blocks trying to get through the bridge will be delayed for so long that timeouts will expire and the transmissions fail.

The splitting of the rings was a major undertaking, principally because of the many changes which had to be made to the communication software. It was a successful exercise, however, and the perceived performance improved as a result. The processor bank now has over 30 minicomputers in it and a second file-server has been added.

The point-to-point bandwidth of slotted rings is very closely related to the number of slots on the ring and this is, in turn, related to the number of stations. As the ring becomes larger, so it becomes slower and if it becomes too slow the only solution is to split it as described above. Splitting implies a bridging mechanism and if the bridge is slower than the rings then careful division of hosts between the rings is necessary. The Cambridge Ring bridge is complex, both in hardware and software. It uses three microprocessors and needs to interact with name-servers on each ring. It is vulnerable to overload and malicious traffic and expensive enough to prevent its duplication for reliability reasons. A much simpler bridge would be preferable. Operating at the minipacket level would be better but the Cambridge Ring architecture will not support this. A new network based on similar principles to the Cambridge Ring could incorporate such a facility.

7.3.8 Changes to the Cambridge Ring

One of the facts to emerge from the study detailed earlier is that when a disk drive is connected to a network like the Cambridge Ring, the network limits the performance that may be had from the disk. A modest disk drive can move data at rates in excess of 5 Mbps and high-performance drives are capable of several times this rate. The Xerox distributed system based around an Ethernet gets round this problem by having local disks on its hosts, in addition to file-servers on the network. The disk is used as a cache and in certain circumstances, can speed file-based operations. On the ring system it was the speed of the ring interfaces on the processor bank machines which limited their transfers with the file-server.

Current basic block protocol implementations are such that multiplexed reception of minipackets from different sources is not possible at a host. Thus, the bandwidth into a station is limited to the point-to-point bandwidth, as opposed to being able to approach the system bandwidth. While this protocol works well for most machines on the ring, it does preclude multiplexed reception which could improve performance at servers such as the file-server. The Ethernet does not suffer from such problems and moreover, the whole of its channel capacity is available to a transmitter once it has gained access to the network.

If a slotted ring is made faster by increasing its minipacket size (in terms of data) and possibly also increasing its clocking rate, then not only would the performance increase, but the way in which the ring was used might change. If a minipacket could now hold what was previously a small basic block a number of improvements would ensue. First, the transmission time of such blocks would be considerably reduced. If an N minipacket block were previously used then the transmission time would be at least N ring revolutions whereas it would now be 1 revolution, provided the minipacket is accepted. Second, there would be a considerable saving both in host software and processing time, since the data no longer needs to be split over several minipackets.

If the minipacket were able to carry a significant amount of data in addition to any protocol information, then the need for basic blocks up to a certain size would disappear and multiplexed reception would be made possible. The minimum minipacket data field needed to efficiently support existing protocols and still allow some data to be carried is about 8 bytes.

Thus a larger minipacket would improve the efficiency of some existing applications and also lead to a simplification of protocols. A larger address field would allow many more stations and make network interconnection by minipacket bridges a possibility. It is assumed that suitable host interfaces to the network could be designed. As was seen in an earlier chapter, existing fast interfaces are costly and complex.

7.4 References

Birrell, A.D. and Needham, R.M., 1980. 'A universal file-server'. *IEEE Trans. Software Engineering*, **SE-6 (5)**, 450–53.

Leslie, I.M., 1983. 'Extending the local area network'. PhD Thesis, Computer Laboratory, University of Cambridge, February.

Needham, R.M. and Herbert, A.J., 1982. *The Cambridge Distributed Computing System*. London: Addison-Wesley.

Ody, N.J., 1980. 'Logging of ring transactions at the basic block level'. Systems Research Group Note, Computer Laboratory, University of Cambridge, September.

Shoch, J.F. and Hupp, J.A., 1979. 'Performance of an Ethernet local network – a preliminary report'. *Local Area Communications Network Symposium*, Boston, May, 113–25.

Chapter 8 **A high-speed ring network**

This chapter describes a network known as the Cambridge Fast Ring (Temple, 1984). The Fast Ring is currently being developed at Cambridge as a successor to the Cambridge Ring. As its name suggests, it is faster than its predecessor and data rates in the range 50–100 Mbps are being planned for it.

The first part of this chapter describes some of the topics which were considered when the network was being designed. Later, the network architecture is described and, finally, one of the novel features of the network is discussed.

8.1 Design considerations of the Cambridge Fast Ring

The initial aim of the designers of the Cambridge Fast Ring (CFR) was to develop a network which was substantially faster than currently available networks. All of the usual network types were considered and the final choice was not unexpected given the experience gained with the design of the Cambridge Ring. Slotted rings do have certain properties which make them good candidates for high-speed networks and, in particular, the ability to have several slots in existence on a ring simultaneously was appealing. In this way, slots could be marked to distinguish them from each other and this would pave the way for bandwidth allocation schemes. This would then allow different hosts to have different transmission strategies so that hosts which needed to transmit video or voice data which required guaranteed bandwidth could do so.

As already mentioned, high speed was one of the main goals of the design. Other factors which were considered were the cost of implementation and connection and the reliability of the network. Implementation in VLSI is a major step in achieving low cost and, to a lesser extent, a means of increasing reliability.

8.1.1 Bandwidth partitioning

By definition, the bandwidth of a fast local network should be high. A secondary requirement which was thought to be important is that it should be partitionable. In terms of speed an increase by a factor of two would make existing applications run faster but a factor of ten increase would be much more interesting, opening up new fields of application. Thus, a clocking rate of 100

MHz was selected as a target speed and the rest of the design process assumed that this rate was achievable. It was also recognised that operation at lower speeds was likely and should be catered for. When varying the speed of a slotted ring, it is wise to vary the slot size in proportion to the speed to keep a reasonable number of slots on the ring. Just what a reasonable number is will depend on the environment in which the ring is used. Current uses of rings suggest that the number of slots will generally be less than ten, a more likely figure being two or three.

Being able to vary the slot size to suit the conditions of use is a useful facility and was included in the LSI implementation of the Cambridge Ring which was described in Chapter 5. In that system the slots could carry between 1 and 8 bytes of data, a range of slot size from 32 to 88 bits. In a ring with several slots there is no reason why all the slots must be of the same length and the mixing of long and short slots may be advantageous if there are a number of different traffic types on the network. A network with both computer data and voice traffic could benefit from such a scheme. The segregating of the two traffic types means that an appropriate slot size may be chosen for each and the two sets of traffic will not interfere with each other. Voice data would be carried in short (1 data byte) slots and other traffic, requiring more bandwidth, in longer (8 data byte) slots. Separating the traffic in this way makes the performance for a given traffic type more predictable. In networks which allow variable packet sizes such mechanisms are unnecessary but the segregation of the different traffic types is not generally possible.

One thing which few local networks provide is the ability to guarantee a user a given amount of bandwidth or a given access time. The slotted ring lends itself to a mode of operation which is analogous to time division multiplexing. In this mode a time slot is allocated to a user who has exclusive use of that slot until he no longer requires it. Applied to a slotted ring this means allocating a slot to a source for its exclusive use. This mode of operation has been named **channel mode**. When a slot is not allocated for channel use it will be available for use in the usual way. A problem associated with this style of operation is that in a ring with a small number of slots it is possible that all of the slots may be allocated and thus starve other stations of bandwidth. This may be overcome by marking certain slots to indicate that they may be used in this way, while all other slots may only be used in **normal mode**. Therefore, if at least one normal slot is available, there will always be bandwidth available to all stations.

A further problem is the allocation and deallocation of a channel slot. A reasonable approach to allocation is to give a station two types of transmission method, one for normal mode and another for channel mode. Channel mode transmissions may only take place in channel slots. When the first transmission takes place the slot is marked allocated and is subsequently only used by the station which claimed it. Stations must know the slot structure of the ring for this scheme to work. This method of working is practical but potentially wasteful if the slot is used only infrequently during the allocation period. A further problem arises when the slot must be deallocated. The host could ask the station to do this but some mechanism must also exist in case the host forgets to release the slot. The monitor station could perform this function or it could be provided in all stations. The slot could be deallocated if it had not been used in the last ten ring revolutions, for example.

An alternative scheme is to insist that the transmitter supplies data at a rate sufficient to keep the slot filled. In this mode the slot is filled once per ring revolution and so the bandwidth is greater than would be achieved in normal operation. Deallocation is automatic in this method when the transmitting host stops supplying data. Allocation of the channel slot may be performed either by explicitly asking to use a channel slot, or by simply transmitting in the normal way and always having data ready when the slot returns. If this latter strategy is used then the transmitter may use a uniform transmission protocol for placing data on the ring and will get a channel slot if one is free.

The channel slot approach partially solves the problem of guaranteeing and partitioning bandwidth. However, it is somewhat inflexible in the amount of bandwidth which is partitioned. Having two or more different slot sizes gives a wider range of choice. A prototype system which embodies the concepts of differing slot sizes and channel mode transmission has been built (Hopper and Williamson, 1983). This system uses the LSI Cambridge Ring implementation to make a ring with two sizes of slots. Short slots contain only 1 byte of data while long slots contain 8 and may be used in channel mode.

Channel mode transmissions provide the highest bandwidth that may be obtained from a slotted ring when slots must return to their source. Still higher bandwidth may be obtained from a slotted ring by allowing a station to have more than one slot in use at once. Imposing a limit on the number of slots that a station may have in use will prevent hogging. The station logic will have to keep track of the number of slots in use and a limit of 2 to 4 seems feasible. Sequencing problems could arise in such systems if data from one slot is rejected, since the station may well have already sent another slot before learning of the rejection. Straying still further from the Cambridge Ring style of working, a possible scheme is to have the destination mark slots empty. This would provide a point-to-point bandwidth equal to the system bandwidth on an unloaded ring but with attendant hogging problems.

A reasonable solution to dynamic bandwidth allocation is the provision of a variety of slot sizes, two being a good start, and the ability to use certain slots in channel mode. Such a system would offer four levels of performance, the two levels using channel mode being stable, the two using normal mode dependent on other traffic on the ring.

8.1.2 Addressing

There are good reasons why a LAN should not be allowed to grow too large. There are also good reasons why a large network is desirable. The ability to connect many hosts together is clearly advantageous but the reasons why they should not all be on the same LAN are less obvious.

The hardware of a network must be designed to cope with its maximum size. Ethernet transceivers must be able to drive up to 255 others over 1 km of cable. If the Ethernet allowed four times as many hosts on the network, the tranceivers would need to be more powerful and hence more expensive. On rings, where the ring delay is dependent on the number of stations, the performance may fall to an unacceptable level if the network grows too large and there may also be instability problems with phase-locked clocking systems. There may be administrative problems in dealing with large numbers of hosts since name translation tables will become large and slow. Reliability too is an issue, placing 200 hosts on a single network assumes a great deal about the reliability of the network. Dividing the network up into autonomous **sub-nets** improves reliability, as well as increasing performance on the sub-nets. The data rates achievable between hosts on different sub-nets may be lower than that between hosts on the same sub-net. The division of hosts among sub-nets may therefore have to be done with some prior knowledge of their likely communication requirements.

Thus, while single LANs may not be allowed to grow arbitrarily large, it is possible to interconnect large numbers of hosts by the interconnection of LANs, provided a suitable addressing scheme can be devised. This leads naturally to a hierarchy of networks in which a host may be addressed by specifying the sub-net on which it resides and also its address on that sub-net. In the past, LANs have been interconnected in an *ad hoc* manner, for example, the Xerox Internet is a collection of Ethernets connected together by serial lines running at rates between 2400 and 56000 bps. On each Ethernet, host addresses are just 8 bits and so each packet which conforms to the Internet protocol carries additional addressing information within the data field of the packet. An Internet address is hierarchically structured and consists of an 8-bit net number, an 8-bit host number and a 32-bit socket (port) number. Packets destined for another network are sent explicitly to a gateway host which forwards the packet via other gateways to its destination. The Internet is like a store and forward network but with an Ethernet at each node rather than a single host.

The Universe network is an interconnection of Cambridge Rings by satellite and high-speed land lines (Adams *et al.*, 1982). Here again a hierarchical address scheme is used, the base networks having no provision for interconnection. Newer networks, such as IBM's token ring network, include provision for interconnection of rings by providing a large address with fields for both ring and host numbers.

A characteristic of all interconnected LANs is the existence of a bridge or gateway on each sub-net, which is responsible for receiving and passing on packets destined for other sub-nets. There are two extremes of LAN interconnection. At one end of the scale is the Xerox Internet, in which no attempt is made to keep performance the same for traffic within an Ethernet and between connected Ethernets. The interconnection is over long distances, typically hundreds of miles, and is largely a convenience rather than a necessity. At the other end of the scale is the IBM ring, where the interconnection of rings is intended to be transparent to the hosts and there may be functional dependence between hosts on different rings. The distances here are small, a few miles at most between rings. Between the two extremes lies the Universe network in which the bandwidth available between two rings is high, around 1 Mbps over the satellite channel, and the distances between rings large.

High-speed land lines, such as British Telecom's Megastream, offer bandwidths of up to 1 Mbps over distances of hundreds of miles. Their introduction means that widely distributed connection of LANs will be possible which exhibit properties similar to those of a single LAN.

When designing a new network it would seem sensible to allow for the possibility of connecting networks together, either over quite short distances or over longer ones with a consequent increase in delay. There are a number of ways of organising the addressing mechanism to allow packets to pass between sub-nets rapidly and so avoid the store and forward effects which reduce performance.

One method of organising addresses is in a hierarchical arrangement so that the bits of the address are split into fields, for sub-net and host number for example. IBM's ring uses this form of two-level hierarchy. An alternative is simply to have a flat address space where hosts are numbered without regard for their position in the network hierarchy. There are other schemes which might be employed, such as Saltzer's (1980) source routing method, but the two already mentioned are the most suitable for incorporation in a new design.

The hierarchical scheme has the advantage that no central address allocator is necessary, addresses on a sub-net may be freely assigned without conflicting with those on any other sub-net. The fields of the address may also make routing packets particularly simple in some networks. There are also disadvantages to this scheme: the relative sizes of the fields must be decided at the outset and may prove unsuitable in certain cases. Making the address large will alleviate this problem. Another drawback is that if a resource moves its physical location between sub-nets then its address must be changed.

A flat address space requires that addresses be allocated rather more carefully if several agents are allocating them. However, there is nothing to stop conventions being applied to the flat address to form fields for the purposes of allocation or whatever. Moving resources in a flat address space means that the address may move with the resource. The principal difference between the two schemes is that the flat address scheme requires the whole address to be inspected to perform routing, while the hierarchical scheme requires just part of the address to be looked at. The hierarchical scheme may impose restrictions on the topology of interconnection which a flat space would not.

Broadcast addressing

Broadcast addressing is a means of addressing a single packet to all hosts on a network and many current local networks have this facility. Generally, a special address is allocated for the purpose and when this address is used as a destination all stations may receive the packet. This can be a very useful facility, particularly for resource location in a distributed environment. For example, it could be used to allow a newly switched on host to locate a name-server. When LANs are interconnected a decision must be made whether or not to allow broadcast data to spread over the whole interconnection. If there are loops it is possible that the broadcast packet may be propagated indefinitely throughout the system and steps would have to be taken to avoid this.

Source selection

Source selection allows a host to receive packets from selected sources only. The Cambridge Ring allows no sources, all sources, or one particular source to be selected by means of a register which the host may update. A useful extension to this might be to allow a certain group of sources to be selected by means of a table look-up on source addresses. A possible use of this mechanism is to mask troublesome sources which send unwanted messages. A problem with the masking of a source in this way is that it is difficult to know when to start listening to it again. A timeout mechanism would solve the problem but would be complex to administer.

8.1.3 Error detection and correction

The fundamental operation performed by most local area networks is the transfer of blocks of memory from one computer to another and there are many stages in this process at which errors might occur, the network being just one of them. Thus, the most effective means of checking is on a memory to memory basis, and a checksum could accompany each data block and be checked when the data is in the destination host's memory. In some circumstances this may be too much trouble to perform and a less thorough method is preferable, such as checksumming individual packets as they are received.

The network should do its best to detect errors which arise during transmission and report them to the appropriate authority. At this level it is possible to distinguish between two types of network error. Both types may have a common cause but their implications are rather different. The first type of errors are those which occur in the data portion of a packet and the second are those occurring in the control portion of the packet. The latter may have implications both for delivery of the packet and for correct operation of the network. Corruption of a destination address may result in a packet being wrongly delivered and further packets to the true destination being out of sequence.

Local area networks are usually constructed of transmission media with a low error rate and the error-checking and protocol systems will be designed with this in mind. Errors on the network will occur however and it is thus common to have some sort of error-checking field in packets. This is often a Cyclic Redundancy Checksum (CRC) of some or all fields in the packet. Whilst it may be useful to know that the data field has been corrupted at the network level, it is rather more important to know that control information is in error. Since the CRC contributes to the overhead in a packet it should be kept as small as possible, while still providing the required level of error detection. Using the

CRC to check just the control fields may be a useful strategy, provided that adequate checking of the data occurs at higher levels.

In all networks it is desirable to check packets when they arrive at their destination and refuse to accept them if they appear to contain an error. In ring networks, where packets return to their source carrying a response, it is also necessary to know whether or not the response is correct. It may be possible to mark the response to indicate that the packet was rejected due to error and thus facilitate a low-level retransmission method. The action taken by a destination on receiving a packet containing an error may vary according to the protocol in use. The data will not be used but a number of courses of action might be taken. Reporting the error to the source might be useful in some cases, but there is the possibility that the source address field may be incorrect. Reporting the error to some central logger could be useful and aid maintenance of the network.

In certain types of ring the packet may be altered by various legitimate means on its way around the ring and recomputation of the error-checking field will be necessary. Cambridge Ring minipackets may be altered at the monitor station and also at the destination station where the response bits are marked. In such systems it may be difficult or expensive to recompute the error-check field and parts of the packet will have to go unprotected. In the case of response bits this is particularly unfortunate and means that sequence checking of packets is essential if packets are not to be lost or duplicated due to errors in the response bits. Alternatively, a simpler error-detection mechanism, such as parity, may be used to guard a small number of bits with some confidence. Having responses means that a destination can signal its rejection of a packet due to error back to the source, which can then retransmit the packet. This prevents having to pass the error up to a higher level and thus is more efficient.

Maintenance

Another important aspect of error detection is that it enables a maintenance system to be constructed. Whilst a station receiving a bad packet might not report it to the source, it would be useful if the error were reported to a centralised logger, where the information would be available to maintenance staff. In this way an overall picture of the error rate of the network could be built up and parts of the network which are particularly error prone identified. Faulty components may be isolated and links which pass close to sources of electro-magnetic interference located. In loop networks, each station on the loop has the potential to look at all packets passing through it and report any errors it sees. If each error message contains its source address then it will be possible to localise the source of the error to a single link. The Cambridge Ring performs such a function by means of a parity bit in each slot which is checked and corrected at each station. Such a mechanism also locates a broken ring cable since a stream of error messages will be generated by the station after the break. This method of testing is most effective in systems such as the slotted ring where all slots, whether full or empty, can be checked and the network is therefore under continuous test.

When deciding on a suitable error-detection scheme for a LAN it is necessary to have some idea of the types of error which are likely to occur and their frequency. Error rates for transmission systems used in LANs are frequently quoted as being in the range 1 bit in 10^9 to 1 in 10^{12} but little work has been done in finding out just what types of errors actually occur. Any transmission system has an associated signal-to-noise ratio. The noise comes from random thermal effects in the transmission and reception circuitry and is the source of a basic level of errors. External phenomena, such as Electro-Magnetic Interference (EMI), will cause additional errors. EMI is generated by the switching of large currents in the vicinity of LAN cables. Fibre-optic cables are unaffected by such phenomena but the very low signal levels encountered in fibre-optic receivers mean that they are much more susceptible to EMI than their wire cable counterparts. While thermal noise may cause corruption of 1 or possibly 2 bits, EMI will generally persist for anything from a few microseconds to a few milliseconds and many bits may be corrupted in what is called a burst error.

Another kind of error occurs in systems which use a phase-locked loop for clock recovery and jitter removal. If the degree of jitter is high, the phase-locked loop may skip a bit time either backwards or forwards, with the result that a bit may be lost or a random bit inserted into the data. All subsequent bits in the data are thus shifted by one place and this amounts to a long burst error.

Error detection must thus cope with a wide range of errors and an effective check is a CRC. This is a fixed-size check field and is easy to compute, yet detects a wide variety of errors. A single parity bit is very easy to implement but is incapable of detecting all errors. It may be useful in a maintenance system where it is not necessary to detect all errors, but just sufficient to allow the maintenance mechanism to function. A parity bit applied more frequently, say to every byte in a packet, would be a much stronger check for long burst errors and could possibly be propagated throughout the entire transmission process, giving an end-to-end check on the transfer. The overhead in doing this is significant, especially since all data paths in the system would need to be enlarged to hold the extra bit.

8.1.4 Reliability

Local networks are vulnerable to failure in many ways. An Ethernet will fail if the cable breaks, since the resulting segments will be incorrectly terminated. Certain modes of failure of an Ethernet transceiver may cause it to jam other transmissions. A Cambridge Ring will fail if a link is broken or if a repeater malfunctions. Failure within a station may prevent a particular host communicating via the network, while failure of a host such as a name-server may prevent other hosts from functioning correctly. Thus, as with error handling, there are many levels to be considered when discussing reliability.

At all levels there are two complementary approaches to improving reliability: partitioning and redundancy. Partitioning involves dividing the network into sub-units which will be unaffected by the failure of one of their number. Redundancy implies the provision of alternative resources to be used in the event of failure, two name-servers, for instance, or two network interfaces for a host or two rings. Providing redundancy means that some means of detecting failure must be provided. Systems vary in their requirements for switching to backup equipment: in some it should be performed automatically, in others it may be sufficient to inform an operator.

Practical work on redundancy techniques for LAN hardware has so far only been performed on ring systems. Redundant cabling techniques have been suggested as a means of allowing a ring to survive certain types of cable break. Recently, rings have been constructed with dual cables which are able to survive a cable break or repeater failure by using a 'loop back' method to reconfigure the ring and exclude the broken element. An example of a network using this mechanism is the Silk ring described in Chapter 4.

Closely allied to reliability is the maintenance system of the network. It should detect and report equipment failure and take any corrective action that the network is capable of. It should also make the location of faulty equipment as easy as possible. Making a network sufficiently redundant to survive cable failure, station failure and network monitor failure is a very complex process and is only attempted in applications which demand exceptional operational reliability such as aircraft control systems and process control applications.

Reliability may also be enhanced by the use of high-quality components and high standards of construction in the network. Reducing the component count, for example by implementing in LSI circuits, will also improve reliability. Practical experience has shown, however, that the main causes of failure of LANs are events such as lightning striking part of the network or accidental cutting of the cables.

A general purpose network will use partitioning to isolate faulty sub-nets until they can be repaired. Partitioning implies that a suitable addressing mechanism exists on the network and that bridges between the sub-nets can be constructed.

8.1.5 Cost

It is frequently the case that the major cost in installing a local area network is that of cabling. Running cables around a building or multi-building site is a labour intensive, disruptive and hence expensive process. There is still a good case for reducing the cost of network interface devices and when this is done the overall network cost will fall. It will also be economically viable to connect cheap computers to the network.

The circuitry which is required to interface a computer or similar digital device to a network generally divides into two parts, the station and the access box. All stations on a network are very similar, while the access box is specific to a certain type of computer system. The complexity of the access box can vary from a few gates and latches to a large microprocessor-controlled system. The station is the obvious first candidate for cost reduction and this topic is now discussed further.

The only way to significantly reduce the cost of digital logic systems which run at high speeds and are traditionally constructed in MSI logic is to implement them in LSI. Until recently only the large semiconductor manufacturers were able to design and build such circuits. Methods of simplifying the design process have been developed and many manufacturers now undertake the fabrication of LSI circuits from designs supplied by clients. Two methods of simplifying the design process are prevalent, gate arrays and semi-custom cell-based logic. Gate arrays are silicon chips containing a regular arrangement of devices such as transistors, gates or flip-flops. The designer specifies an interconnection pattern for these devices which the manufacturer can then place on the chip, using one or two layers of metallisation. Semi-custom design involves the designer using a small set of predefined circuit elements such as latches, multiplexers and gates to realise his circuit. The cells on the chip which perform these functions are of regular shapes with predefined contact points so that they will tile together on the chip without wasting space.

Development cost for a gate array design is lower than for a semi-custom design but the cost per chip is higher and so gate arrays are better suited to low-volume production of a few thousand chips and semi-custom to higher volumes of tens of thousands. At present only Metal Oxide Semiconductor (MOS) chips can be produced in semi-custom while faster bipolar chips are made as gate arrays.

The design of a LAN station in LSI will involve considerations of speed, power consumption and the size and complexity of the circuit. The design may require more than one chip, in which case the partitioning of the logic amongst the various chips must be decided. A single-chip implementation is likely to be cheaper than a multi-chip one and so it is desirable to try to fit the whole design onto a single chip. The loss of some features of the design may be considered worthwhile in order to do this. Pin count is also a consideration. Chips with many pins are expensive, yet a LAN station will probably require a parallel interface of at least 8 bits leading to a requirement for at least 40 pins and possibly more. The LSI implementation of the Cambridge Ring required 1000 gates and was implemented using two 40-pin bipolar gate arrays. Advances in technology now allow several thousand gates on a gate array and semi-custom designs are limited in size only by the area of the chip, 10,000 gates being an economic maximum.

In many chip technologies power consumption is related to the actual or expected maximum speed of operation and if several chips are being used it may be possible to place all the high-speed logic on the same chip. Part of a LAN station will have to work at the clocking rate of the network and this is likely to be the highest speed encountered. It may be possible to divide the clock rate in other parts of the logic and handle data in parallel, an obvious choice being to divide the clock by eight and deal with bytes of data. This approach has several advantages. If power consumption is related to clocking rate then the overall consumption will be reduced and if the whole design is on the same chip then timing tolerances will be increased in the slower parts, making the design process easier and operation more reliable.

Rough estimation suggests that a station will require between 1000 and 5000 gates to implement the control logic and if a clock division method is used no more than about 10% of the logic will have to function at full speed. With a slotted ring, where the amount of data carried in each slot is quite small, the provision of transmit and receive buffers on the chip might be considered.

Buffer sizes in the range 1 to 100 bytes could be expected, which would require up to several thousand more gates, bringing the total requirement to a maximum of around 10,000 gates. The provision of buffers on the chip may be unwarranted as the silicon area of the chip and hence its cost, will be increased. Buffers are just memories and readily available at low cost in a variety of forms.

Considering now the integration of a station for a slotted ring running at 100 MHz, computer simulation suggests that gate delays of not much more than 1 ns will be required in those parts of the circuit clocked at 100 MHz. Gates as fast as this are only available on bipolar gate arrays, the largest of which have about 2500 gates. Generally only about 70% of the array may be utilised and so only about 1800 gates will be available for use in the design. Larger gate arrays are available but at the cost of increased gate delays. With gate delays of 10 ns we can consider using MOS processes and semi-custom design. Therefore, an alternative strategy is to use a small, fast bipolar chip to interface to the ring's serial data stream and divide the clock of this device to a level suitable for use with a slower and much larger chip. A parallel interface would be necessary between the two and this might cause problems in that the pin count of the slower chip could be high.

Thus a slotted ring station might be approached in one of two ways. Placing the entire circuit on a single fast chip might restrict the complexity and hence the number of features that could be provided. Using a small fast chip in conjunction with a large slow one would be more expensive, but allow a much more complex system to be implemented.

8.2 The Cambridge Fast Ring

The CFR is made up of three kinds of nodes: **stations**, which transfer data between devices attached to the ring; **bridges**, which copy minipackets between rings; and **monitors**, one of which is required on each physical ring to set up and maintain the slot structure. There is a global address structure with which it is possible to make arbitrary connections of rings such as that shown in Fig. 8.1.

The slots (minipackets) of the CFR are divided into two types, according to the way they can be used for transmissions. The two types are called **normal slots** and **channel slots** and they are distinguished by a bit in the slot. Slots form a train round the ring with a gap to fill out the excess delay. Transmissions can be made as on the Cambridge Ring, with each slot being passed on empty after use (normal mode), or they can be made in channel mode where once a slot has been marked full it can be replenished for an indefinite number of revolutions. The implementor of a particular CFR system can choose which slots may be used in this way and which may only be used for normal mode transmissions. A typical system might have a number of channel mode slots for bulk data transfers and at least one normal slot to guarantee that some bandwidth will always be available regardless of the usage of the channel slots. The minipacket format is shown in Fig. 8.2.

The control bits at the front of the minipacket occupy four bits and

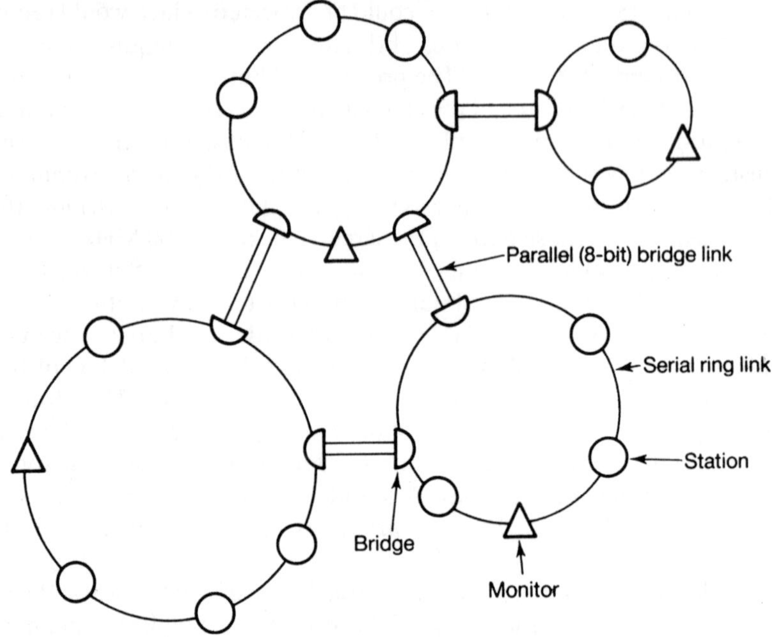

Fig. 8.1   A Cambridge Fast Ring network

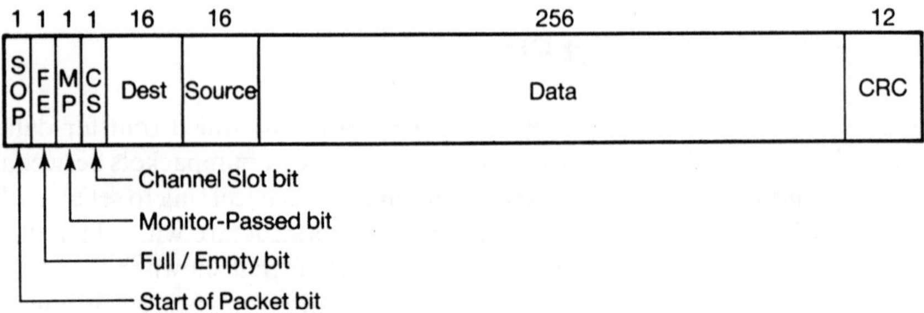

Fig. 8.2   Minipacket format of the Cambridge Fast Ring

comprise a start bit, the full/empty bit, the monitor-passed bit and a channel
slot bit. The latter is set in slots which may be used in channel mode and unset in
normal slots. The monitor is responsible for setting up the slot structure and so
it must be programmed with the number of each type of slot that a ring is to
contain.

Following the control bits in a slot are the destination and source
addresses. These are 16 bits long and they are followed by 256 bits (32 bytes) of
data. At the end of the minipacket is a 12-bit CRC of all the bits in the
minipacket. Encoded in the CRC is a single response bit. The minipacket is

therefore 304 bits or 38 bytes long. An early version of the CFR allowed for different sizes of slots, but this proved to be cumbersome to implement and a compromise size was chosen.

8.2.1 Hardware

An early attempt at implementing the CFR was made using a bipolar gate array to contain the majority of the logic and external FIFOs for minipacket storage. Problems with the manufacture of this chip caused that line of attack to be abandoned and another one sought. The method which was chosen uses two special chips, a fast ECL gate array and a slower CMOS semi-custom chip. The ECL chip interfaces to the ring cables and converts the serial data on the ring into 8-bit wide paths which feed data to and from the CMOS chip.

ECL chip functions

In order for the system to function at high speeds the ECL chip must divide the line clock by a suitable factor to provide a clock for the CMOS chip. A factor of 8 is suitable and this allows the CMOS chip to clock within its capabilities. Data must therefore be passed between the two chips in groups of 8 bits. This requires 16 pins since data must flow bidirectionally between the two chips.

The primary function of the ECL chip is to interface to the serial lines of the ring and convert the serial ring data into bytes which it then passes to the CMOS chip. The CMOS chip accepts the bytes, processes them and then passes them back to the ECL chip. The ECL chip converts them back into serial form and transmits them to the next node. The ECL chip is limited in size (300 gates) and the only other function it is able to incorporate is to detect the start of the slot train and signal its arrival to the CMOS chip. This means the ring does not have to be a whole number of bytes long. A variety of line-driving options are provided and the ECL logic fits comfortably in a standard 40-pin dual-in-line package. The line inputs and outputs are ECL-level signals which will drive twisted-pair or coaxial cables directly. The signals which interface to the CMOS chip are level shifted within the ECL chip to interface directly to CMOS logic.

CMOS chip functions

The CMOS chip must interface to the ECL chip and also to a 64K dynamic RAM chip which forms the select map and bridge routing table. It must also interface to the host device and contains minipacket buffers for transmission and reception. Interfacing to the ECL chip and RAM requires 30 pins and, for reasons of cost, it was required to use a package with at most 68 pins. Power and other ancillary pins require around 15 pins, leaving 25 available for the host interface. The ECL and CMOS chips and the way in which they are connected are shown in Fig. 8.3.

Connecting the ECL and CMOS chips together uses 18 pins on each device. If the ECL chip is not present, then these pins on the CMOS chip may be used for another purpose. The logic of the ECL chip is therefore duplicated

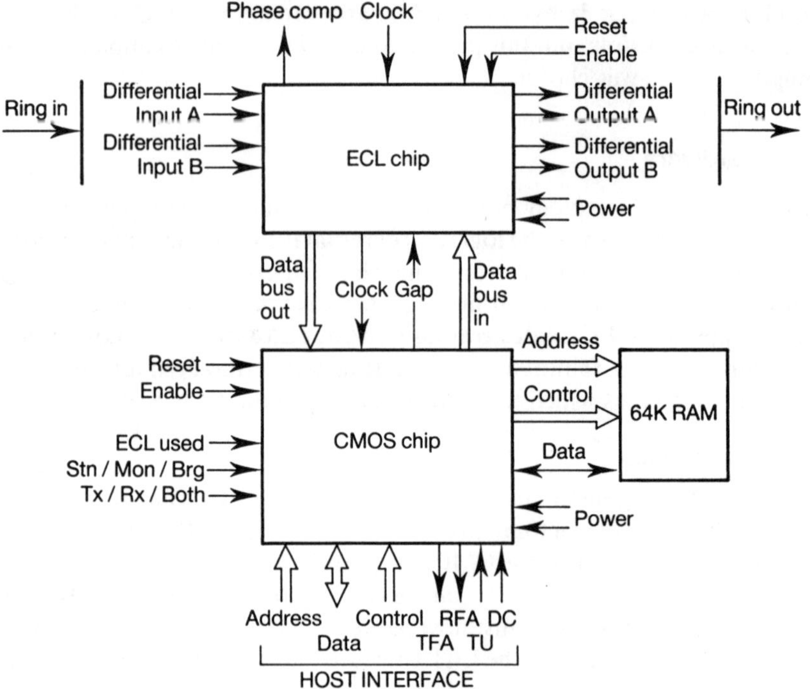

Fig. 8.3   Components of a Fast Ring node

on the CMOS chip and the 18 pins are used to perform the function of serial interface to the ring. This results in a single-chip network controller. It will only run at low speeds (around 10 MHz) in this mode, but will make for a very low-cost network.

Another facility is the ability to use just one ECL chip with several CMOS chips. This is useful when many network connections have to be made close together, for example within a single cabinet. There are two advantages to this. First, the number of chips is reduced and second, the delay inserted in the ring is less than if several pairs of ECL and CMOS chips were used. The delay inserted into the ring by the ECL chip is 24 bits and by each CMOS chip is 16 bits. When using several CMOS chips with one ECL chip the gap must be long enough to span all of the CMOS chips connected to a particular ECL chip. Where the distance between all the nodes in a network is small it is possible to dispense with the ECL chip and design a high-speed switch where the ring datapath is 8 bits wide.

Host interface

The number of pins available on the CMOS chip which makes up the host interface is very small compared with the number used on the Cambridge Ring. This means that the interface is much less general than is desirable and simultaneous access to the receive and transmit sides is not possible. The interface does, however, have the advantage of simplicity and it is trivial to interface it to devices such as microprocessors. More complex interfaces for faster, more sophisticated hosts require extra logic and hence are rather more expensive.

The CMOS chip is controlled by the host writing and reading registers contained within it. The structure of the host interface is shown in Fig. 8.4. An 8-bit data bus and 5 address lines allow the host to access the registers. To allow effective control by hardware of the most common functions, transmission and reception of minipackets, four pins are provided to monitor the state of the minipacket buffers and to force transmissions and receptions. Less frequent operations must be performed by addressing data to the appropriate register. The transmit buffer appears as a single 8-bit register and successive writes to it cause data to be added. The receive buffer works in a similar manner. The chip may also be programmed to provide an interrupt to the host on a variety of events, such as the reception of a minipacket.

The problem of the chip being only half-duplex may be solved by using two CMOS chips per station (or bridge). In this case, one of the chips is configured for reception only and the other for transmission only. A single line is required to connect the two chips so that they operate in harmony and there is a constraint in that the receiver must be before the transmitter on the ring. A single ECL chip can connect the two CMOS chips to the ring as described above.

8.2.2 Transmission and reception

Two transmission buffers for minipackets are provided with the CMOS chip. The automatic retransmission of minipackets relies on the original contents of

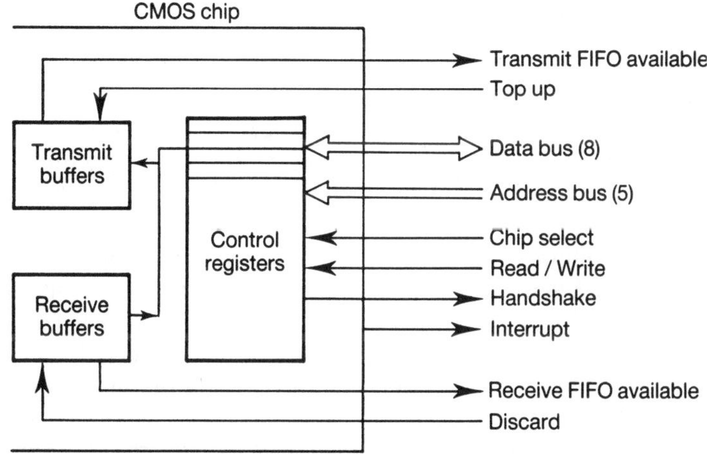

Fig. 8.4   Host interface of the Cambridge Fast Ring

the minipacket being retained in the transmitter and it is convenient to be filling a second buffer while the first is being transmitted. The reception side also has two buffers for minipackets.

In order to transmit a minipacket a host simply has to write 32 bytes of data into a transmit buffer, having previously written a destination address into a separate buffer. Transmission takes place as soon as the 32nd byte is placed in the buffer. An output pin on the chip called Transmit FIFO Available (TFA) indicates when a transmit buffer is free. The host uses the TFA signal as a prompt to place more data in the buffer and is unaware of the fate of previously transmitted minipackets. If the buffer is not to be filled with the entire 32 bytes before being transmitted, the host can use the Top Up (TU) input to force the transmission of whatever is in the buffer at the time.

Receive buffers are managed on a similar basis. A signal to the host called Receive FIFO Available (RFA) indicates that there is a full buffer waiting to be read. Reading all 32 bytes initiates the reception of another minipacket. There is a Discard (DC) input with which the host may force the emptying of a receive buffer. There are also receive address buffers into which the source addresses of received minipackets are placed for reading by the host.

8.2.3 Addressing

The CFR uses unstructured (flat) 16-bit addresses. The addressing mechanisms built into the node hardware allow local transmissions to occur and also cater for minipackets directed to nodes not on the ring on which they were transmitted. To allow for this, certain nodes can be configured as bridges and these nodes are able to recognise which minipackets should be received by the bridge and retransmitted on another ring.

The destination address 65535 (all bits of the address are one) is the broadcast address. Minipackets sent to this address may potentially be received by all stations on the network.

Address filtering

Each station of the CFR contains a 16-bit select register and a 64K bit select map which are used when receiving minipackets. The select register and map contents are set by the host. Selection operates by looking at the source address field of arriving minipackets. When the select register contains 0, the station rejects all minipackets addressed to it. When the select register contains a station address, minipackets from all addresses other than that in the register will be rejected. When all the bits of the select register are set to 1 then the source addresses of minipackets addressed to the station are used to index the map. If the addressed map bit is 0 the minipacket will be rejected, otherwise the minipacket is eligible for reception. The mechanisms outlined above allow a receiver to choose from whom to receive minipackets – no stations, just one station or a group of stations. It is expected that, initially, the map will be set to allow reception from all addresses and that certain addresses will be marked to prevent reception as time goes by. The term 'hate-list' has been coined for the select map.

Inter-ring addressing

Nodes which are configured as bridges use the map in a rather different way to that described above. At a bridge the map is indexed by the destination address of passing minipackets. Thus, for a given address, the map bit should reflect whether the address can be reached through this bridge or not. The bridge itself does not have an address and thus cannot be transmitted to directly. In some implementations it may be configured as a low-level hardware bridge with the map in ROM. The bridge can be processor-controlled, however, to allow the map to be configured when the network starts up. In this case the processor must be connected to the network via its own station.

Care must be taken with broadcast minipackets in networks which contain a circular path through bridges. If a broadcast minipacket follows such a path it will circulate forever. The bridge maps can be configured to constrain broadcast minipackets to selected areas of the network and thus avoid this problem.

8.2.4 The response bit

As mentioned earlier a single response bit is encoded within the CRC. It can therefore encode two states of the receiver and inform the source which of these states is applicable. These states have been chosen to mean 'Try Again' and 'Don't Try Again'. Unlike the Cambridge Ring, the response is not passed back to the host but is used within the station to govern whether an automatic retransmission should be attempted. Whenever the try-again response is seen the transmitter will retransmit the packet, subject to some maximum number of retries.

The destination will give the try-again response if its receive buffer is full or if it detects a CRC fault in the slot. It will give a don't-try-again response if the select mechanism prohibits reception or if it receives the packet. This means of using the response is far removed from that of the Cambridge Ring and reflects the fact that a CFR may be made up of interconnected rings across which it is not possible for a response to be sent from destination to source. That is, a response is something which is local to a ring, while CFR minipackets may traverse several rings before reaching their destination.

It would have been possible to allow the host to see the response but, to make use of it, it would need to know the location of the destination and, in particular, whether or not that destination was on the same ring as itself. It was thought that this was an undesirable state of affairs since it would require two sets of protocols, one for on-ring traffic and another for off-ring traffic. It would also mean that addresses could not move from ring to ring without requiring changes to the address look-up mechanism.

The low-level protocol on the CFR will therefore have to use explicit acknowledgement minipackets to indicate the arrival of data at a destination.

The response bit is now just a hint to a station or bridge that a retransmission would be worthwhile. The automatic retransmission is likely to be of use in two ways. The first is the case of a fast transmitter sending to a somewhat slower receiver on the same ring. The receiver will mark try-again those minipackets which arrive while the host is still busy emptying the receive buffer. The source will automatically retransmit the marked minipackets and the whole process will occur efficiently without intervention from either host.

The second use of this mechanism is at bridges. It is possible that there will be an appreciable number of minipackets passing through bridges. This means that there is a good chance that a bridge will be busy for an appreciable proportion of the time and that automatic retransmission to a bridge would be a very good thing.

The number of retransmissions that a station makes before giving up may be altered by the host. The number may be set to 0, 1, 3 or 7 and the interval between attempts at retransmission can be 0 or 4 ring revolutions. The host might set these numbers according to the prevailing conditions.

8.2.5 Channel mode

Channel mode works as follows. Each station or bridge has two transmit buffers and so the host may be filling a second one of these while the contents of the first filled buffer are in transit around the ring. If, by chance, the slot originally used was marked for channel use, then the slot will be replenished from the second buffer and channel mode will be entered. If the slot was not a channel slot then it will be passed on empty and a normal transmission started from the second buffer. If the host continues transmitting and there is a free channel slot on the ring, then it will soon be used by the host's station and channel mode transmission will commence. In this case the bandwidth out of the station will be constant and unaffected by other traffic on the ring.

The host cannot tell which mode is being used and will generally not need to. For channel mode to have the same overall effect as normal mode, transmission in channel mode must stop if the destination sends back the try-again response. There is a problem with this because the slot will already have been replenished and be on its way around the ring before the source gets to see the response from the previous minipacket. The problem is solved by sending the response out to the destination the opposite way round to normal. The destination takes this to mean 'disregard this minipacket' and then all is well. The response is thus used as a directive on the forward path.

8.2.6 Error checking and maintenance

The maintenance mechanism detects bit corruptions and line breaks near where they occur and forwards a maintenance minipacket reporting the fault to an error logger. Two types of maintenance minipacket are sent by stations and bridges. One type is sent when the node detects a line break. It does this when it has not received a slot for a certain length of time. Under these circumstances the node must generate a slot in which to place the maintenance minipacket. The second type of maintenance minipacket is sent when a node detects an error in the CRC of a passing empty slot. In this case the node will correct the CRC and wait for an empty slot to arrive and use that for the maintenance minipacket. Because the response is encoded in the CRC it is not possible for a node to correct the CRC in a full slot since it does not know which response to generate. The CRC of a full minipacket is, of course, checked and corrected at its source and destination. A failing of this scheme is that full minipackets do not take part in the maintenance function.

Maintenance minipackets contain the source address of the station which sent them and are sent to destination 0. It is the latter which distinguishes them from normal minipackets. The type of error they are reporting is encoded in the data field. Any station with address 0 will receive maintenance minipackets. By default, the monitor has address 0 and so will receive maintenance minipackets in the absence of an error-logging station. The monitor removes maintenance minipackets using the mechanism which detects full minipackets circulating around the ring twice. On finding such minipackets the monitor marks them empty and thus a maintenance minipacket may pass an error-logging station twice.

8.2.7 Bridges

When a CFR node is working as a bridge, minipackets can be routed between rings according to the destination address. Thus, when a source sends a minipacket it uses a 16-bit global address. This address will be recognised by a bridge node which will receive the minipacket. The response passed to the source will indicate how the minipacket was handled at the bridge. If the minipacket is received it is passed from the bridge node to another bridge node on an adjacent ring. This bridge node then transmits the minipacket on its ring. This may be the ring containing the destination station or the minipacket may have to pass through further bridges.

The response received by a bridge node will therefore be local to the ring on which the minipacket is being transmitted. The minipacket may not be accepted and the bridge node may try to send it again a number of times before giving up and discarding it. This may pose a problem because the original source will not know from the local response whether a minipacket has been accepted at its final destination. This is the normal problem with store and forward networks and one way of solving it is to adopt some end-to-end flow control procedure which notifies the sending station about the progress of the transmission.

A bridge can also be designed to cope with channel mode minipackets. These have to be handled with care because delay fluctuations and interactions on the two rings may cause minipackets to be lost. When the first such minipacket is received at a bridge, a channel slot has to be found on the next ring and the minipacket transmitted in it. Provided that this can be done before the next minipacket arrives from the source, then the transmission will continue successfully. Any other traffic trying to use the bridge is likely to upset the channel mode traffic and such operations are only likely to succeed with cooperation from all stations on the network.

8.2.8 Monitors

The functions performed by the monitor are to set up and maintain the required slot structure, monitor the ring for errors and generate error minipackets accordingly. The monitor has address 0 and can be used to receive maintenance minipackets.

The slot structure required on the ring is specified to the monitor by an associated processor which need only be very simple, a single-chip micro-processor, for example. When the monitor initialises the ring it goes into a mode known as **start mode** and puts out the slot structure which was specified, with each slot marked as full. It then waits for the incoming gap to end and repeats this operation until it detects no errors on the incoming slot train. While this is going on, stations and bridges on the ring will be synchronising to the slot structure. When the monitor has detected no errors for a complete revolution it sends out a slot train consisting of empty slots and then enters its normal mode of operation – **run mode**. When in run mode the monitor checks for a variety of errors and sets and checks the monitor-passed bit in slots. Certain catastrophic errors cause it to re-enter start mode, while other types may be corrected less drastically. For the latter the monitor generates maintenance minipackets which are marked to indicate a monitor error.

8.3 Linking Fast Rings

This section discusses the bridge facility which is provided in CFR networks. The ability to send minipackets to destinations on other rings is implicit in the design of the CFR. A station can be unaware of the location of the destination of the minipackets it is sending and minipackets will cross bridges automatically to reach their destination.

This has implications for the protocols in use on the network since the time taken for a minipacket to reach its destination will vary widely. There is also a finite chance of a minipacket being thrown away (lost) at bridges on its path. The maps which control the routing of minipackets through bridges must be set up and maintained in a consistent state.

8.3.1 Modes of use

There are a number of ways in which the facilities of a bridge may be exploited. It may be used to connect two otherwise autonomous rings for convenience reasons only, or it may be used to allow a large slow ring to be split up into smaller and hence faster rings. A further reason is to allow the division of a network into small units for geographical or administrative reasons. Finally, the splitting of a large ring into small ones will improve the reliability of the network.

From these classifications two extremes of bridge use can be predicted. One will be on systems where the majority of data flow occurs on rings and very little passes through bridges. The other has much traffic passing through bridges, there being no distinction made between on-ring and off-ring minipackets. This suggests that a wide range of traffic handling capability may be required from bridges and that a number of different designs may be needed to cope with the various requirements. If the very fastest bridge that can be built is not adequate then it is possible to place two or more of them between two rings. Care must be taken in this case to ensure that their maps are configured so that minipackets for a given destination will pass through only one bridge. If this is not the case then minipackets may arrive at their destination in a different order to that in which they were transmitted, making the reassembly of messages from minipackets more difficult.

8.3.2 Ring bridge design

A bridge node is a CFR node which receives minipackets on the basis of their destination address being in a 64K bit map. When a minipacket passes a bridge node its destination address is used to address the map and the addressed bit says whether or not the destination can be reached through the bridge. If it can and the bridge node has a reception buffer free, then the minipacket will be received. Not only is the data field of the minipacket buffered, but also the source and destination addresses. All of these items are placed in a 36-byte reception buffer. The bridge node can also transmit these 36-byte structures. Writing 36 bytes to a bridge node's transmit buffer will cause them to be interpreted as addresses and data and therefore to be transmitted. Two bridge nodes are required to construct a ring bridge which connects two rings and transfers minipackets between them.

The simplest bridge which will transfer minipackets bidirectionally consists of two bridge nodes connected back to back. Some arbitration circuitry is required to ensure that only one transfer is attempted at once on the data bus connecting the two nodes. In addition, a means of initialising and updating the bridge maps is required. A single-chip microprocessor, the **bridge processor**, will be adequate for this purpose. It must be attached to one or both rings to enable it to communicate with whatever service provides the necessary information to keep the maps in order. Since bridges cannot transmit and receive in their own right, the bridge processor must have a station on one of the rings to allow it to communicate. A more symmetrical arrangement is for the bridge to have a station on each ring and this may be useful when traffic cannot flow through the bridge. This situation may arise during network initialisation or while updating the maps. An example of such a configuration is shown in Fig. 8.5. This design takes advantage of the ability to use more than one CMOS chip with a single ECL chip.

Because the CMOS chip can be configured to act as a transmitter only or a

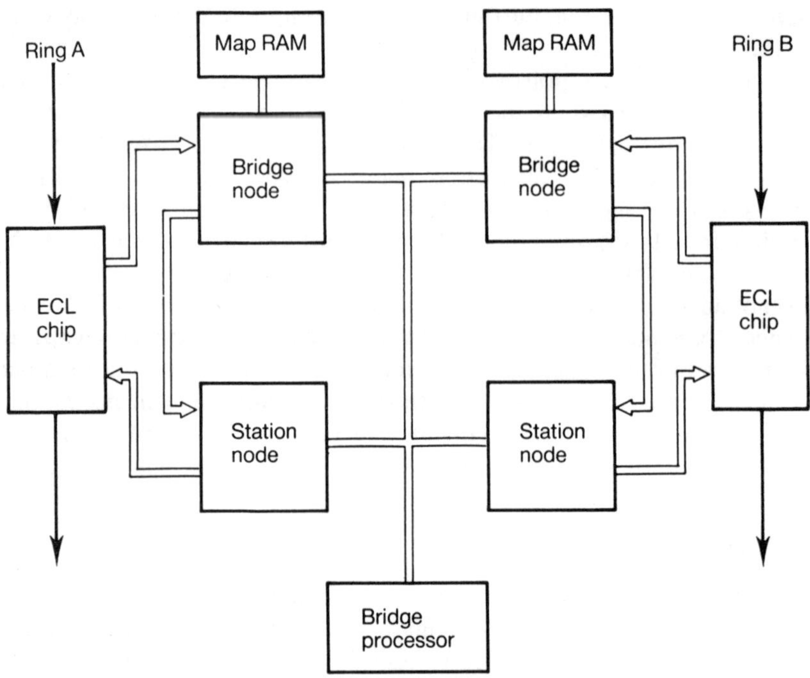

Fig. 8.5   A simple Fast Ring bridge

receiver only, pairs of chips can be used to construct a fully duplex bridge. The throughput of such a bridge under heavy load will be higher than the previous design, since minipackets may cross the bridge in both directions at the same time. Similar considerations to those of the simple bridge apply to the updating of the bridge maps. In this case the map RAMs will be attached to the receiver chips and no RAMs are needed for the transmitting nodes.

It has been assumed so far that bridges will be bidirectional. A unidirectional bridge is also easily constructed. It will require a bridge node configured as a receiver on one ring and a transmitter node on the other ring. A station node and microprocessor are associated with the receive side to maintain the map RAM. This configuration could prove to be a useful building block, since, with minor changes, it could behave as the simple bridge described earlier. Using two of these blocks would allow the construction of the full-duplex bridge, while on its own it would function as a unidirectional bridge.

Unidirectional bridges may be of use in relieving traffic congestion problems where the flow of minipackets is predominantly in one direction. A ring with a continuous large influx of minipackets might have one unidirectional bridge taking minipackets off the ring and two or three bringing minipackets on to it.

8.3.3 Bridge maps

There are two fundamental operations which must be performed on the maps at bridges. The first is initialising the map when the bridge becomes active and the second is updating the map as a result of changes to the network structure. The changes which are relevant are the addition and removal of stations and the movement of addresses from ring to ring. It should be borne in mind that the bridge works only in terms of physical addresses and these are generally closely bound to a particular station. Frequent moves of addresses are unlikely under normal circumstances, although it is possible to conceive of situations where movement could occur quite often. For example, in systems which use redundancy of hardware to improve reliability, the failure of a node or ring might cause alternative hardware to be used. The replacement nodes might well duplicate the addresses of the failed or isolated nodes. This would necessitate changes to the bridge maps if the replacements were on different rings to the original stations.

In general use, the contents of bridge maps are likely to be fairly static, with the time between updates being measured in days rather than seconds. In this case updating might best be performed by a complete reinitialisation. If updating is necessary on a more frequent basis then a more subtle approach can be used. Cooperation between bridge processors will be required to keep the maps in a consistent state. Inconsistency could lead to minipackets circulating indefinitely if there were a loop in the network. Algorithms for updating the maps are well known, having been devised many years ago for use with store and forward networks.

The initialisation of the maps will be done from some record of the system configuration kept on stable storage such as a disk. The following method uses broadcast minipackets to help with the initialisation process. On powering on, each bridge processor sets the maps so that no minipackets can pass through the bridge. This means that broadcast minipackets will be constrained to the ring on which they are transmitted. The bridge processor now sends a broadcast minipacket requesting the address of the machine which will supply map information, the **map-server**. It repeats these requests at intervals until it receives a reply. The map-server will receive these requests from bridge processors on its own ring and will respond by sending them its own address. The bridge processors can now send a request to the map-server asking for their maps. The map-server gives them the appropriate maps and these processors now reply to requests for the map-server's address coming from bridge processors on adjacent rings. These bridge processors can now request their map from the map-server via the recently set up bridges. This process continues until all bridge processors have obtained their maps.

A recent development in memories is the Electrically Alterable Read Only Memory or EAROM. This is a read/write memory which retains its contents when power is removed. Writing is somewhat slow, but reading takes place at conventional speeds. Using this memory for bridge maps would remove the need for initialisation every time a bridge was turned off and on again, though clearly it would need setting up at some stage.

8.3.4 Factors influencing bridge performance

Whilst high-speed traffic is expected through bridges, it seems unlikely that channel mode will be effective through general purpose bridges. This is because any minipacket arriving at a bridge and having to be retransmitted on the other side will hold up the channel packets and cause normal mode to be resumed. This may be satisfactory in some cases, but if a guaranteed channel transmission is required across two rings a dedicated bridge will be needed. The bridge map must be set to pass minipackets only for the channel destination. A duplex bridge would allow bidirectional channel mode conversations between the two stations, assuming that they were duplex, too.

The main objective of a bridge is to transfer minipackets from a variety of sources to a variety of destinations. The bridge is equipped with two transmit buffers and two receive buffers in each direction. The speed at which data may be passed from the reception buffers on one ring to the transmit buffers on the other will influence the delay experienced at a bridge.

Having received a minipacket, a bridge node must transfer 36 bytes of data and addresses to the adjacent bridge node. Preliminary figures for the speed of the buffers on the CMOS chip suggests that they can be read and written, via the external interface, at the rate of 150 ns per byte. The whole 36 bytes will therefore cross in 5.4 μs. Assuming rings to be lightly loaded, the average time before transmission can take place will be half a slot time, or just over 3 μs on a 50 MHz ring. The minimum delay from the reception of a minipacket at a bridge to its retransmission on the next will therefore be around 9 μs. Minipackets sent across bridges will need explicit acknowledgement. The delay through bridges is sufficiently large to make acknowledging each minipacket very wasteful of bandwidth and, if possible, minipackets passing through bridges should be acknowledged in groups.

When the rings to which a bridge is attached are heavily loaded, the bridge may have to wait some time before transmitting and a backlog of minipackets may develop. Four minipackets can be buffered in a bridge in each direction, two in receive buffers and two in transmit buffers. When these buffers are full the bridge will start rejecting incoming minipackets, marking their response try-again. Judging from the traffic patterns seen in the study of Chapter 7, there will be bursts of activity, during which bridge congestion is most likely to occur, and longer spells of low activity. If the bursts can be readily handled by the bridge then there are no problems. If not, then additional buffering at the bridge may enable the burst to be endured.

A further consideration, under conditions of heavy load, is the way in which retransmissions are made. The issue here is what to do when a bridge is transmitting to a destination which does not receive the minipacket. If the response says 'don't-try-again', then the bridge stops transmitting and throws the minipacket away. In the case of the response saying 'try-again', the transmitter will attempt a number of retransmissions. This will hold up the passage of minipackets through the bridge far more seriously than heavy load on the destination ring. This means that the retransmission algorithm must compromise between not occupying bridges too long and being sufficiently prolonged to allow slow receivers to receive effectively. When rings of widely differing speeds are interconnected by bridges the problem becomes even more acute. The CFR includes options to allow the retransmission algorithm to be altered. The number of retransmissions and the interval between them may be chosen from a limited range.

8.3.5 Discussion

Bridges bring with them a number of useful facilities and a number of potential problems. Partitioning a large network into many rings is possible and brings higher reliability and higher data rates than if the network was made with a single ring. The problems arise when bridges carry a lot of traffic. Their limited buffering capability means that it is likely that minipackets will get thrown away because they cannot enter a bridge. This problem will be particularly apparent when bridges connect rings of different speeds. Because the retransmission rate is related to the ring's clocking speed, minipackets will be retransmitted much more slowly on a slow ring than on a fast one. At times of heavy load many minipackets sent to the bridge from the fast ring will be thrown away because the bridge spends a long time performing retransmissions on the slow ring. A larger buffer at bridges may help to reduce this problem if the average level of bridge traffic is much smaller than the peak level.

8.4 References

Adams, G.C., Burren, J.W., Cooper, C.S. and Girard, P.M., 1982. 'The interconnection of local area networks via a satellite network'. In *New Advances in Computer Systems*, ed. K.G. Beauchamp, pp. 201–10.

Hopper, A. and Williamson, R.C., 1983. 'Design and use of an Integrated Cambridge Ring'. *IEEE Journal on Selected Areas in Communication*, **SAC1 (5)**, 775–84.

Temple, S., 1984. 'The design of a ring communication network'. PhD Thesis, Computer Laboratory, University of Cambridge, January.

Saltzer, J.H., Reed, D.P. and Clark, D.D., 1980. 'Source routing for campus-wide internet transport'. In *Proc. IFIP WG 6.4 on Local Networks, Zurich, Switzerland*, eds. A. West and P. Janson, pp. 1–24. Amsterdam: North-Holland.

Chapter 9   Concluding remarks

The last chapter considers some aspects of the way LANs are developing and being extended.

9.1 Extending local area networks

The number of local area networks in use over the last few years has grown by several orders of magnitude. As has already been seen, these networks have been of many types and provide many levels of service. However the local area network is often only one part of a more general communications system and it is the issue of providing a single general purpose networking facility that is now beginning to be addressed. This should improve the most important parameter by which the network is measured which is the service it provides. The cost of generality is normally greater complexity and it is only if that complexity can be hidden from the user, for example by integration, that the more general communication problem can be addressed. The wall socket in the lab, office or home should provide a standard way of communicating with the rest of the world.

Haphazard connection structures have been useful up until now. For example, it is not necessary for a microprocessor controlling a garage door to be able to talk to other digital devices around the home. However, this changes as soon as other control functions in the home are incorporated into the system. This can also be dealt with using a haphazard solution but at a certain point, for example when control is to be also exercised remotely via the telephone network, the standards issue must be faced. While the home example may seem trivial it has its counterpart in the office or factory. It is interesting to consider the possibility of designing a large network which connects many local networks and retains some of the performance benefits of LANs and provides a service transparent to the user. The general network should provide at least a transparent data switching capability to provide a minimum general communications standard. This is primarily a software protocol problem but it also descends to the hardware level in that a solution can be attempted using specialised hardware.

An example of this kind of system is Project Universe (Kirstein *et al.*, 1982). The aims of this project were to try and extend the most attractive properties of local networks (high bandwidth, low error rates and small delays) to a wider area. The networking system consisted of a number of local networks at geographically distant sites (Cambridge, London, Loughborough and others). The local networks were primarily Cambridge Rings and the medium for linking them was a satellite providing a low error rate channel at 1 Mbps. The problem of communication across satellite links is that the round trip delay can be large and that the delay through bridges can be significant, especially under high load conditions. The local networks themselves supported a number of protocols for exchanging files, sharing peripherals and distributed computing and it was the extension of these services that was the aim of the project. The main aims of the Universe experiment were met in that a number of the services available on a single network were made to work across the satellite links. In particular, various rings supported diskless workstations running a simple operating system called Tripos (Richards *et al.*, 1979). The filing system for these machines was provided by a set of file-servers. A special machine, the filing machine, provided a cache between the target Tripos machines and the file-servers to smoothe some of the performance limitations of the file-servers. This service was made available to workstations on various sites with access to the filing machine via the satellite and was found to work well. Another application that has been successfully accomplished is to transmit video images between a frame store and a monitor both on local rings and across the satellite link. A more recent experiment called Unison uses land-based 2-Mbps lines as the long-distance communications medium.

Universe is an example of the way differences between remote and local networks can be blurred. While performance across the satellite in Universe is not as good as on the local net, the protocol changes have been minimised and most of the performance characteristics of the local network have been maintained. The Fast Ring system mentioned in the previous chapter is an attempt at similar goals by pushing some of the complexity into the bottom-level hardware units of the network.

9.2 Flexibility in LAN architectures

As well as observing how the differences between local and remote networks have been blurring, it is interesting to note the way in which the various local area network architectures are being developed to make them more adaptable to different types of traffic and in particular to real time traffic such as process control and voice.

The broad performance characteristics of a token ring are that it can be used to send long packets efficiently. However, under load, the time to send a short packet can be considerably longer. With an empty slot ring the opposite is the case. Short packets can be sent with little delay even under saturation conditions while long packets may take a substantial period of time. Thus, in a token ring the recent architectural emphasis has been to introduce a second mode of operation during which the token cannot be used except by special users who send short packets. The time to move into this mode can be minimised and so the short time-critical applications can be serviced. Another way of achieving this is to combine an empty slot with the token in some way so that, in effect, two transmissions can take place on the ring at once, one short, based on the empty slot and one long, based on the token. Indeed, it would be possible to have several such fixed-length slots circulating with the token (or packet header) or to make this structure change dynamically.

In the case of the empty slot ring the architecture can be extended to allow a slot to be reused at the source, or to configure the ring so that various sizes of slot are circulating. While these sizes are fixed it is possible to use the longer slots to send bulky traffic. This is not necessarily a general solution because the difference between a long slot and a short slot is unlikely to be great and in any case the long slots may not be used efficiently. It is possible to make this data structure change dynamically with demand but this level of complication may not be worthwhile. Possibly a better scheme is to have a ring with lots of very short slots which can be used in contiguous sets by a transmitter. To do this, an extra bit, called the continuation bit, is added at the front of each slot to indicate that the contents are part of a transmission which started earlier. On transmission, a sender marks a slot full and places the destination and source addresses in the first slot together with some data if there is room. The source then continues to fill slots with data and mark the full/empty and continuation bits until the transmission is completed or there is an incoming full slot making continuation impossible. The packet structure is shown in Fig. 9.1. The full slots now make their way to the destination and then back to the source where the full/empty and continuation bits are cleared. In this system both short and long transmissions are catered for, the worst case performance can have a well-defined (and low) threshold, and the efficiency of transmission is good since, for longer packets, the address and control overhead is minimal.

The examples above show how the designs of two types of LAN can be adapted so that real time traffic is catered for and both long data packets and short control packets are treated in an optimum fashion. To the user these augmented token and empty slot networks have very similar characteristics and

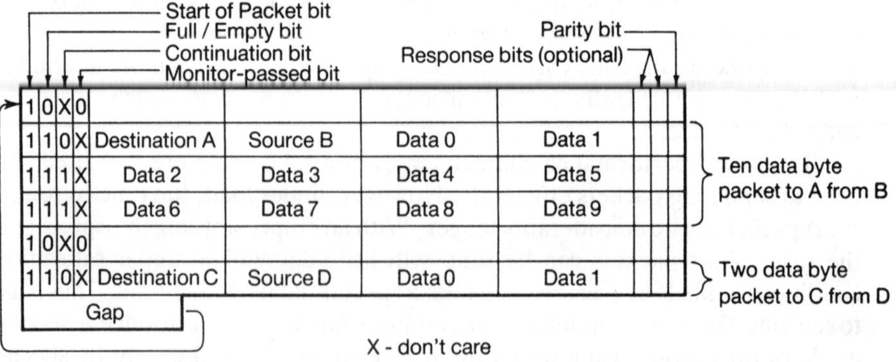

Fig. 9.1   Empty slot ring with continuation bits

it is likely that they will work well in most applications. This suggests that a standard can be devised in which it is not important what the underlying network is. The choice of network will then be made on very specific issues like the availability of cheap hardware, transmission systems or interfaces and will not have an impact on higher levels.

9.3 Integrated services LANs

One of the areas where it is likely that a lot of progress will be made is integration of voice, data and perhaps video on the same communications system (Weinstein and Forgie, 1983). The attraction is that by integrating these services, the same switching and control equipment can be used, leading to lower total system cost. Also, additional services can be provided, for example voice annotation of documents, incorporation of video images in computer-based teaching systems, PABX applications and others.

From an information transfer point of view, using voice for communication is very inefficient. For a power-to-noise ratio of about 100, an analogue voice channel using about 3 kHz of bandwidth is capable of transmitting about 3000 log (100) or 20 Kbps. At the other extreme the information content of the words that are being spoken assuming a rate of speech of about three 5-letter words per second is equivalent to about 75 bps. Where a digital channel is being used as the communications medium, the apparent waste of bandwidth is even worse. Thus, integration of voice has only become practical as the speeds of local networks have increased, not only because that enables many connections to be supported, but also beause it is then possible to treat bandwidth in a more cavalier way and trade its use for design simplicity. Using a digital representation of the voice samples with the encoding and decoding being done in the handsets is precisely the characteristic which makes integrated services LANs feasible.

Because voice is a special application it is also possible to design hardware to make handling it easier. When transmitting speech, an initial compression technique is to detect silence periods and stop transmitting at those times. Secondly, only differences between samples need be sent, thus further reducing the bandwidth requirement. If the LAN bandwidth is plentiful it may not be necessary to compress at all. However, if the samples are to be stored, some form of compression is normally required and by using these simple techniques a factor of about ten is possible.

Important issues when implementing a voice system are the choice of packet size, time stamps and sequence numbers. Packet size controls the voice sample size while time stamps and sequence number are useful for the reconstitution process. An interesting area still to be investigated is the design and use of algorithms for scheduling control, voice and data packets together. The natural gaps in voice lend themselves to be exploited for other transmissions, these being perhaps restricted in some way so that the threshold of service is not affected. Voice traffic is normally given higher priority than data traffic although a bimodal system could be designed which alternates these priorities. Short control packets are likely to use the spare bandwidth during the voice silent periods efficiently, while long data packets are likely to cause unacceptable pauses in the voice.

Many LANs have architectures which do not guarantee delivery of every packet but, because of the nature of the human ear, the loss of an occasional short sample may not pose problems. If a packet is dropped during an active conversation period it is better to fill the gap with some sound, often the previous sample, rather than complete silence. The ear can cope with gaps of up to 2 ms and with end-to-end delays of about 100 ms with little difficulty. A 10 Mbps local network can support about 100 simultaneous conversations using 5 ms samples. This can be improved by using longer packets or if the activity of the attached voice devices is reduced. While using longer packets allows a greater number of transmissions to be supported, the probability of a packet exceeding some maximum delay or being lost also increases.

9.4 Cost of connection

The availability and use of cheap VLSI network controllers is making the use of local area networks possible in many new applications (Taylor *et al.*, 1983). Such controllers exist for the Ethernet, token and empty slot rings amongst others. These devices often use a low-level modem or repeater for interfacing to the transmission medium. In the case of Ethernet controllers this consists of a line transmitter and receiver and a collision detection circuit. For ring controllers the collision detection circuitry is not necessary but normally some mechanism for helping with clock recovery is provided. The modem or repeater chip normally talks to a network controller chip through a serial interface. For higher-speed systems this interface can be 2, 4 or 8 bits wide so that the amount of logic working at high speeds is minimised.

The functions of the network controller are to implement the network protocol, transmit and receive packets, perform error checking and provide a user interface. The most important criterion for such chips is to hide the network complexity from the user and thus the design of the user interface is of considerable importance. The complexity of the user interface is influenced by a number of factors including the style of the network architecture, the buffering strategies, and the availability and constraints on the use of registers available to the user bus.

The network architecture can be broadly categorised in two ways: packets either have a guarantee of having been delivered or they only have a high probability of having been delivered. An example of the former is any ring network which provides a direct response path in the hardware to the user. Providing no complex fault has occurred the response path directly informs the user about the status of the receiver or the receiving agent. This makes it easy to implement a repeat-on-busy or similar strategy for delivering data. Examples of the latter are an Ethernet-type system in which no direct response path is available and a system of linked rings where low-level responses do not pass back through bridges and therefore do not get back to the sender. This approach makes it more difficult to implement a service which is transparent to the user because the timeout periods are less constrained and performance is subject to greater variation.

Some VLSI network controller chips implement complex buffer management and DMA facilities which can be used for high-speed scatter read and write of data in the hosts memory. There is a tradeoff in the buffering between implementation of a large FIFO buffer on the controller and providing lots of registers for storing DMA addresses. In a simple design the DMA registers store the actual addresses to be used for DMA and when a particular block of DMA finishes, chaining onto the next one can take place directly. The FIFO registers are used to smoothe the flow of data to the network as this switch takes place, the average data rate on the memory bus being about 1.25 Mbps for a 10-MHz controller chip. However, because there are dead times on the user bus during which no transmissions are taking place, the peak data rate to the memory is higher. A more complex scheme is for the DMA registers to store pointers to locations in user memory which, in turn, store the DMA addresses. This allows a more structured approach and can have performance benefits if the access speed to the user memory is high. However, because of the extra indirection, transmission of many short packets may be a problem and may increase the maximum required memory bandwidth considerably.

While a simple interface can be designed which is based on simple use of a network controller, the future is likely to bring a single integrated device consisting of a microprocessor, a buffer and the network controller integrated onto one chip. Such a device should be able to implement a virtual circuit protocol and have sufficient performance to make the use of the network transparent to the user. This is particularly likely to be true if the target devices are slow, making the network controller a high-speed device in comparison.

9.5 Local area network standards

The Institute of Electrical and Electronic Engineers has drafted a family of standards for LANs (IEEE, 1982). A general purpose document (802.1) describes the relationships between these standards and the way they fit with the International Standards Organisation reference model. The standards are shown in Fig. 9.2 and are comparable to the physical and data link layers of the OSI reference model described in Chapter 1. As the figure shows, four standards have been adopted at the physical layer and these are the CSMA/CD system (802.3), a token bus system (802.4), the token ring system (802.5) and a standard for metropolitan area networks (802.6). The token bus and metropolitan area networks have not been described in this book. The common logical link control standard (802.2) can be used with all four physical standards below it.

The IEEE standards are under consideration by ISO under the numbers

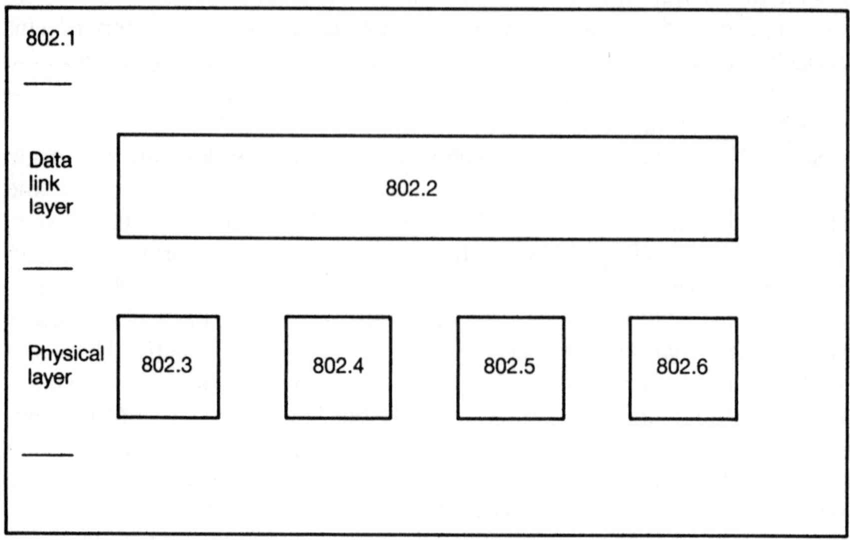

Fig. 9.2   Family of IEEE 802 local area network standards

8802/2-5. In addition, the Cambridge Ring is being considered as standard 8802/6 (not to be confused with IEEE 802.6). In order to make the Cambridge Ring comply with the data link layer standard above it an extension is proposed which incorporates longer address fields and other minor modifications. The Cambridge Ring has also been accepted as British Standard 6531 and 6532.

9.6 References

IEEE, 1982. *IEEE Computer Society Project 802: local area networks standards*. Draft C. IEEE Computer Society, Silver Spring, MD, October.

Kirstein, P.T. *et al.*, 1982. *The Universe Project*. Proc. Sixth International Conference on Computer Communication, September. Amsterdam: North-Holland.

Richards, M. *et al.*, 1979. 'Tripos – a portable operating system for minicomputers'. *Software Practice and Experience*, **9**, 513–26.

Taylor, D., Oster, D.L. and Green, L., 1983. 'VLSI node processor architecture for Ethernet'. *IEEE Journal on Selected Areas in Communications*, **SAC-1 (5)**, 733–9.

Weinstein, C.J. and Forgie, J.W., 1983. 'Experience with speech communication in packet networks'. *IEEE Journal on Selected Areas in Communications*, **SAC-1 (6)**, 963–80.

Suggested reading

In this section we recommend publications which have proved to be useful to us in our research into local networks. We also list some recent books on the subject which are basic introductions to the field, aimed at the non-specialist. They provide information on specific commercial products and guidance on how to employ them.

Books

A useful guide to early research literature on LANs is gathered together in

J.F. Shoch, *An Annotated Bibliography on Local Computer Networks*, XEROX PARC Technical Report, Xerox Corporation, 1980.

For a good grounding in network fundamentals the first book to be consulted should be

A.S. Tanenbaum, *Computer Networks*. Prentice-Hall, Englewood Cliffs, NJ, 1981.

Further reading on the early computer networks such as ARPANET and the Aloha system may be found in

N. Abramson and F.F. Kuo (eds.), *Computer Communication Networks*. Prentice-Hall, Englewood Cliffs, NJ, 1973.

A good introduction to network architectures with good coverage of the IBM view of the world is provided by

R.J. Cypser, *Communications Architecture for Distributed Systems*. Addision-Wesley, Reading, MA, 1978.

Further information on this topic is provided by Green, whose book looks at layered network architectures and provides details of various implementations for each layer

P.E. Green (ed.), *Computer Network Architectures and Protocols*. Plenum, New York, NY, 1982.

A detailed introduction to the transmission systems employed in local networks and other telecommunication systems is given by

P. Bylanski and D.G.W. Ingram, *Digital Transmission Systems*. Peter Peregrinus Ltd, Stevenage, 1976.

The application of a local network in implementing a distributed computing system is described by two of our colleagues in

R.M. Needham and A.J. Herbert, *The Cambridge Distributed Computing System*. Addison-Wesley, London, 1982.

It is only recently that books explicitly describing local networks have been published and we list some of them below. These books are mostly concerned with the exploitation of LANs, rather than their implementation and will be useful to those considering using a local network.

W. Stallings, *Local Networks*. Macmillan, New York, NY, 1984.

V.E. Cheong and R.A. Hirschheim, *Local Area Networks*. John Wiley, Chichester, 1983.

D.N. Chorafas, *Designing and Implementing Local Area Networks*. McGraw-Hill Book Company, New York, NY, 1984.

K.C.E. Gee, *Introduction to Local Area Computer Networks*. Macmillan, Basingstoke, 1983.

Proceedings

Possibly the most fruitful reading for those interested in the design of LANs comes from the proceedings of conferences where such matters are discussed. The following are particularly interesting.

A. West and P. Janson (eds.), *Local Networks for Computer Communications*, Proc. IFIP WG6.4 Workshop on Local Networks, Zurich 1980. North-Holland Publishing Company, Amsterdam, 1981.

P.C. Ravasio, G. Hopkins and N. Naffah (eds.), *Local Computer Networks*, Proc. IFIP TC6 Symposium on Local Area Networks, Florence, 1982. North-Holland Publishing Company, Amsterdam, 1982.

I.N. Dallas and E.B. Spratt (eds.), *Ring Technology Local Area Networks*, Proc. IFIP WG6.4 Workshop on Ring Technology Local Area Networks, Canterbury, 1983. North-Holland Publishing Company, Amsterdam, 1984.

A detailed description of three of the networks described in this book may be found in

D. Hutchinson, J. Mariani and D. Shepherd (eds.), *Local Area Networks – An Advanced Course*, Lecture Notes in Computer Science, no 184. Springer Verlag, Heidelberg, 1985.

Another useful proceedings is

Proc. Local Networks and Distributed Office Systems. Online Publications Ltd., Northwood, U.K. 1981.

Journals and magazines

There are a number of journals devoted to communications and these often contain articles of relevance to local networks. The IEEE publishes *Transactions on Communications* and also *Communications Magazine*. Both of these appear monthly. The ACM publishes the quarterly *Computer Communications Review* and Butterworths publishes the bimonthly *Computer Communications*. The more commercially oriented *Datamation* and *Electronics* also contain articles on LANs from time to time.

Some specific articles are worth mentioning. A basic introduction to LANs may be found in

D.D. Clark, K.T. Pogran and D.P. Reed, 'An introduction to local area networks', *Proc IEEE*, **66**, Nov. 1978, 1497–1517.

An interesting collection of state of the art research papers was published in

K. Kumerle, B.W. Stuck and F.A. Tobagi (eds.), *IEEE Journal on Selected Areas in Communications*, Special Issue on Local Area Networks. **SAC-1**, No. 5, Nov. 1983.

Index